PROGRESS OF NEW YORK IN A CENTURY.

1776–1876.

AN ADDRESS

DELIVERED BEFORE THE

NEW YORK HISTORICAL SOCIETY.

DECEMBER 7, 1875,

BY

JOHN AUSTIN STEVENS.

NEW YORK:
PRINTED FOR THE SOCIETY.
1876.

THE PROGRESS OF NEW YORK IN A CENTURY.

1776-1876.

Mr. President and Members
of the New York Historical Society:

The members of this Society will remember that early last winter a petition was addressed by it to the Governor and Legislature of the State of New York, praying for authority to prepare a Memorial Volume, showing the growth of the State during the last century; and it was respectfully urged that no more fitting contribution could be made by the State to the International Exhibition, to be held at Philadelphia, than a faithful record of the progress of this great community in political, civil, and social life. Other and more pressing duties have, no doubt, hindered the Governor of the State from paying any regard to this request, and the petition left in his hands by the Committee of this Society has never been presented to the Legislature. A further effort will be made at the approaching session, though the time is short for such an exhibit as the extent and nature of the subject demand.

It has not been the habit of New York to pause in its march to count the milestones which mark its progress. In the many new duties which perpetually crowd themselves upon this busy community, there has been little time for such considerations, and only here and there sketches like those of Duer, Francis, and King have attracted passing notice; but now that in the depression which almost inevitably follows a period of unusual activity, there is a moment of pause and discouragement, the thought may be profitably turned backward, new hope be derived from a retrospective view, and new courage drawn from the example of that wondrous activity which, from a depth of misery unparalleled in the history of any other of the colonial cities, has lifted New York to its undisputed pre-eminence as the metropolitan city of the Western Continent, and its rank among the few cosmopolitan cities of the world.

Early in the war the British Government recognized the importance of occupying the city of New York as a military post and a basis of supplies. Repeating the strategy, old as war itself, of dividing the hostile territory by seizing the great rivers which serve at once as lines of separation and easy avenues of transportation, the plan of subjugation included the occupation of Quebec and New York, and the establishment of a line of almost unbroken water communication by the Hudson and St. Lawrence, navigable high up for vessels of the largest size, which should isolate the great and populous New England colony from those of the Middle region. With these magnificent harbors, at which all her fleets could ride at easy anchor, Great Britain was sure of safe and convenient bases for the operation of her troops; and her vessels could patrol the long broad streams as safely as the warlike vessels of the old Northmen the streams and lakes of Southern Europe, from the Seine to the Mediterranean. A similar policy adopted by the great Union commanders during the late war held the Ohio and the Tennessee with gunboats, and again dividing the Confederacy by the broad and rapid course of the Mississippi, insured the final triumph of the national arms. The failure of Great Britain was not a consequence of her strategy, but inherent to the condition of the two countries. A careful perusal of the journals of the day, which abound in papers of remarkable vigor and sagacity, amply shows that there was never a doubt in the minds of the colonists of their ability to achieve their independence. Nor is it at all probable that, even with entire union in the councils of Great Britain, there could have been any other result. Indeed, as early as 1740 serious alarm had been felt in England by the Ministry, and a defection of the colonies feared.

Great Britain, rich in every appliance of civilization, whose foundries and manufactories had increased many fold her manual force by mechanical contrivance, was poor in men. The complaint of Goldsmith, made in the "Deserted Village," in 1770, was still fresh in the ears of his countrymen, and his sigh of regret over the time

> —"Ere England's griefs began,
> When every rood of ground maintained its man,"

had been wafted across the Atlantic to those of a race who knew no such sorrow. In the land struggles of the Continental powers, where men were abundant and the material of war was scarce, the wealth and resources of Great Britain had always turned the scale, and on the sea she had proclaimed a policy of exclusion and imperial assumption which, since the defeat of the Dutch fleet, had never received more than temporary check. But the contest with the colonies was to be of man to man with a race to whom the very struggles for mastery of the continent with the old enemy, France, had taught the secrets of military science. In this contest no ingenuity or contrivance could make up for numerical inferiority, nor could the British Government hope for any serious advantage from local divisions or dissensions. With but few inconsiderable exceptions the colonists were of one mind, and though there were many, particularly in New York, of direct or near English descent, who were unwilling to take up arms against their immediate kindred, yet their secret sympathies were all with their old companions and friends. The American spirit was already strong. The king had said, "the test of the colonies is submission." But the colonies had been founded by men who would not submit to arbitrary rule, whether priestly or regal. The first act of repression crystallized resistance, and consolidated hesitating opinions into firm and set resolve.

It was the misfortune of New York, to whose sagacity and inflexible resolve the union of the colonies was chiefly due, that she should be, from her position of natural and central advantage, the seat of hostile occupation. The American leaders foreseeing, if not informed of the strategy of the enemy, had failed in their first efforts to thwart its accomplishment.

The attack upon Quebec had been repulsed, and the St. Lawrence lay open from its mouth to the Lakes. The line of the Hudson became now of the utmost importance, and while the northern army was slowly gathering for its defence, Washington moved from the eastward to New York, to cover the city and prevent the landing of Lord Howe. His efforts were fruitless; on the 22d August, 1776, the British troops were safely landed on Long Island, under the guns of the fleet, and Washington, defeated in a disastrous battle on the 27th, retreated across the river and prepared for the abandonment of the city.

It is hardly possible for those who have never personally witnessed the capture of a great city to realize the anxiety and gloom which fall upon the unfortunate population—an anxiety and gloom to which civil war adds double horrors. The result of the battle of Long Island filled New York with alarm, the apprehensions of the citizens being heightened by the memory of their struggles in the past with the royal troops, who had many a discomfiture to avenge. Numbers hastily followed the retreating army, including many sick and helpless, for whom Gen. Washington had provided with humane foresight.

On the 15th of September, 1776, the British troops took possession of the city, and in their train were refugees from all sections. Later, traders and speculators came in hordes by every transport fleet from Great Britain, and a large business sprung up in the purchase and sale of army supplies, but the city itself found no profit in this abnormal traffic. Its legitimate occupation as the outlet and inlet of product and supplies for a large section of country entirely disappeared, and its merchants, one by one, gave way to hucksters and petty traders whose interest was limited by and dependent upon the British occupation. The streets and buildings were allowed to go to decay, with the exception of temporary repairs for sanitary reasons, and the glories of the once thriving city were but a story of the past. Two terrible conflagrations added to the measure of distress and ruin. Hardly had the British troops taken possession ere (on the 21st of

September, 1776) a disastrous fire, breaking out in a small wooden house on the wharf near Whitehall, occupied by dissolute characters, spread to the northward, and consumed the entire city westward of Broadway to the very northernmost limit. In this terrible calamity, which owed its extent to the desertion of the city and the terror of the few remaining inhabitants, 493 houses were destroyed, including old Trinity and the Lutheran Church. Another destructive fire broke out on Cruger's wharf on the 3d of August, 1778, and burned about 54 houses.

At last the fortune of war changed. The thunder of the American artillery at Saratoga, where the sons of New York were in full force on her own battle-field, and at Yorktown, where the same gallant corps vied in friendly and not unequal rivalry with the trained officers of France, had cleared the sky, and beneath the smoke of battle peace was dawning in the near horizon. On the 24th of March, 1783, Robert R. Livingston, the Secretary of Foreign Affairs, notified Washington, then at West Point, of the agreeable intelligence of a general peace, and on the 9th of April following, at 12 o'clock, peace was proclaimed from the steps of the City Hall by the Town Major. The patriots were in glee, the English occupants and their friends in alarm. Oliver de Lancey, the Adjutant-General of the Royal army, issued a proclamation a few days later, offering transportation to all those who wished to withdraw from the city, and measures were taken to establish a refugee colony in Nova Scotia. During the summer there was a constant departure by the fleets, and the Whigs began to pour into the city and take possession of their deserted homes and estates. Feeling ran high, and the remaining loyalists awaited in terror the hour when the final withdrawal of the British forces should leave them helpless at the mercy of the irritated patriots. The prudent foresight of Gen. Washington, counselling "moderation and steady behavior," and the wise precautions of Gov. Clinton, happily arrested any disposition to excess, and in this they were nobly seconded by the Whig leaders, who at the meeting to prepare for the reception of the American troops, after a signification of their opinion of those who had remained in the city during the British occupation, by a request that any such withdraw from the room, pledged themselves to "prevent any confusion that may arise on and after the day of evacuation." On the 25th day of November the American army, under the command of Major-Gen. Henry Knox, marched from Harlem to the Bowery lane, where they remained until 1 o'clock, when, the British posts being withdrawn, the American column marched in and took possession of the city. Nothing could have been more grateful to New York than this disposition, for in Knox's artillery command was the favorite regiment, commanded by Col. John Lamb, and officered by men who like himself were of the earlier Patriots and Sons of Liberty. The new era began upon this day; henceforth New York is to move on her marvellous career. Stripped of everything, her streets in decay, her halls in dilapidation, her churches burned, desecrated, or abused, whole sections charred and blackened ruins, her shops empty—the retiring tradesmen having conveyed away their goods as well as their profits—her tenements vacant, her citizens in poverty and rags; a city of desolation; yet like the athlete who has thrown aside every external trapping, and stands stripped to the loins for the contest which is to strain every nerve and draw each muscle to the utmost tension, a contest of which fame, and wealth, and honor are the reward, she is the stronger for her nakedness. In a few years she appears reorganized, rebuilt, with new architecture, new institutions, *facile princeps* the imperial city of the continent.

Though New York had suffered the change in its physical surface and interior life, which is in every city the result of foreign hostile occupation, varying its purpose and pursuits, diverting its channels of industry, and disturbing its social organization, the limits of the city itself were the same in 1783 as on the outbreak of war in 1775. The area of the city at this time may be described as comprised within a line drawn from the North River at the foot of Reade street across the island in an easterly direction to the East River at the foot of Catharine street. Within this surface, which was divided into six wards, known from the time of the charter granted by Gov. Montgomerie in 1730 as the West, South, Dock, East, North, and Montgomerie Wards, was the principal seat of population; beyond, on a part of what was called the Out Ward, was an irregular parallelogram, with Division street as a base, extending easterly as far as Norfolk, and northerly to Hester, through which ran the Old Bowery Lane to Kingsbridge—a total surface averaging about three-fourths of a mile in width, and embraced within a circumference of about four miles. Broadway was then, as now, the ridge or back-bone of the lower end of the island. From it the land fell in easy slope to the East River, but to the westward a steep embankment, with occasional breaks, separated it from the Hudson, presenting an appearance from the river not unlike that of the Brooklyn Highlands within our own memory.

The water line on the East River, where the greater part of the shipping lay at this period, and a great depth of water was found at every pier, extended from Whitehall to the ship-yards at the foot of Catharine street, a distance of one and a half miles, passing in its easterly course Coenties slip, or the Albany Basins; the Great Dock at the foot of Broad street; Cruger's Wharf, a broad land projection on the line of present Front street, with extending piers, and Burnet's Key on the line of Water street; and running with numerous other irregularities, and intersecting piers and slips, of which Coffee-House slip and its extension, Murray's Wharf, at the foot of Wall street, and Burling's, Beekman's, and Peck slips were the most important. From the Fly Market, at the foot of Maiden lane, a ferry communicated with Long Island. On the water-line of the Hudson, extending from the Battery to the foot of Reade street, one and a half miles, there were no wharves below Little Queen (now Cedar) street, and but few and inconsiderable structures above, as far as Murray street. From the rear of the houses on Broadway gardens were laid out on the slope, which ended in a sandy beach. Mr. Duer relates in his interesting sketch of old New York, that his mother was wont, in her youth, to amuse her-

self fishing from a summer-house or garden-wall overhanging the water in the rear of one of these Broadway houses. Cortlandt street was the principal street, cut through the green embankment; at its foot were the Bear (now Washington) Market, and the ferry to Powles Hook (now Jersey City), then as now the thoroughfare to the Jerseys. There was a third ferry from Scotch Johnnie's tavern at Whitehall to Staten Island.

The streets were irregular and of great diversity, the better houses being built of brick, after the English manner, except that the roofs were tiled. They were mostly painted. Water and Queen (now Pearl) streets were low and narrow, with insufficient sidewalks, in some parts with none. They were the chief business streets. Broad street, which extended from the Exchange at the water side to the City Hall, on the corner of Wall street, was the main avenue, a street of sufficient width and well inhabited. Wall street was a wide and elevated street, and the buildings in it large and elegant. The upper part, toward Broadway, was a fashionable residence, the lower end exclusively given up to stores, auctioneers' rooms, and offices, here and there interspersed with lodging-houses. Broadway was already beginning to be thought the most agreeable and convenient part of the city, being unincumbered by traffic, and from its high situation free from the nuisances with which the imperfect system of drainage afflicted the streets near the East River. Beginning at the Bowling Green, there were buildings as far as St. Paul's Church. The lower end facing the green was a favorite residence. The street numbers began here. No. 1 was the Kennedy mansion. On the corner of Stone street (now Thames street) was the famous tavern, afterwards replaced by the City Hotel. The great fire stopped with the destruction of Trinity Church, and spared the buildings to the northward on the front of the street. There were only two brick houses at the upper end of Broadway opposite St. Paul's, both of which have now disappeared. They later made part of the Arden estate, and one of them was for a long period occupied by the Chemical Bank, and, with its neighbor, is now the site of the Park Bank building. On the opposite side of Vesey street there stood on the corner a building of two stories. A sign-board affixed upon it bore the inscription "Road to Albany," while on the opposite corner, on the house which has been replaced first by the American Museum, and since by The New York Herald building, a similar board pointed the traveller the "Road to Boston," through Chatham street, which ran as far as the Fresh Water, a street so called after the great Earl, who for so long stood first in the affection of the Colonies for his manly support of American rights and liberties. Thence the Boston Road ran through the Old Bowery lane to a point (present corner of Broadway and Twenty-third street) where it forked, and took the direction to King's Bridge, which it crossed.

Beyond lay the open space known as the Commons or Fields, and later as the City Park—a spot celebrated as the scene of many a public gathering during the colonial days. Here was held the great popular meeting on the evening of Friday, the 1st of November, 1765, which protested against the Stamp Act, burned the lieutenant-governor in effigy, and here also rallied the "prodigious concourse of people," as the journals of the day termed the armed multitude which, on the 5th of November, marched upon the fort and compelled the royal authorities to surrender the obnoxious instruments into the hands of the popular representative, the mayor of the city. On the western border of the Fields, opposite to what is now known as No. 252 Broadway, between Warren and Murray streets, and nearly opposite the latter, was planted the famous liberty pole about which many struggles took place between the British soldiery and the people. The fourth pole was planted here on the 19th of March, 1767, and a flag flung to the winds with the motto of "King, Pitt, and Liberty," which was maintained with many vicissitudes until the British occupation. This was the rally-point of the Sons of Liberty, an organization originated in the Stamp Act period, and revived, in November, 1773, to prevent the landing of the tea from the ships of the East India Company, which were announced as on the way; this was also the scene of the great popular rising known as the "Great Meeting in the Fields," on the 5th of July, 1774, at which the youthful Hamilton, then a student at King's College, is said to have made his first appearance in public life. When Washington occupied the city, a part of the troops were quartered on the Commons, and here the Declaration of Independence was proclaimed and read to the army on the 9th of July, 1776. Later, on the entry of the British, the liberty pole was cut down, and the Commons became a scene of imprisonment and torture as the site of the new jail, the building now known as the Hall of Records.

Above the line of the Commons, on the west side of Broadway and north of Reade street, built upon the grounds of the old Ranelagh Garden, was the New York Hospital, extending from what is now known as Duane to Worth street, and opposite to Pearl street, where was then a broad green. Upon this beautiful site a building was begun by private subscription, the corner-stone of which was laid by Governor Tryon in 1773. It was hardly completed when in February, 1775, it was nearly destroyed by fire. During the war it was occupied in an unfinished condition as a military hospital by each army. Later completed, the New York Hospital was long a model of admirable curative art, but like other landmarks of the city, gave way in 1869 to the march of population, and has lost something of its old prestige. To the northward of the hospital grounds stood the Ranelagh House and Gardens, a summer resort. Beyond were farms and country residences, and to the westward the Church farm, the property of the already wealthy corporation of Trinity Church.

The only other open space in the city proper which served as a park was the ancient Bowling Green, sometimes called the Royal Bowling Green. This little green, now hardly noticeable save as one of the few open spots which has been left for public uses in the lower part of the city, was in the days of Dutch rule one of the most conspicuous features of the town. It was then part of the spacious green in front of the fort, where a market was daily and fairs occasionally held; here the Train bands made their usual parade. In March, 1753, the corporation leased the ground to some of the inhabitants of Broadway, "to be enclosed as a Bowling Green, with walks therein for the beauty and ornament of the street," and it has since been known by this name.

In the centre of this green, on a white marble pedestal fifteen feet high, stood the equestrian statue of George III., erected by the Assembly, Thursday, the 16th of September, 1770, the anniversary of the birthday of Prince Frederick, second child of George III. This statue is described as made of metal, richly gilt, and the workmanship of the celebrated statuary, Mr. Wilton, of London. The same artist made a statue of George III. for the Royal Exchange of London. The erection in the Bowling Green was the occasion of a grand public display, the members of the Colonial and City Governments, the Corporations of the Chamber of Commerce and Marine Society, and the officers of the army and navy, waiting upon the Lieutenant-Governor at the fort near by, where toasts were drunk to the accompaniment of military music and artillery. To protect it the corporation in 1771 built an iron railing around the green at a cost of £800. The statue stood upon the green in all its gilded glory, the object of loyal admiration and patriot contumely until the evening of the 9th of July, 1776, when, after the hearing of the Proclamation of Independence, it was overthrown by the soldiery, an act of vandalism for which they received the rebuke of Gen. Washington in general orders the next morning. This was another instance of that disposition for destruction which unfortunately is not confined to the excited populace, but is shared by deliberative bodies. But too often the first act of a new order of government is the overthrow and ruin of even the artistic emblems of the old. The mutilated statue, the material of which was lead, is said to have been taken to Litchfield, Conn., and run into bullets for the use of the American army. Fragments of it still exist, one in the possession of this Society, and a bullet-mould to which a similar romantic story is attached. The slab on which the statue rested was taken to Powles

Hook in 1783, and was used as a memorial stone for the grave of Major John Smith, of the 42d Highland regiment. Later it served as a door-step for the residence of Mr. Cornelius Van Vorst in Jersey City, and has now a resting-place in the vestibule of this Society. The marks of the hoofs are still visible. The pedestal remained for some years in its original position, but was removed when the green was remodelled. It is to be regretted that there is no discrimination in these acts of barbarism. No complaint would be made by the present generation if some modern iconoclasts should destroy the hideous objects which now disgrace our public places, and are even invading the National capital, *proh pudor*, in the name of art.

At the intersection of Wall and Smith (now William street) stood the pedestrian statue erected to William Pitt " for the services he rendered America in promoting the repeal of the Stamp Act "—a peaceful victory as dear to the Colonies as ever conquest celebrated by triumphal pageant or memorial arches in the streets of ancient Rome. The statue is described in the journals of the day as of " fine white marble, the habit Roman, the right hand holds a scroll partly open, whereupon we read, Articuli Magna-Charta Libertatum ; the left hand is extended, the figure being in the attitude of one delivering an oration." On the south side of the pedestal there was a Latin inscription, cut on a tablet of white marble. This statue (like that of George III., the workmanship of Wilton) was erected on the 7th September, 1770, by the Assembly of the Colony, " amid the acclamations of a great number of the inhabitants, and in compliance with a request of a public meeting of the citizens held 23d June, 1766," when the news of the repeal of the Stamp Act reached the city. This statue stood in its original position until 1787, when it was removed by city ordinance on the " petition of a majority of the Proprietors of the Lots of Ground in Wall street, as an obstruction to the city." It was then a deformity, having been beheaded and otherwise disfigured in 1776, during the British occupation. It lay for many years in the corporation yard, then in that of the arsenal, after which it stood for a long period in front of Riley's Museum, or Fifth Ward Hotel, corner of West Broadway and Franklin street. It was later purchased by Mr. Samuel F. Mackie, one of our members, and by him presented to this Society, in the refectory of which it may now be seen. It is hoped that some liberal member will restore it to its original beauty, as its counterpart, which may serve as a model, is still in existence in Charleston.

The ground in front of the Trinity Cemetery was at this time, and for many years after the Revolution, the fashionable promenade, and was known as the "Church Walk," and the Mall. During the war seats were arranged for the public, and music was given every evening by military bands, while the army officers and such city belles as "loved the military" paraded up and down in pleasant discourse. In the present day, when the rights of the sexes are matters of discussion by the indignant of both in the public prints, it is amusing to notice a protest from a British officer in The Royal Gazette, 1780, against the "want of politeness and decorum in the masculine gender" in monopolizing the seats in the Mall. He remarks, with sense and sensibility, in the elegant language of the day, "that this must be very disagreeable to the fair sex in general, whose tender, delicate limbs may be tired with the fatigue of walking and being denied a seat to rest them." The Central Park to-day repeats in its broad and beautiful Mall and adjacent musicstand these features of the life of the city a century ago.

The public buildings were not striking either for size or beauty. The City Hall, which stood at the head of Broad street, where the elegant white marble structure occupied by the United States Treasury Department now stands, was a three-story brick building with wings. The ground floor was open as a thoroughfare. The site of the building was laid in the year 1700, on a bastion and line of stone fortifications which extended across the northern boundary of the city from the East to the Hudson River, whence the name of Wall street is derived. First occupied by the Common Council in 1703, the edifice was for a long time the most magnificent in the city, and was frequently improved and embellished until the Revolutionary War. While in possession of the British it was occupied by the main guard, and, escaping the ravages of the enemy, remained entire, although much injured, until the evacuation in 1783. The Legislature of the State and the courts met here after the war. The city bell was here. A curious notice in The New York Packet of 1784 warned the inhabitants "not to be alarmed by the ringing of the court bell;" and informed them that "the said bell will be rung daily, at a quarter before ten o'clock in the forenoon, for the meeting of the Legislature," and other papers were requested to copy. It was renovated in 1784, and extensive additions made in the rear, for the use of the Congress, which had adjourned to New York from Philadelphia; in the spring of 1789 the first Congress under the new Constitution met in the new edifice, which took the name of Federal Hall; and here it was that on the 3d of April, 1789, George Washington was inaugurated the first President. The building was demolished in 1812.

The Exchange, at one time called the Royal Exchange, at the foot of Broad street, below the intersection of Dock (now Pearl street), was a building raised upon arches in the middle of the street. Built upon or near the site of a structure which had served as a market-house as well as meeting-place of merchants, from the beginning of the century, it was sometimes called the New Exchange. A subscription was made by the merchants, in 1752, for its erection, but it was assumed and finally completed by the city corporation. At times its lower arch-covered surface seems to have been inclosed. Above the arches was a large hall sixty feet by thirty, with walls fourteen feet high, arching to a height of twenty feet, surmounted by a cupola. It was provided with a stove, then a modern invention, and a clock. In 1754, the lower story was used as a coffee-house, and the room above as a ballroom. The Chamber of Commerce hired and repaired it in 1769, and occupied it until their sessions were interrupted by the breaking out of hostilities in 1775. During the war it was used by the British as a market. When the City Hall was undergoing repairs after the peace, the State Legislature and courts of justice held their sessions here. In 1795 it passed into the hands of the Tammany Society for use as a museum, and was so used under the direction of the eccentric Gardner Baker. In 1799, in consequence of numerous complaints, the city authorities ordered it to be taken down and removed. At the time of its erection, the streets in its neighborhood had been greatly improved, and the commerce of the city for a few years gathered about it, but it gradually lost its prestige from the nuisances which were allowed to accumulate about the water edge near by. Then, as now, the system of sewerage was a crying disgrace to the city, and the river banks had become intolerable nuisances. Comparing English and American cities with those of Continental Europe, the thought forces itself upon the mind that the Anglo-Saxon race, neat as it may be in personal habits, has no special " vocation " for public cleanliness.

At the south-west point of the island stood the Fort in a square with four bastions, facing the Bowling Green ; within it a building which was the residence of the colonial governors until destroyed by fire in December, 1773. The Fort itself was removed in 1790, to make way for the Government House erected for the use of the State Government. Below the Fort, on the water line, were fortifications of considerable extent. A stone battery was laid here by Governor Cosby, in 1735, and called after his son-in-law, the " George Augustus Royal Battery." Hence the name of the Battery, which was before and for many years after the war, in the summer season, a delightful promenade, cooled by the sea breeze, and presenting a bay view unparalleled in beauty and extent. It is not improbable that this charming spot may again become a favorite residence. The other public buildings were the new jail called the " Provost " during the war, and " The Bridewell," both in the fields now the City Park.

Of the three Episcopal churches founded under one royal charter in 1697, Old Trinity, the most stately edifice in America, had fallen a victim to the terrible fire which swept the city after the British entry in 1776. St. George's Chapel, finished in 1750, stood in Beekman street. It was destroyed by fire in 1814, again rebuilt, and finally taken down in 1868. St. Paul's Chapel, on the corner of Broadway and Vesey street, completed in 1766, is the finest relic of colonial architecture, and for beauty of design is not excelled by any later structures. Its elegant and graceful spire was added in 1794.

There were three houses of worship belonging to the Presbyterians. The First Presbyterian, or Wall Street Church, a modest building of rough stone, stood at the upper end of Wall street, near Broadway. It was originally erected in 1719, enlarged in 1768, rebuilt in 1809, and finally removed in 1844, and reconstructed in Jersey City. The second or Brick Meeting-house, a branch of the Wall Street Church, was built, in 1768, on the Vineyard lot opposite the Common, rebuilt in 1797, and was demolished in consequence of the widening of Beekman street. The present New York Times building occupies its site. The last service was held here in May, 1856. This was for a long time, with the exception of a few small wooden houses, the only building on Chatham row. The third or Second Presbyterian church was built in 1768, in Little Queen (now Cedar street), between Nassau and Broadway. This congregation originated about the year 1756, in a separation of the Scottish members from the Wall Street Church, in consequence of changes in the form of worship and a difference of opinion as to psalmody. All these three churches were occupied by the British troops as hospitals and barracks, and were left behind them in ruins and dilapidation.

There were three Dutch Reformed churches. The Old South, or Garden Street Church, which stood in the present Exchange place, was built in 1693, rebuilt in 1766, again in 1807, and was destroyed by the great fire in 1835. The New or Middle Church, built in 1729, and remodelled in 1764, still remains. From its cupola one of the best views of the city and surrounding country was to be seen. It was here that Dr. Franklin made some of his experiments in electricity. Indeed the only steeples high enough to be seen to advantage, after the destruction of Trinity, were those of this church and St. George's Chapel. During the occupation it was used by the British as a riding school for dragoons. Public worship ceased in it in 1844, when it was sold to the United States Government, the merchants of New York contributing to its purchase by subscription, for the use of the Post-Office Department. It has been this fall abandoned, and is now being demolished. The North Dutch Church was erected in 1769, on the corner of Fulton and William streets, remodelled in 1842, and has been this year taken down. It had become famous, in latter years, as the seat of the Fulton street prayer-meetings.

The Methodists erected a church in John street in 1768, which is still standing on the south side of the street, near Nassau. The Moravians began their worship in a small frame building which they put up in Fulton street, between William and Dutch streets, in 1751. The old house was taken down and rebuilt in 1829, and finally removed in 1843. The Baptists had their place of worship in Gold street, between Fulton and John streets, in a small building erected by them in 1760. It was rebuilt in 1802, and finally taken down in 1840. The Friends, who had occupied a modest structure in Little Green street (now Liberty place), a small street running from Maiden lane to Crown (now Liberty street), from the early part of the century, in 1775 built a second house of brick in Pearl street, between Franklin square and Oak street, which was taken down in 1824. In 1794 the old building was destroyed and a new one erected, fronting on Liberty street. This continued to be used as a meeting-house until 1826, when it passed into the hands of Mr. Grant Thorburn, who occupied it as a seed store for many years. The French congregation, L'Eglise du Saint Esprit (Church of the Holy Ghost), which had existed from an early day, in 1704 erected a building, which was long the oldest of the New York churches, in Pine street, fronting the rear of the present United States Sub-Treasury, with a burial ground running back as far as Cedar street. Here the descendants of the French Huguenots continued their worship, according to the tenets of the old faith, for 130 years. The building was "low, grave and sombre, and its tower heavy and monastic." The Jewish house of worship was built in Mill street, about 1706. This was taken down, and the first Synagogue erected on the same site in 1729. This building, in turn, was rebuilt in 1818, and occupied till 1833, when the property was sold, and the congregation removed. The first Roman Catholic public worship was held at the Vaux Hall, at the foot of Warren street; this was the origin of St. Peter's Church in Barclay street, built in 1786. The corner-stone was laid by the Spanish ambassador, Don Diego de Gardoqui, and the building fund contributed to by both the Spanish and French official representatives. It was later rebuilt.

Education had not as yet been considered a matter for legislative interference. It was held, indeed, to be a matter with which the Government had no right to interfere, and was chiefly in the hands of the clergy. Early in the history of the Dutch colony teaching in Latin had been fostered by the Government. In 1710 the first free school was opened by Trinity Church, under the teaching of William Huddlestone. In 1754 King's College was established, and a year later the Dutch, tenacious of their old language, imported a schoolmaster for instruction in the Dutch language. During the seven years of war these schools and the college were closed. The first to reopen was the Dutch, many months before the evacuation by the British. King's College (now Columbia) occupied the beautiful square, well remembered, bounded by Church, Chapel (now West Broadway), Murray and Mortlike (now Barclay street). This was an elegant stone structure three stories high, with a chapel, hall, library, museum, anatomical theatre, and school for experimental philosophy. The edifice was surrounded by a high fence, which also inclosed a large court and garden. The students resided in the building. The fire of 1776 burned all the houses west of Broadway up to this limit.

There were no public collections of art in the city before 1800; a few occasional portraits, but of a low order of merit. An example may be seen in the portrait of Lieut.-Gov. Cadwallader Colden, painted for the Chamber of Commerce by

Matthew Pratt, a picture 46 × 78, for which the artist received £37.

In the year 1791, Mr. Archibald Robertson, an artist, organized "The Columbian Academy of Painting," but this was a private institution. In 1801, the American Academy of Fine Arts was organized under the advice of Robert R. Livingston, then Minister to France, with the active co-operation of Aaron Burr. It opened its rooms with numerous donations, prominent among which were several gifts from the Emperor Napoleon, and in 1808 was incorporated, with Edward Livingston as President. It ceased to exist in 1841, and its valuable collection is scattered.

The theatre was on the north side of John street, about half-way between Broadway and Nassau street. The building stood, as described by Mr. Duer, about sixty feet back from the street, and was entered by a covered way. It was opened on the 7th of December, 1767, by "The American Company," with Farquhar's comedy of the "Stratagem," and Garrick's farce or dramatic satire, "Lethe." A curious incident is connected with the history of the theatre at this period. Some Cherokee warriors arrived in the city from South Carolina with Capt. Schermerhorne, among whom were Attakullakulla, or the Little Carpenter; Ocounostola, or the Great Warrior; and the Raven King of Tougooloo, who expressed a desire to see the performance of the 14th, which was the play of Richard III., not the most appropriate entertainment, certainly, for the instruction of savage chiefs. Attakullakulla was a noted Cherokee chief. He had visited England and signed the treaty of peace at Westminster, in 1730. The general depression which resulted from the sullen but as yet peaceful struggle of the colonies with the home Government, brought theatrical exhibitions to a close, and no entertainments were given after Aug. 2, 1773. On the 24th of December, 1774, the Provincial Congress passed a resolution recommending the suspension of all public amusements, and no further performances were given. When the British held the city, amateurs reopened the John Street Theatre under the name of "Theatre Royal," and plays were given from January, 1777, to June,

1781, the receipts being for the benefit of the poor of the city. It was here that the accomplished and unfortunate Major André distinguished himself both as an actor and scene painter. After the peace, in spite of strong public sentiment, which took shape in articles in the newspapers and speeches in the Legislature, the theatre was reopened on the 24th of August, 1785, with a prologue and pantomime, which continued until Oct. 14 of the same year. The legitimate drama was not resumed till the 21st of November, 1785. The last performance in the John Street Theatre was "Wives As They Were and Maids As They Are," on the 12th of January, 1798. The New, or Park Theatre, which stood in Park row, near Ann street, was opened on the 29th of January of the same year.

The principal tavern was the City Arms, a large house on the west side of Broadway, at the corner of Stone, now Thames street. This famous house was a part of the Delancey estate, and until 1754 was the residence of James De Lancey, the Lieutenant-Governor of the colony. On the 15th April of that year it was opened as a tavern by Edward Willet, a noted host, under the name of the Province Arms. In the newspapers of the day it is sometimes called the New York Arms, the York Arms, the City Arms, or, as was often the case, by the name of the proprietor. Willet's opening notice describes the house "as not only the best accommodated with stables and all things necessary to the entertainment of travellers, but the best situated of any house in that business in this city, being nearest the centre; and in a direct line with the eastern road, and very handy for both the North River, Staten Island, and Long Island Ferries." The New York tavern-keepers were in the colonial days an itinerant class, and moved from house to house with the regularity of lawyers on a circuit. Crawley, Burns, Bolton, and Hull all kept it in turn. It was here, while in the keeping of Burns, that the famous non-importation agreement was signed the 31st October, 1765, by the merchants of the city. Burns succeeded Crawley in 1763. John Adams, delegate to the first Continental Congress, stopped here on his way to Philadelphia in 1774. During the earlier part of the war it was kept by Hicks, who seems to have been displaced in an arbitrary manner in 1781, to make way for Roubalet. It was a favorite resort of the military, on account of its proximity to the fashionable promenade. On its piazzas and balconies were "coigns of vantage" for the review of the loyalist belles "walking down Broadway." Later it passed into the hands of John Cape, and was called the "State Arms of New York" (No. 18 Broadway), in his advertisements of May 31, 1784. The house was provided with a large ball-room, where concerts were given and dancing assemblies held. These assemblies were subscription balls under the direction of managers. They were renewed immediately after the war. The first was held on the evening of Thursday, the 18th of December, 1783, at 6 o'clock. Rivington, the editor of the newspaper which advertised this ball, announced in the same paper that he had "for sale a supply of white dancing gloves for gentlemen, silk stockings, dress-swords, and elegant London cocked hats." As he was a loyalist, this was probably the stock of the outgoing officers of the British army. Cape does not appear to have met with success in his venture. In 1786 Joseph Corre, a Frenchman by birth, took the house, and in 1788 he, in turn, made way for the veteran Edward Barden, who had returned to the city from Jamaica, Long Island, where he kept the inn opposite the Episcopal Church. Broadway was already the favorite street, and the old tavern became the chosen spot for the meetings of societies and great public entertainments, and acquired a popularity which it uninterruptedly maintained for a long period. In 1793 the old building, which was still owned by the De Lancey family, was taken down, and the Tontine City Tavern or City Hotel, erected by a company who organized for its purchase on the Tontine plan. The City Hotel has been taken down within our recollection.

There was another tavern largely patronized by the officers of the British army and navy, on Brownejohn's Wharf, at the Fly Market, as it was called. This was kept by James Strachan until 1781, when he changed his quarters. Not far distant, in Water street, Ephraim Smith kept a house known by his name—Smith's Tavern. He had previously kept a tavern under the same sign in Philadelphia. The Bull's Head was in the Bowery lane. But of all, the most famous for its historic associations was the house on the south-east corner of Broad and Dock (now Pearl street), which is still standing. It was built in the early part of the last century, by the De Lancey family, on land conveyed by Col. Stephanus Van Cortlandt to Estienne de Lancey, his son-in-law, in 1700. It was for some time occupied as a residence by Col. Joseph Robinson; then by Delancey, Robinson & Co. as a store, and later passed by sale into the hands of Sam Fraunces, the most noted publican of the day (later the steward of General Washington's household), who here opened a tavern in 1762, under the sign of Queen Charlotte. This was in honor of the charming and popular queen of George III., who had already, although only in her eighteenth year, earned the name of "The Good Queen Charlotte." A record of the interesting incidents connected with this old house would fill a volume. The Chamber of Commerce organized here in 1768; the clubs and societies often met at its hospitable board. This was the building which was struck by the shot upon the city by the "Asia" man-of-war, but it is most dear to the heart of the patriot as the spot where, at a dinner given to him on the 4th of December, 1783, Gen. Washington bade a touching and affectionate farewell to his officers. Before the war it was known as the Queen's Head; later, as Fraunces's Tavern. It is now kept as a lodging-house by W. Stübner, under the sign of Washington's Headquarters, in memory of the incident related.

On the new road, a continuation of Broadway, there were several mead-houses and tea-gardens, and opposite the Park, where Peale's Museum stood later, was the celebrated garden and public house of de la Montagne, where the Liberty Boys had their rendezvous. The Liberty Pole was near by. The Vauxhall was a large garden at the foot of Warren street, extending as far as Chambers street, overlooking the Hudson, and commanding a beautiful view. This had been the residence of Major James of Stamp Act memory, and had later passed into the hands of the enterprising Fraunces.

Besides these, there were billiard tables at de la Montagne's, in the fields, and near by Walker's Fives Alley, about the corner of Murray street, where Sir Henry Clinton was wont to play with his officers. There was also a Fives alley in John street, near the theatre. In summer the ladies visited the tea-gardens, but then, as now, the men at times preferred to enjoy themselves without the restraining influence of the fair sex.

Before the war, coffee-houses, kept on the English plan, were places of great resort. A notice of a Coffee-House appears on the Assembly Journal of 1705, and occasional mentions of it occur until 1737, when the Exchange Coffee-House is noticed in an advertisement in Bradford's Gazette. A few years later (1744) one appears of "The Merchants' Coffee-House," which stood on the south-east corner of Wall and Water streets, on the site later occupied by The Journal of Commerce. Coffee-House slip and Coffee-House bridge, which occupied the centre of Wall street, running from Queen (now Pearl) to Water street, derived their names from their proximity to this Coffee-House. The Bridge was the place where the "vendues," as auctions were then called, were held. A notice in Parker's Post Boy of August 27, 1744, shows that this was the favorite resort of captains. It was for a long time kept by a Madame Ferrari, until a new building was erected on the opposite cross corner, when she removed to the new house. John Adams, recording his walk about the city in 1774, mentions a visit to the coffee-house, which he found full of gentlemen, and his reading of the newspapers there; but for some cause coffee-houses gradually declined toward the close of the colonial period, probably because of the depression in trade and general want of ease in the fortunes of the population, as the next year a long article appeared in Holt's New York Journal calling on the inhabitants to support these useful institutions, and complaining that those who did take advantage of their many conveniences, did not, as was the custom in England, do their part to the support of the house by ordering a cup of coffee, a glass of wine, etc. Cornelius Bradford opened the Merchants' Coffee-House after repairs in May, 1776, but his stay was of short duration. A warm patriot, he went out with the American army on its retreat, and remained near Rhinebeck during the war. It then passed into the hands of a Mrs. Smith, probably the person who kept the building next door, where the Insurance Office was. Later, James Strachan moved from the tavern on Brownejohn's wharf, and tried his fortune here, but without success, as appears from a piteous appeal to his debtors, March, 1783. In October of the same year, Cornelius Bradford returned, and the Merchants' Coffee-House under his admirable management became a noted resort. He established in 1784 the first Marine List ever publicly kept in New York, from which the newspaper notices were daily taken. He also opened a register where "gentlemen and merchants" were requested to enter their names and residences. This was the first approach to a city directory. The first directory was published by David Franks, in 1786, and contained the names and addresses of 933 persons. Trow's City Directory for 1875 contains 233,971 names. It must be observed, however, that the first of Franks was very incomplete. The Chamber of Commerce and the Marine Society entertained Congress at the Merchants' Coffee-House in February, 1784. Bradford died the next year, but the house remained in the keeping of his widow for some years, until the building of the famous Tontine Coffee-House, on the northwest corner of Wall and Water streets (the opposite cross angle), when the widow withdrew. The Merchants' Coffee-House was destroyed in the great fire of 1804, and rebuilt as the Phœnix Coffee-House the next year. The Tontine was projected on the 30th of March, 1791, by an assemblage of gentlemen who met at the Coffee-House, with John Broome, at that time President of the Chamber of Commerce, as chairman. The corner-stone was laid with ceremony on the 5th of June, 1792, and the building formally opened by a great public dinner, at which 120 gentlemen sat down, the 5th of June, the following year (1793). The Tontine became celebrated under the management of John Hyde, its first host. A letter on emigration, published in London by a "gentleman lately returned from America," recommends the house as having "as elegant accommodations as any in London," and as considered to be the best in the United States. He states the cost of living in a handsome apartment at £70 to £80 per annum, wine and porter excepted, and speaks of it as frequented by all genteel strangers and the superior gentlemen of the town. Hyde died of the yellow fever in 1805. During the war a Mrs. Treville kept the London Coffee-House at the Exchange.

Of the two private houses of note, the chief was the Kennedy Mansion, at No. 1 Broadway built for Capt. Archibald Kennedy of the British Navy, who had married a daughter of the wealthy colonial family of Watts. This house was the headquarters of Gen. Putnam in 1776, and afterward of the British commanders. The other famous dwelling was the Walton House, an edifice of Holland brick, 50 feet front, and three stories high, still standing, though shorn of its architectural ornaments, and known as No. 324 Pearl street. This old house was illuminated for the repeal of the Stamp Act in 1766.

Of the four sugar-houses three were in the hands of persons of Dutch descent, by whom this lucrative business was then as now almost monopolized. The old sugar-house in Crown street (now Liberty street, near the Dutch church), built by the Livingstons, is best known as the British prison during the Revolution. That built by Henry Cuyler, Jr., for his heir, Barent Rynders Cuyler, in 1769, is still standing, a massive structure on the corner of Rose and Duane streets. It later passed into the hands of the Rhinelanders, who continued the same business. The Van Cortland sugar-house was on the north-west corner of Trinity churchyard. The Roosevelts also had a sugar-house, in Skinners street, near the Walton House. The Bayard sugar-house, which stood in Wall street, close to the old City Hall, from 1729, had been in 1773 turned into a tobacco manufactory. The Bayards introduced what they termed the "mystery of sugar refining" in New York.

Water was supplied to the inhabitants from the Tea Water Pump. Kalm, in his account of New York in 1748, says: "There is no good water to be met with in the town itself, but at a little distance there is a large spring of good water which the inhabitants take for their *tea* and the uses of their kitchen:" hence the name which the spring and pump long retained. The Tea Waterworks, as they were called, stood in the Out Ward, on a lot 75 by 120, which made, in 1784, part of the estate of Gerardus Hardenbrook. This lot fronted on the Bowery road, at what was then the head of Queen (now Pearl street), now the west side of Chatham, nearly opposite Roosevelt street. It was said to receive its supply of water from never-failing springs, but in reality drew it from a pond not far distant, known as the Collect Pond or Fresh Water, which lay where the present Tombs building stands in Centre street. This pond had an outlet on the North river, through what was called the Canal, over which a stone bridge was erected on the line of Broadway, and another on that to the East river. The Collect was unfortunately filled up by the authorities of the city instead of being enlarged and made a water communication between the two rivers, a plan at one time proposed, which would have afforded excellent basin accommodation for river transports, and a safe winter harbor. Nature seems to have indicated this in her original design. The water still runs through the Canal street sewer. The well which supplied the famous Tea Water Pump was about twenty feet deep and four feet in diameter, and supplied an average daily drawing of from 14,000 to 15,000 gallons. In summer sometimes as many as 28,000 gallons were taken, yet the depth of water never fell below three feet. The water was sold at the pump at three pence the hogshead. In 1796 there was a rumor that the supply of water was failing, but it was immediately contradicted by the proprietor. At this time the water was sold at the pump at four cents the hogshead of 140 gallons. The water was carted through the streets and retailed from door to door. Two years later its reputation became bad, the Collect was reported as being "a shocking hole, where all impure things centre together." An article in The Daily Advertiser of September 6th, 1798, urged the citizens, "every man for himself, to leave no stone unturned to provide aqueducts."

As early as 1774 Christopher Colles, with his usual sagacity, had proposed to erect a reservoir and to convey water through the several streets, and with the aid of the corporation erected a steam pumping engine near the Collect, but the war caused an abandonment of this plan. This enterprise was completed in March, 1776. The newspapers describe the engine as carrying a pump eleven inches in diameter and six feet stroke, which lifted 417,600 gallons daily. There is a curious notice of these works in the journal of Dr. Isaac Bangs of the New England troops, who was quartered in the city in 1776. He describes the works as consisting of a reservoir on the top of a hill, from which wooden pipes distributed it through the city (the reservoir a quarter of an acre in extent). His astonishment was excited by the working of the machine which lifted the water through a wooden tube. With his native curiosity, however, he mastered the problem and gives a lucid description of the steam-engine. In 1799 the Manhattan Company was chartered to supply the city with water, and the Bronx river was proposed as the source of supply. A pump was built near the Collect and wooden pipes laid through the streets, and the inhabitants served with water for a long period. It was not until the completion, in 1842, of the Croton Aqueduct, that colossal and beneficent monument of New York enterprise, that there was assured to the population a never-failing supply of pure water, the first condition of prosperity and health, an enterprise so eloquently and prophetically described by the late John Romeyn Brodhead at the fortieth anniversary of this Society in 1844—"the stern and majestic ruins that frown over the desolate Campagna are not more impressive monuments to the Emperor Claudius than will the aqueduct of New York be an enduring memorial of the far-reaching philanthropy of those who projected and advocated this noble work."

Even before the Revolution the city provided itself with the purely American luxury, ice, the use of which is only at this late day becoming general in Europe by the example of American travellers. There were several ice-houses, all of which took their supply from the fresh water. The principal of these buildings was situated on the North River, near Trinity Churchyard.

The principal market was the Fly Market, so called from Vly, or valley, its site having been originally a salt meadow. It stood at the foot of Maiden lane, and was supplied, as New York has always been, with an endless variety of fish and shell-fish of the most delicious kind, and with meat, poultry and fruit—the latter in abundant profusion. The other markets of importance were the Bear Market, now Washington, on the west side of the city, between Greenwich street and the Hudson; the Oswego Market, which was built on the site of the old Broadway, in 1771, and stood in Maiden lane, between Broadway and Nassau street, until removed as a nuisance in 1810, when its stalls were transferred to the Bear Market. There was also a market at Peck slip, built in 1763, occupied as a storehouse by the British, again restored after the war, deserted when Catharine Market was built, in 1786, and finally removed in 1792. Still another was opened at the foot of Broad street, at the Exchange, on the petition of the inhabitants during the war, there being no other convenient to the population in this locality.

Besides the Trinity Church Cemetery, which was the city burying ground from an early period, and the graveyards attached to the churches, there was a Jewish cemetery at the corner of Oliver and Chatham streets, and a negro burying ground on the spot immediately north of the common now occupied by A. T. Stewart's dry-goods store.

Bradford's New York Gazette and Zenger's New York Weekly Journal, the one the organ of the Colonial Government, and the other of the Opposition party, make frequent mention of a club named the Hunc Over De, which met at the houses of four gentlemen, where lively discussions seem to have taken place. A letter of one Andrew Merrill to Zenger says, that "the members were merry enough; but they had like to have demolished the ladies' tea-table at whose house the club was. They had not much party till supper came, and then they were as warm as scollopt oysters." Politics ran high at this time, 1735-1736, when Colonel Lewis Morris, afterward Governor of New Jersey, and James De Lancey, later Lieutenant-Governor of New York, were struggling for the control of the province of New York.

A Whig Club was formed in 1752, which met once each week at the King's Arms Tavern. Of this William Livingston, William Smith and John Morin Scott, the Presbyterian leaders, were members and as they were not of the order of men who consent to take secondary places, no doubt the founders. The King's Arms Tavern was at this time in Broad street, opposite to the Royal Exchange, and kept by George Burns.

Before the war the Social Club met every Saturday evening in winter at Sam Fraunces' Tavern, and enjoyed themselves after the usual manner. In summer the members met at Kip's Bay, where they built a neat and comfortable house. It was at this point the British landed, September 15, 1776. The club dispersed at the time of the war, and never reassembled. An account of the club and a list of its members were found among the papers of Mr. John Moore, and presented to the New York Historical Society by his son, T. W. C. Moore. Among its members were John Jay, Gouverneur Morris, Robert R. Livingston, Egbert Benson, Gulian C. Verplanck, Morgan Lewis, the Ludlows, Watts, Lispenards, Bards and others. The lawyers had a club which they called the Moot, organized in 1770, where disputed points of law were formally debated. Such veteran lawyers as William Smith, John Morin Scott, Richard Morris, and among the younger, Samuel Jones, John Jay, R. R. Livingston, James Duane, Gouverneur Morris, and Peter Van Schaack, need only be named to show the character of the society. The Moot was held at Barden's Tavern, on the evening of the first Friday in every month. Barden's Tavern was in 1770 at the corner of Murray and Broadway.

After the war the Belvedere was organized by thirty-three gentlemen, and a building erected on the corner of Cherry and

Montgomery streets, in the year 1792. The club building comprised a ball-room with a music gallery, bar-rooms, and bedrooms, and had a large balcony from which there was a beautiful view of the East River and Long Island. Attached to the house were bowling-alleys, coach-houses, a green, with gravel walks and shrubbery, elegantly laid out and cared for. This was a celebrated club, and included such members as Babcock, Constable, Fish, McEvers, Kemble, Ludlow, Seton, Hoffman and Van Horne—all leaders of fashion and the beaux of the day. They met on Saturday nights, also evenings specially set apart for social gatherings, and the strangers in the city were generally invited guests. The Sub-Rosa was another club of thirty gentlemen, who met on Saturday evenings at a tavern kept by Rebecca Gere, at Corlears Hook. This dame bore the sobriquet in the club of "Our Hostess of the Garter." This club, organized in 1794, was essentially a dining club; no cards were allowed by the articles until two hours after dinner, and no discussions during or after dinner. Such men as Robert Lenox, Thomas Roach, Buchanan, Bayard, Winthrop, Henry Cruger, Walton, Gouverneur, Sherbrooke, and Laight composed this solid band of good livers. The minutes of their proceedings show that the proposal of an unfortunate member, that the bill of fare consist of cold beef or lamb, was voted down by the conclusive majority of eleven to three.

New York had always been celebrated for the elegance of its life. When, in Parliament, the poverty and exhaustion of the colonies after the French war was given as a reason why they should not be taxed, the " plea was rebutted by an appeal to the elegant entertainments given by the city of New York to the officers of the British army, and the dazzling display of silver plate at their dinners, equal, if not superior, to any nobleman's." John Adams, in his diary, constantly refers in terms of wonder to the luxury of life in the city, to the plate, the damask, and the choice luxury of the food. Even the butter did not escape his notice and his praise. He complains, however, that the gentlemen did not wait for him to finish his sentences before interrupting him with their remarks. The New Yorkers were then, as now, a mercurial people, a quality they derived from the large intermixture of foreign element in their blood, and perhaps John Adams was himself a little prosy and pompous. New England has always been declamatory.

Of the numerous foreign National Societies now in existence, only one was incorporated in the Colonial period, that of St. Andrew, which was instituted on the 19th November, 1756, as a society for charitable purposes, with Philip Livingston as president. The English, Welsh, and Irish born residents were in the habit of meeting at Sam Fraunces', Bolton's, Barden's, or Burns's Taverns, on their Saints' days of St. George, St. David, St. Patrick, and contributions were then made for the poor of their nationality. The St. George's Society was established in 1786; the St. Patrick's later.

The St. Tammany Society, or Independent Order of Liberty, was first organized in 1789. It announced itself as " a National Society, consists of Americans born who fill all offices, and adopted Americans who are eligible to the honorary posts of warrior and hunter. It is founded on the true principles of patriotism, and has for its motives charity and brotherly love." In 1792 its members formed a Tontine association, under the name of the New York Tammanial Tontine Association, to expire in May, 1820, whose primary object was stated to be " the building of a hall, with a view to accommodate the Tammany Society ; " but so far as a building was concerned the plan does not appear to have been successful. The Society was incorporated under the name of the " Society of Tammany, or Columbian Order," on the 9th April, 1805, for the purpose of affording relief to the indigent and distressed." It is needless to state how widely its practices have diverged from its original purpose, unless upon the principle that charity begins at home.

The Black Friars was a society established for social, charitable, and humane purposes, on the 10th November, 1784.

The Society of the Cincinnati was organized at the Cantonment of the American Army on Hudson River, May 10th, 1783, by the officers of the Army of the Revolution, as a

Society of Friends, with a provision that its future membership should be limited to their male posterity. The New York branch organized the 5th July following, at New Windsor; their annual meetings are always held in the city.

Besides these societies may be mentioned the Society for the Manumission of Slaves, and protecting such of them as have been or may be liberated, organized in February, 1785, with John Jay as president and John Keese as secretary. Their articles of association were published in Loudon's New York Packet of 21st February, 1785. The General Society of Mechanics and Tradesmen was originally designed in 1784, and appeared before the Legislature in application for a charter in the following year, failing which it was formally instituted on the 4th August, 1785. It obtained an act of incorporation March 14, 1792, which was renewed in 1810. This Society built the well known Mechanics' Hall, corner of Park place and Broadway, and is still in existence. A Society for the Promotion of Useful Knowledge was formed, of which George Clinton was President. This was a revival of the old New York Society, which was formed before the war for similar purposes. They met on the 13th July, 1785, at Cape's Tavern.

The first directory of 1786 makes mention also of a Gold and Silver Smiths' Society in existence in 1786, and of a Society of Peruke Makers and Hair Dressers, which met at Mr. Ketchum's, No. 22 Ann street, the same year. Hairdressing, when perukes and queues were in fashion, was a business of importance.

The physical, popular, and social features of New York, at the close of the colonial period, and during the war, have been presented. It only remains to give some account of the commerce of the city, to establish a basis for the comparison of New York as it was in 1776 with the New York of to-day.

The preparation of flour for export had always been a chief industry of the city and colony. An old document in the English records of 1698 speaks of "grain as the staple commoditie of the Province of New York," and adds that "the citizens had no sooner perceived that there were greater quantities of wheat raised than could be consumed within the said Province but they *contrived and invented the art of bolting*, by which they converted the wheat into flour, and made it a manufacture, not only profitable to all the inhabitants of this Province, by the encouragement of tillage and navigation, but likewise beneficial and commodious to all the plantations, and the improvement thereof is the true and only cause of the growth, strength and increase of buildings within the same, and of the riches, plenty of money, and rise of the value of lands in the other parts of the Province, and the livelihood of all the inhabitants of this city did chiefly depend thereon." The Minutes of the Common Council of 1692 record that the Supreme Court were of the opinion that the City of New York had the charter or privilege of bolting or packing flour. Gov. Andros prohibited the transportation of wheat " that the same might be improved by the inhabitants of this city in bolting it into flour, and to bake 'bisketts' for transportation." Of this privilege New York was deprived by Act of Assembly in 1694. The writer complains that the City of New York, which had been called the granary of America, where never less than 40,000 or 50 000 bushels of wheat were in store, suffered greatly in consequence of this legislation, and the supply fell off to scarce 1,000 bushels, insufficient for the supply of the inhabitants. The sketch closes with the remarkable statement that of the 983 houses then in New York, 600 depended upon "bolting;" while in the three counties of Kings, Queens, and Ulster, there were not over 30 "bolters." Notwithstanding the careful attention paid by the Assembly of the Colony to the inspection of flour, as its minutes abundantly show, and in fact compulsory inspection was not abolished until 1843 (April 18), both Pennsylvania and Maryland had excelled New York in this product, and the superfine flour of their manufacture commanded higher prices than that of New York. In 1768 New York exported 80,000 barrels of flour to the West Indies, and received in return rum, sugar, and molasses. Provisions also were exported to the Spanish Main, wheat, flour, Indian corn, and timber to Lisbon and Madeira—and before the Revolution the manufacture of pot and pearl ashes had become an important industry. There was also a considerable export of flaxseed to Ireland, in return for which linens were received. In addition to these there had been from the earliest history of the Colony a large and profitable trade in peltry. All Northern and Western New York was a fur-yielding country, and thousands of hunters traversed the great interior in pursuit of skins.

The old seal of the Province itself gives evidence of the importance of the two great interests of the Colony, the beaver and flour-barrel being both borne upon the arms. The beaver figured upon the seal of New Amsterdam from 1654; the flour-barrel was added after the English conquest in 1686. The fur trade had declined after the capture of the Canadas, but was again to revive with the new-born sympathy of the Canadians, French, and Indian half-breeds for the Americans. Already young Astor, who arrived here in 1784, was traversing the wilderness and organizing the vast trade which was the foundation of the colossal fortune which attracted universal notice a few days since as it passed, quintupled in magnitude, to a second generation, a fortune in itself the most remarkable witness of the growth of the city which alone has swelled it to its enormous magnitude.

With the close of the war with France and Spain, in 1763, began the period of greatest commercial activity in the Colonies. In May of that year the lighthouse at Sandy Hook was lighted for the first time. The lucrative business of privateering, in which New York largely indulged whenever there was an occasion, and to which the rich galleons of Spain, heavy with the freight of the Indies, contributed many a prize, had of course fallen with the general peace.

In the year 1773, the importations by New York from England reached the sum of £531,000, and her exports £529,000, the chief export business being, as has been shown, with the West Indies. In the year ended January 5, 1776, the customs books report among other exports from New York in 705 vessels, 104,357 barrels flour and 19,033 tierces and barrels bread, 700,689 bushels wheat, 66,045 Indian corn,

111,845 flaxseed, 99,949 casks of beef and pork, 3,057 casks of butter.

Such were the conditions under which New York began her new career. It will not be possible to measure the gigantic strides of her progress in every walk of life through the century, or give more than a faint sketch of the innumerable details which fill its history. In the preceding an endeavor has been made to present New York as it was in 1776, and to show the changes caused by the war in its physical appearance. The returning patriots who left the city on the entrance of the British troops found it on their departure not only deserted, but, as Dunlap describes it, a mass of "black unsightly rubbish."

The population of the city at this period (1783) cannot be accurately ascertained. A great change was then occurring with the outgoing of the loyalists and the incoming of the patriot population, and the arrival of large numbers of new settlers who, attracted by the natural advantages of New York, proposed to make it their home; among these many New Englanders, whose energy and enterprise contributed largely to its growth and prosperity. In 1768 the city was estimated by Noah Webster, a competent authority, to contain 3,340 dwelling-houses and a population of 23,614 souls. This little city was then the second in importance of the Western Continent—Philadelphia, the first, had at this period 40,000—Boston, owing to her inferior situation and climate, had been already outrun by her more fortunate rivals, and her population did not exceed 15,000. Baltimore followed with 14,000, and Charleston, which at one time had ambition equal to any of her sisters, 10,000. New York had already begun to feel within her broad loins the throes of empire, and was looking forward to her magnificent destiny. Already it commanded the trade of the larger part of New Jersey, of Connecticut, and part of Massachusetts, besides the vast interior country to which its imperial river gave it access, and the eye of enterprise was measuring the distances from sea and river to the interior lakes, over which connections might be made, to lock the whole in one grand system of internal communication which should open an avenue for the commerce of a continent. The road to the Canadian provinces and the great North-West was up the banks of the Hudson, and at its mouth lay the matchless land-locked harbor, safe anchorage for fleets of untold magnitude. The mission of New York was commerce, and she early understood it. Philadelphia had at this period outstripped her sister cities in manufacturing of all kinds, and New York seems never to have undertaken any serious rivalry in this branch of industry. She recognized that commerce was her vocation.

During the colonial period New York had always been extremely careful of her credit, and her issues of paper money were never in excess of the absolute demands of trade. The first issue was made in 1710, but no such bills were made a legal tender after 1737. Later, when a new issue was consented to by Lieut.-Gov. Colden, in 1770, they were only made a tender at the Loan Offices and Treasury, a well-regulated sinking fund prevented depreciation, and New York bills were at par all over the country, and equal to silver.

For some time after the war the currency was expressed in pounds sterling. Hamilton, in his famous report to Congress, January 28, 1791, on the establishment of a mint, says: "The pound, though of various value, is the unit of the money account of all the States. But it is not equally easy to pronounce what is to be considered as the unit in the coins, there being no formal regulation on this point." "But," he continues, "the manner of adjusting foreign exchanges would seem to indicate the dollar as best entitled to that character." Before the Revolution, the debasement of coin by clipping and washing had become a general and annoying evil. As all the coins were foreign, and the Lyon dollar, introduced by the Dutch, was the only legal tender of coin in the Colony, the Provincial authorities had been powerless to remedy the evil; the Lyon dollar, the value of which was fixed as early as 1720 as "seventeen pennyweight for fifteen pennyweight of Sevil pillar or Mexican plate," having almost disappeared. The proclamation of the King,

June 24, 1774, had directed the breaking up of all British coins which should reach the Treasury deficient in weight; but this rather increased than abated the evil in the Colonies. The dollar was, therefore, only a money of account, and—like the marc banco of Hamburg—a fictitious symbol of value by which all others were measured.

After the adoption of the State Constitution in 1777, but two laws were passed making bills of credit. The first, March 27, 1781, was for $411,250 to pay the proportion called for by Congress toward the expenses of the war. The bills of the Provincial Congress as well as the Continental bills were made a legal tender. The only other law passed making bills of credit was one of April 18, 1786, for £200,000, which provided that they be received in all payments to the State Treasury, and limited their circulation to the year 1800. On the 30th of March 1780, an act was passed fixing the rates at which the Continental issues should be taken. By the act it was declared that $146 of Continental issue of June 1, 1778, was the equivalent of $100; $679 of the issue of Jan. 1, 1779; $2,932 of the issue of Jan. 1, 1780, and $4,000 of that of March 16, 1780, showing a depreciation in the value of the last issues to two and one half per centum of the face of the bill. In 1781 an act was passed repealing all laws making bills of credit a legal tender, and four years later all such bills in the Treasury were destroyed. Such were the sound principles upon which this mercantile community began its career.

During the Colonial period there was no such institution known as an incorporated bank. The Bank of North America, the first of this nature in the United States, originated in the efforts of the merchants and citizens of Philadelphia to supply the wants of the army in 1780, and the honor of its conception was due to the distinguished financier and patriot, Robert Morris. The bank was incorporated by an ordinance of Congress Dec. 24, 1781, and by act of the Legislature of Pennsylvania April 1, 1782. On the 10th of the same month the Legislature of New York, then sitting at Poughkeepsie, passed an act to prevent the establishment of any bank within this State, other than the Bank of North America, during the war. The importance of a local institution became evident soon after the peace. On the 12th of February, 1784, a plan of a bank appeared in The New York Packet, and on the 28th a notice was issued in the same journal "inviting all gentlemen disposed to establish a bank on liberal principles, the stock to consist of specie only, to meet at the Merchants' Coffee-House the next evening." Every effort was made to attract subscribers by notices in the newspapers, public placards on the street corners and personal application. The capital proposed to be raised was $500,000. When about one-third of that sum ($150,000) had been taken, it was resolved to commence operations. On Monday, the 15th of March, 1784, the Bank of New York was organized, with Alexander McDougall as President and William Seton as Cashier. An application for a charter was refused by the Legislature, and the bank did not become a corporate body until the 21st of March, 1791, with a capital of $1,000,000. This was the only bank in New York before 1800. The Manhattan Company, originally organized in 1799, to supply the city with water, only availed itself of its banking privileges at a later period. The next, the Merchants' Bank, commenced operations without a charter in 1804. In 1815, Mr. Isaac Bronson, in a pamphlet entitled "An Appeal to the Public," stated the active capital of the banks of the city to be $13,515,000. On the 31st of December, 1874, there were 59 banks, with a capital of $85,166,100, deposits of $165,918,700, and a circulation of $24,977,300. The transactions of the Clearing-house, in which the banks are associated, for the year 1874 reached the enormous sum of $2,226,832,247.89.

This is not the occasion for a history of banking in this city or a eulogy of the banking laws of this State under which this difficult business was carried on for so many years with safety and success. Nor is there room for an account of its vicissitudes and trials. In all financial disasters the banks of this city have borne themselves with credit and courage. Whatever opinions may be entertained of the wisdom of their policy, on occasions of grave emergency, it cannot be denied that they have always kept in view the best interests not only of their stockholders, but of the community at large. By common consent the financial centre of the country, New York has always led the way to resumption when suspension of specie payment became inevitable. Such was the case in 1817, in 1839, in 1857. In 1861 the scheme was here devised which associated the banks of the four great commercial cities in support of the Government, and enabled them to make to it the colossal loan of $150,000,000 in coin. It may be truly said of the New York banks that they spared no effort to keep the country on a specie basis and to avert the calamities which have fallen upon it from excessive issues of paper money—a dark disaster to which the well-worn quotation may be applied with perfect fitness—"*Facilis est descensus Averni, sed revocare gradum, hic labor, hoc opus est.*"

The first savings bank was the Bank for Savings of the City of New York, incorporated on the 26th of March, 1819. Its plan was devised in the rooms of this Society by John Pintard, to whose sagacity New York owes so many of its most useful and thriving institutions, and Thomas Eddy. The deposits from the 3d of July to the 27th of December (1819) reached the sum of $153,378 from 1,527 depositors. On the 31st of December, 1874, there were 44 savings banks in this city, holding $180,010,703 from 494,086 depositors.

Insurance companies, or associations of individuals for the purpose of insurance under the management of a chosen board of officers, are of comparatively modern growth. The old fashion was different. Then any persons inclined to underwrite risks made their undertaking at some public place where the policies upon which insurance was desired were shown, and kept books of their own in which their liabilities upon such policies were entered. In the middle of last century the "Old Insurance Office," as it was called in 1759, was kept at the Coffee-House, where the clerks of the office, Keteltas and Sharpe, attended every day from 12 till 1 in the day, and 6 to 8 in the evening. A rival office, the New York Insurance Office, with Anthony Van Dam for clerk, was established the same year, and a permanent office taken next door to the Coffee-House. This was the office patronized by the Waltons, Crugers, Jaunceys, and other city capitalists. In 1778, when the destruction of vessels and convoys by the adventurous American privateers had greatly enhanced the risk of navigation, "the New Insurance Office" was opened at the Coffee-House. The mode in which this business was done is shown by an announcement of Cunningham & Wardrop, "Insurance Brokers," who advertised in 1779 that they had opened a "Public Insurance Office," where policies are received and offered to the merchants and underwriters generally. Each underwriter subscribed his name for the sum he engaged. An interesting hand-book of the insurances of William Walton, in sums varying from £400 to £50, is still preserved. All these offices were for marine insurance. The first marine insurance company organized after the war was the United Insurance Company, founded in 1795, or early in 1796, and chartered March 20, 1798, with a capital of $500,000. The charter allowed fire as well as marine risks. The second was the New York Insurance Company, founded in 1796, and incorporated April 2, 1798, with a capital of $500,000. The first company which confined itself wholly to sea risks was the Marine Insurance Company, which commenced business Nov. 19, 1801, with a capital of $250,000. To-day there are nine marine insurance companies, with assets reported Dec. 31, 1874, at $25,035,785.62.

The first proposal for insurance against fire seems to have been a motion made in the Chamber of Commerce by Mr. John Thurman on the 3d of April, 1770, that "as it is the desire of a number of the inhabitants of this city to have their estates insured from loss by fire, and that losses of this sort may not fall upon individuals, the Chamber take into consideration some plan that may serve so good a purpose." The consideration of the subject was postponed, and no action taken. On Feb. 16, 1874, a notice appeared in The New York Packet: "Some gentlemen have now in contemplation to form a company for insuring houses in this city against fire.

Such houses as are insured will be of course received as security in the bank;" and a further attempt was made by Mr. John Delafield in April, 1785, to establish a "fire insurance office," but they do not seem to have been successful. The first fire insurance company was organized by John Pintard (who became its secretary), June 15, 1787, under the name of the Mutual Assurance Company. An act of incorporation was obtained March 28, 1809. To-day there are 74 fire insurance companies in the city, with assets reported Dec. 31, 1874, at $44,696,827.

The first notice of a life insurance company appears in an act of incorporation of the Mechanics' Life Insurance and Coal Company on the 28th of February, 1822, "with power to make insurance upon lives or in any way depending upon lives, to grant annuities and to open, find out, discover, and work coal-beds within this State."

To-day there are in the city 21 life insurance companies, with assets reported, December 31, 1874, at $191,683,513. These companies issued 59,261 policies last year, for the sum of $178,389,450, and had outstanding at its close 272,803 policies, for the amount of $994,151,329.

In these figures no account is taken of the large business done in this city by insurance companies of other States having branch offices here.

A recapitulation of these sums gives the amount of capital employed in banking and insurance at $692,501,627. The recapitulation is as follows:

```
Bank capital............................$85,166,100
Deposits ...............................165,918,700
Savings................................180,000,703
                                       ───────────
       Total..........................$431,685,503
Insurance— Marine...................$25,035,785
           Fire ....................  44,696,827
           Life ....................191,683,513
                                    ───────────  261,416,125
                                                ───────────
       Total...........................$692,501,627
```

The commerce of the city was under the watchful care of two important societies during the colonial period. The

Chamber of Commerce was founded the 3d of May, 1768; chartered 13th of March, 1770, and revived 13th of April, 1784, by an act of the Legislature confirming its charter. This institution established the rates of commission, settled the usages of trade, fixed the value of coins, and otherwise supervised the mercantile interest. The other commercial society was the Marine Society, chartered April 12, 1770, and rechartered by the State Legislature in May, 1786. The business of this corporation was the "improving of maritime knowledge and the relief of indigent and distressed masters of vessels and of their children."

No sooner was the treaty of peace signed than the great Continental powers hastened to stretch forth a hand of welcome to the infant Republic, and ambassadors were appointed to the seat of government. France, the Netherlands, and Spain were all represented by first-class Ministers as early as 1785. As was remarked at the time, "every nation in Europe solicited to partake of her trade." Great Britain alone, chafing under her defeat, remained for a long period sullen, and endeavored by navigation acts and other adverse legislation to cripple the commerce of the States. The West India trade, the most profitable in which New York was engaged, was prohibited in American vessels, and all intercourse forbidden, except in British bottoms, the property of and navigated by British subjects. She only consented to a treaty of amity and the sending of an ambassador in 1791, and only then because of the fear of a closer alliance of America with the French Republic. Nor was this the only obstacle to the development of the trade of New York.

On the 3d of February, 1781, the Congress of the United States had passed an act recommending to the several States as indispensably necessary that they vest a power in Congress to levy for the use of the United States a duty of five per cent. ad valorem, at the time and place of importation, upon all goods, wares, and merchandise of foreign growth and manufacture, to take general effect when the States should consent. On the 19th of March of the same year (1781) the Legislature of New York passed the required act, suspending its operation until all the States not prevented by war should vest similar powers in Congress. Here, again, as in the act authorizing the legal tender of Continental bills as money in this State, New York had without delay waived its settled opinion and undoubted interest for the benefit of the whole. On the 15th of March, 1783, the Legislature, after reciting in a preamble that several Legislatures of other States have passed laws " dissimilar to the true intent and meaning of the act of 1781," repealed the same, and passed a new act granting to Congress a duty of five per cent. ad valorem, as in the preceding act, but ordered the duties to be levied and collected by officers under the authority of the State. To the provisions of this act the merchants of New York took exception, and on the motion of Isaac Moses, one of the most intelligent and respectable of the Jewish merchants of the city, the Chamber of Commerce memorialized the Legislature to abandon the vicious system of ad valorem duties, which opened every man's invoices and trade to the inspection of his neighbors, and adopt in lieu a specific tariff. The Legislature listened to this petition, and on the 18th of November, 1784, passed an act levying specific duties, and established a custom-house the same day. The veteran Col. Lamb was appointed the first Collector of the Port. When the State adopted the Federal Constitution in 1789, it was compelled to surrender its preference for specific duties, among other and valuable privileges. From that day to this each succeeding generation of merchants has urged upon Congress the importance of a change to the specific system.

Almost immediately upon the return of the merchants exiled by the war, new avenues were sought by them for the extension of commerce. In the fall of 1783 a ship was purchased by some of the most enterprising, in association with their neighbors of Philadelphia, and dispatched to China laden chiefly with ginseng for exchange for tea and Chinese manufactures. This ship—the Empress of China, Capt. John Green—sailed on the 22d of February, 1784 (Washington's birthday), having on board, as supercargo, Major Samuel Shaw of the Revolutionary army, later the first American

Consul at Canton. This was the first American venture in those distant seas. She reached the city (New York) on the 12th of May, 1785, after a voyage of 14 months and 20 days. This venture was one-half for the account of Robert Morris of Philadelphia, and the net profit was $30,727—over 20 per cent. on $120,000, the capital employed. Other vessels followed, and as early as 1789 the United States had 15 vessels, against the 21 ships of the East India Company, in the China seas; and in the six years, from 1802 to 1808, of £12,831,099 in value of bullion imported into India, £4,543,662 was from the United States, and of £22,970,672, the value of goods exported from India, £4,803,283 was to the United States. The Empress of China carried the original flag of the United States, adopted in 1777 as the national flag, "thirteen stripes, alternate red and white, and a union of thirteen stars, white, on a blue field, representing a new constellation." This flag, first shown in the Pacific at the masthead of a New York vessel in 1784, was taken round the world by the Columbia in 1789-1790, and by the Franklin of Salem to Japan in 1799. The French Government was quick to stimulate the commerce of the American States, from whose enterprise it anticipated a counterpoise to the maritime power of Great Britain. In August, 1784, the French Consul-General at New York communicated to the merchants an invitation of the King "to avail of the French ports of the Isles of France and Bourbon in their voyages to and from the East Indies," where they were promised "every protection and every liberty they might wish for or stand in need of." To show the importance of the trade which sprung from these small beginnings, it is only necessary to refer to the amount of the total Asian trade of the city of New York, which, in the year closed June 30, 1874, reached the sum of $36,099,362, of which the imports amounted to $31,275,679, and the exports hence, $4,823,683.

In its inception the young marine had other difficulties to contend with than the simple unfriendliness of Great Britain. One of the greatest was the terror spread over the colonies by the report in February, 1785, of the capture of an American vessel by the Barbary pirates, who then infested the Mediterranean Sea, and even ventured in pursuit of their prey into the open ocean. It is almost impossible for us at this day to comprehend the policy which influenced such a naval power as Great Britain to consent to the ignominy of paying tribute to, and taking papers of safe-conduct from, this petty but audacious power. Probably no better explanation can be given than that she considered it for her interest to have a dangerous sea between the near towns of France and the African coast as a shield to her Indian possessions, the highway to which lay through the Mediterranean. Certain it is that at a later day her agents negotiated a treaty between the Barbary States and Portugal, then wholly under her influence, in which it was stipulated that Portugal should furnish no protection to any nation against Algerine cruisers. This treaty, kept secret both by the contracting powers and Great Britain, in 1793 opened the gateway of the Atlantic to the Moors, and ten American vessels fell unsuspecting victims into their hands. The United States, like the European powers, finally consented to pay the required tribute; but the disgrace at last awakened the pride of the States, a navy was created, and in 1815 Commodore Decatur met and defeated the Algerine squadron, sailed into the Bay of Algiers, and forced the Dey at the mouth of his guns to surrender all American prisoners and all claims to tribute, an example soon followed by the great powers.

The French, though never openly hostile, were never wholly friendly. The French people, who had declared the "rights of man" on the Champs de Mars, and asserted their own freedom in 1789, were dissatisfied with the neutrality of the United States, which they looked upon as signal ingratitude. The Imperial Government in the Berlin and Milan decrees, by which it attempted to enforce a Continental land blockade against British trade, was as indifferent to American rights as Great Britain herself in her Orders in Council, and the adventurous trading vessels of the States had to run a double gauntlet. It was not till after the peace of 1815, and when the gallantry of its youthful navy, led by Hull, Perry, Preble,

Bainbridge, Decatur, and Lawrence, had shown that it was as dangerous an enemy in war as a valuable friend in peace, that the young nation found a fair and unimpeded field for its marvellous activity. Of the rapidity of its movement at this period, the Customs revenue collected by the United States Government is a striking example. From $4,415,362 in 1814, it rose in 1815 to $37,695,625, of which $16,000,000 was taken at the port of New York alone. In the fiscal year ended June 30, 1875, the total amount of Customs revenue for all the United States was $157,167,722, of which $109,207,786 was taken at the port of New York.

The communications with Europe were now largely increased. In 1774 there were only five packet-boats, belonging to the royal service and carrying the mails, stationed between Falmouth and New York, of which one left each port the first Wednesday in every month. They were the Earl of Halifax, the Harriott, the Duke of Cumberland, the Lord Hyde, and the Mercury. Besides these, there were numerous excellent vessels in the merchant service. An instance of the speed of these vessels is to be found in the voyage of the Samson, Captain Henry Coupar, which brought out the act known as the Boston Port bill. This fast ship left London the 10th of April, 1774, Land's End the 14th, and arrived at New York on the 12th of May, making the passage in 27 days. The journals record that this vessel brought an account of the receipt of bills (of exchange) sent from New York to London in one month and 29 days, which was in less time than perhaps was ever known before, considering the distance. The French Government was early in establishing regular packet communication with the young nation. In the fall of 1783, on the 19th of November, before the evacuation of the city, the Courrier de l'Europe, Capt. Cornic de Moulin, arrived from the port of l'Orient, and notice was at once given of the establishment of a line of five first-class ships — le Courrier de l'Europe, le Courrier de l'Amérique, le Courrier de New York le Courrier de l'Orient, and l'Allegator—to make monthly trips. The line was under the direction of Mr. Hector St. John, the

Consul-General of France for Connecticut, New York, and New Jersey, and the immediate supervision of Mr. William Seton as deputy agent. The "noble cabin" of l'Orient was advertised as capable of accommodating forty persons at table. The price of passage was fixed at 500 livres at the captain's tables, and 200 livres for those who chose to take ship's rations, and 120 livres the ton of 2,000 pounds weight, or forty-two cubical feet. This vessel sailed on her return Dec. 19, 1783, and took out a number of passengers, among whom, strange to say, were several officers of the British army. In the commencement of this enterprise the public were informed that the French packet was an immediate channel of conveyance for letters from and to all parts of the continent of Europe, the General Post-Office at Paris having a daily intercourse with all the capitals.

Such was the beginning of regular communication. In 1816, the famous Black Ball line to Liverpool was established, a few years later the Swallow Tail line to London, and in 1824 the Havre line. In 1827, the Liverpool line employed twenty ships, the London line eight, and the Havre line twelve, besides which there were weekly lines to Savannah, Charleston, Mobile, and New Orleans. The average passages outward of the Black Ball line were made in twenty-two days, and the home voyage in twenty-nine days. But steam was soon to change the entire mode of ocean navigation as well as of land travel; and to such an extent that to-day, of all the passenger fleet the only line which continues its regular passages is the old Swallow Tail line.

As far back as 1790 John Fitch had solved the problem of the application of steam to vessels, and is said to have made experiments on the Collect Pond in this city, in which he used the screw as well as the paddle and within a short period from that date practically carried passengers on the Schuylkill at Philadelphia. In March, 1819, the steamship Savannah sailed from New York for Savannah, and leaving that port on the 25th of May, made the first ocean passage, arriving in Liverpool the 20th of June. On the 7th of April of the same year, the Legislature of New York incorporated an "Ocean

Steam-ship Company;" but it was not until 1838 that the arrival of the Sirius and Great Western opened ocean steam navigation. The Bremen line was the pioneer of the American steam lines. In 1850 the "Atlantic" began the career of the Collins line, which was for a long period the pride of the nation as well as of New York, but at last succumbed after a series of misfortunes and disasters. The history of our once splendid steam marine is but an episode in the progress of New York commerce. Of all the large fleet of steamers only one now carries the flag of the United States across the Atlantic. Yet the exhibit of its commerce is none the less wondrous for this absence.

In the year 1770, the ships which entered the harbor of New York were 196 in number, the sloops 431—a total of 627 sail. In the year 1828, the arrivals of vessels at New York were 1,400 from foreign ports and 4,000 coasting vessels. In the year ended June 30, 1874, the number of entrances at the port of New York of American and foreign, ocean, steam and sail, was 6,723—5,044,618 tons, and handled by crews numbering 148,246 men. Of these vessels, 4,290 were foreign and 2,433 American. In this number are included 1,108 steamers; 877 foreign and 231 American. Of the American steam-vessels, every one, with one single exception, was from the coast, the West Indies, or South America, the ocean trade having been wholly abandoned to foreigners. The registered tonnage of the customs district of New York was, at the same date, 6,630 vessels of 1,318,-523 tons; 2,810 sailing vessels of 600,020 tons; 788 steam vessels, 351,686 tons; 546 barges, 123,535 tons; and 2,486 canal boats, 243,281 tons. The coastwise trade engaged 2,742 vessels, 1,774,181 tons, of which there were 1,583 steam vessels, 1,517,481 tons, and 1,159 sailing vessels, 256,700 tons.

The internal trade has progressed with equal rapidity. The project of a canal connecting the great lakes of the interior with tide-water was the first thought of the city after the peace. In 1785 Christopher Colles, an ingenious mechanician, memorialized the Legislature of New York for the establishment of a canal to connect the Mohawk with the Hudson, and in 1792 a company was chartered, which in five years opened the passage from Schenectady to Oneida, and intended to continue it to Lake Ontario, for which extension the route had been surveyed in 1791; but it was not till 1810 that the canal policy found its great advocate in De Witt Clinton. His memorial in 1815 gave a new impulse to the movement. Through his commanding influence, the act establishing the Erie Canal was passed in 1817, and the grand enterprise completed. On October 26, 1826, the sound of cannon commenced at Buffalo, and, repeated from city to town and town to city, announced to New York the completion of the Erie Canal and the final union of the lakes with the Atlantic, the presage of the power and wealth of the city as the great gateway of the western hemisphere. The arrival of the first canal boat on the 11th November following, was the occasion of a grand aquatic and civic pageant, in which the commingling of the waters was typically illustrated by the pouring by Gov. Clinton, the "Father of the Canal," of a keg of fresh water of Lake Erie into the Atlantic Ocean at the Narrows. The measure of this grand improvement may be judged from the amount of produce now brought to market. In 1874 the transportation of produce from the interior of this State and the Western States by canal boats amounted to 3,323,112 tons, and the returns of supplies of various kinds to 753,981 tons. An estimate of the value of the produce brought into this city by the canals and railroads may be made from an examination of the exports from New York in the fiscal year ended June 30, 1874, in which breadstuffs figure to the value of $91,332,669, and provisions to the value of $40,193,947, in all $131,000,000, without estimate of the amounts retained for consumption or traffic with other States. The other principal exports of American product from this port were cotton to the amount of $41,499,597; lard and tallow, $20,319,514; tobacco, $16,117,749; illuminating oils, $23,121,059. A summary of the total foreign trade for the same year (ended June 30, 1874) shows that of the total imports by the United States, of $595,861,248 in value, New York imported $395,133,622; and of the total exports of the United States, $704,463,120, $340,360,260 were by New York; and of a total aggregate of foreign trade, inward and outward, by the whole country of $1,300,-324,368, New York had $735,493,882, or nearly 60 per cent. It may not be without interest to present a summary of the trade of New York in geographical divisions. Its total trade (in the year ended June 30, 1874) with foreign American ports, Canada, South and Central America, and the West Indies, amounted to $163,523,775. Its total European trade, $533,711,992. Its total Asian trade, $36,099,362, and its total African trade to $2,158,753.

In its imports sugar and molasses figured to the amount of $52,360,176; coffee, $33,485,559; tea, $15,024,794.

Soon after the peace, a German society was established under the direction of Cols. Lutterloh and Weissenfels, as President and Vice-President (both of whom had been distinguished in the Revolutionary War, the latter as one of the expedition under Gen. Montgomery to Canada), for the purpose of encouraging emigration to the State of New York, "so that the western part thereof may be settled by those useful members; witness the State of Pennsylvania." So runs the card of "A Friend to Cultivation," in The New York Packet of October 14, 1784; but no considerable movement took place for a long period. In 1824 the total number of emigrants to all the United States was 7,912. The improvement in comfort and diminished risk of the ocean traverse gradually induced a larger movement; but the great impulse to the exodus, which in the last half century has reached nearly ten millions of people, was given by the Irish famine of 1844. The highest rate of emigration was reached in 1872, when 449,042 persons were landed; of these, 294,581 at the port of New York. Since that year there has been a gradual decline in the number; in 1873 it fell to 266,449, in 1874 to 149,762, of which 41,368 were from Germany, 41,179 from Ireland, 19,822 from England, and 7,723 Mennonites—a religious sect from Russia. In 1875 the number landed at this port dropped to 84,544. This decline may be ascribed chiefly to the long-continued financial and business depression throughout the country. The movement will certainly be resumed upon a revival of trade and renewal of prosperity. This emigration has been a large and profitable branch of the carrying trade, now in great distress in consequence of its decline.

It has been observed that New York has never claimed any preëminence as a manufacturing city, yet as a great industrial centre it ranks next to Philadelphia. The United States Census of 1870 showed that there were then 7,624 establishments, with 1,261 steam-engines and sixteen water-wheels, employing 129,577 hands, at an annual outlay in wages of $63,824,262, and a capital of 129,952,262. The raw materials used were valued at $178,696,939, and the annual product at $332,951,520. In addition to these, the ship-building in the year ended 30th of June, 1874, comprised 89 sailing and 60 steam vessels, 196 canal boats, and 51 barges, a total of 396 vessels, 64,001 tons. It is a fact too often forgotten, but of which the increase of the great landed property to which allusion has been made, by accumulation alone without original enterprise, since the death of its founder in 1848, is indisputable evidence, that no ship arrives, no emigrant lands, no railroad or canal brings its freight to this city, that does not pay some toll and add some value to its real estate.

Let us now pass from the review of the commercial and industrial progress of New York to an examination of its advance in social improvement. Before the Revolution popular education was limited, and chiefly dependent on the aid of churches. Indeed, until this century the education of the lower classes was regarded rather as a favor than a right. Universal suffrage has set forever at rest this fallacy in the United States, and if it have no other advantage, it has at least the indisputable merit that it compels capital to educate labor. William Smith, the historian, writing in 1756, says: " Our schools are of the lowest order; the instructors want instruction; and through a long shameful neglect of the arts and sciences our common speech is extremely corrupt."

Noah Webster speaks of the schools in 1788 as " no longer in the deplorable condition they were formerly, and many of them as kept by reputable and able men." But all these remarks apply to private schools. The first action toward general education was in 1791, when the Legislature appropriated the sum of $50,000 for five years for elementary and practical instruction in this State. To-day the public instruction of the city is under the charge of a Board of Education, who reported the number of schools within its jurisdiction, December 31, 1874, as 287, held in 121 buildings, engaging 3,215 teachers, of whom over 3,000 are females, and giving instruction to 251,545 scholars. The system is maintained at an annual cost of $3,475,313. New York may safely challenge rivalry on the part of any community, American or foreign, with this magnificent showing of her system of public education, which includes for the higher branches a Free Academy, a Normal College for the education of teachers, a Nautical school, and a school for the compulsory instruction of delinquents.

The institutions for instruction in letters, science, law, medicine, and art must be passed by in silence; enumeration even would be tedious. Columbia College, the University of the City of New York, and the Rutgers Female College are the principal. Besides these, each religious denomination has its own school system. The College of Physicians and Surgeons heads the list of medical colleges, the Law School that of law—both adjuncts of Columbia College; but every branch of instruction has its special institution. Reviewing the whole, there are found 3,365 instructors, 277,310 students, and an annual expenditure of $3,808,381. In addition to these, all institutions incorporated by the State or making a report to the authorities of the State, there are numerous schools for instruction of both sexes in the higher departments of knowledge, some of which are as extensive as the colleges. Of these, the most famous is the Cooper Institute, the munificent donation of Peter Cooper for the education of the working classes—a model institution, which includes free tuition in engineering and the arts of design and modelling.

The earliest organized library in the city of New York was the City Library, founded in 1729. Its rooms were in the City Hall, where the Society Library, organized in 1754 and chartered in 1772, was also kept. Both of these libraries, as also that of King's College, were sacked by the British and Hessian troops during the war. In 1784 (February 12) Mr. Samuel Bard, by order of the trustees, made a public request in The New York Packet for the return of such volumes as belonged to the Society Library. To-day there are 23 libraries of circulation and reference, of which the Astor is the most valuable, containing 150,000 volumes. This is a free library, under certain reasonable restrictions. Another, which promises to be of great if not equal value, is that projected by James Lenox. The beautiful structure erected for its reception is one of the principal ornaments of the city. The Mercantile Library follows with 158,034, and the New York Society Library is next in order. The New York Historical Society Library, in the rooms of which we are now gathered, has a valuable collection of manuscripts, public and private documents, bound newspapers to the number of 2,319, historical works exceeding 60,000, and includes a fine museum, with the famous Abbot collection of Egyptian antiquities and the Lenox Nineveh collection. The Metropolitan Museum of Art, yet in its infancy, has already brought together a remarkable variety of curiosities, among which is the Cesnola collection of Etruscan antiquities, and the society is erecting a large building in Central Park.

The first newspaper in New York was The New York Gazette, established by William Bradford in 1725. During the war the only journals were Hugh Gaines's New York Mercury, Rivington's Royal Gazette, and Robertson's Royal American Gazetteer, suspended after the departure of the British. In 1784 the newspapers were The New York Packet and The American Advertiser, published by Samuel London; The New York Gazetteer, by Shepard Kollock; and The Independent Gazette, or The New York Journal, revived by John and Elizabeth Holt; The Independent Journal or The General Advertiser, by McLean & Webster. To-day New

York boasts of 444 newspapers and periodicals, of which 28 are daily and semi-weekly, 187 weekly, 22 semi-monthly, 180 monthly, 3 bi-monthly, and 16 quarterly; 32 are in foreign languages, and 99 have a circulation of over 5,000 copies. Of the 10 principal newspapers, one has a daily circulation of 127,000 copies; the lowest, printed in German, of 30,000 copies. Of the illustrated papers, one weekly issues 100,000 copies. Of the newspapers devoted to literature and stories, one has a weekly circulation of 300,000, and another of 180,000. One of the religious papers issues 78,000 copies, and one of the monthly magazines 130,000 copies. The weight of newspapers and periodicals mailed by publishers at the City Post-office to regular subscribers for the first three quarters of 1874, Jan. 1 to Sept. 30, was 17,392,691 pounds, the postage prepaid on which amounted to $249,952.17.

The charities of New York are conducted on an imperial scale. Her cosmopolitan munificence is proverbial. To her the eyes of suffering communities, cities, nations, are first turned, and never in vain. Ireland in its famine, France in its floods and desolation, England in the suffering of its manufacturing districts, Portland, Chicago, Boston, scourged by fire, have all found ready and abundant aid in their day of trial, and at home her charity is no less bountiful. The public prisons, hospitals, asylums, almshouses, and nurseries are 27 in number. The Commissioners of Public Charities and Correction made an expenditure last year of $1,541,685.50; the Commissioners of Emigration gave relief to 51,871 persons, at an expense of $466,108.22. Besides these great public charities there are endless private associations. That for Improving the Condition of the Poor gave relief in 1874 to 24,091 families. There are also 27 hospitals in the city, of which 15 have large and commodious buildings. St. Luke's, the Roosevelt, and Mount Sinai are prominent examples. There are seven dispensaries, chief among which is the New York Dispensary, established in 1790, which supplies an average of 40,000 patients annually. There are two institutions for the deaf and dumb; three for the blind. There are in addition 26 religious, educational, and charitable Roman

Catholic organizations, 51 benevolent societies, 50 trades-unions, and about 50 other charitable institutions, reformatory and educational. The organized local charitable societies receive and disburse about $2,500,000 annually. The Department of Buildings reports 66 hospitals and asylums, 1st January, 1876. Where is the community which contributes so much of its wealth to the improvement and support of the ignorant and indigent of its members?

Clubs have grown to be a marked feature of city life. Those of New York, including literary and sporting associations, number 40. Of these the most celebrated is the Union, with a handsome and costly building, and a full membership of 1,000 members; the Union League Club, an offspring of loyalty during the late civil war; the New York, Knickerbocker, Travellers', the Century, (home of Art and Literature,) the Lotos, and the German Club, all provided with refreshment rooms and restaurants, and largely attended.

The limits of the city in 1783 have been described as contained within the irregular triangle formed by the North and East rivers and a line drawn across the island at Reade street. To-day they include the whole of Manhattan Island, 13½ miles in length, and averaging 1¾ miles in width, an area of 22 square miles, or 14,000 acres; and the recent annexation from the mainland of part of Westchester County, before known as the towns of Morrisania, West Farms, and Kingsbridge, gives an additional area of about 13,000 acres. In addition there are the islands of Blackwell, Ward, Randall, Bedloe, Ellis, and Governor, of which the last three named have been ceded to the Government of the United States for Federal purposes; the other islands have been set aside for correctional, reformatory, and charitable purposes. Of the 27,000 acres comprising the city proper, 1,007 acres, or 8,712,000 yards, are devoted to public parks. The Central Park needs no mention. There is no park to be found in any European city at all comparable to it. It only requires an extension of narrow wings to the river sides near by to combine all possible beauties of location and scenery. Of the other parks, the Battery, Bowling Green, and City

Hall Park are of the last century; Tompkins, Washington, Union, Madison, and Reservoir-square, and at the northern end of the island, Mount Morris, High Bridge, and Morningside parks, complete the admirable provision of breathing-places for the fast-growing population.

The little town which in 1788 contained in its seven wards 3,340 houses with 23,614 inhabitants, had grown in 1870 to a colossal city, with 64,044 dwellings, and 942,292 inhabitants. Of these 419,094 were foreign born,—234,594 British and Irish, and 151,216 Germans. To these considerable additions must be made. The Department of Buildings reports the total number of dwellings at 84,200; of stores, stables, markets, etc., at 16,438; of public buildings, churches, etc., at 524; a total of 101,162 of all kinds, 1st January, 1876. The recent State census of 1875 carries the total number of the population, including that of the two wards lately annexed, to 1,046,037, an increase of 419,707 since 1865. But although this is the actual number of persons residing within the city limits, it is not the measure of its real population: the true location of population is that where it leads its waking not its sleeping life. To the enumeration made should be added the number of those who visit the city daily, or depend upon it for livelihood and support. Those added would carry the population of the city and suburbs within a radius of twenty-five miles from the City Hall to more than two millions.

The lower part of the city is quite irregular in construction, but from Houston street to the northward is laid out upon a regular and well-devised plan, essentially that made by the Commissioners appointed by the Legislature in 1807 (Gouverneur Morris, De Witt Clinton and others). There are broad avenues running in parallel lines to the end of the island, traversed laterally by parallel streets, all of which are designated by numbers. To this recent changes have added extensive boulevards which connect with the Central Park and offer long and pleasant drives. Broadway, the most famous of New York, and, indeed, of American avenues, is an exception to the general rule of regularity and runs across five of the parallel avenues in a north-westerly direction. This is the great shopping street, and is lined with enormous retail stores and hotels. Fifth avenue, extending northward from Washington square and skirting the eastern limit of the Central Park, is, with its splendid private residences, churches and clubs, one unbroken series of architectural display.

The public buildings are numerous, and some of them grand as well as graceful. For massiveness, the Custom-house in Wall street, originally built for the Merchants' Exchange, and the new Post-Office, are the most noted : for grace and beauty, the old City Hall, and the Sub-Treasury in Wall street. A new order of architecture has recently sprung up, of which the Tribune building with its tall tower, and the Western Union Telegraph building, are the most aspiring examples. Structures are being erected all over the city of great size and costliness, both for stores and as private residences. The fourteen churches in which the little city worshipped in 1788, have expanded, with their adjuncts of mission organizations, into 470, of which there are 344 distinct edifices, providing seats for 350,000 persons. Connected with the Protestant churches are 356 Sabbath-schools, which give instruction to 88,327 scholars. Many of the churches are large and imposing. Those most marked for their beauty are Trinity, Grace, St. George's, the new Fifth Avenue Presbyterian, the Reformed Collegiate, and the Jewish Synagogue. The Roman Catholics are erecting a cathedral in the Gothic order, with all the emblems of the new cardinalate, which will surpass all other New York churches in architectural beauty and grandeur

The Croton Aqueduct has been alluded to. The supply of water is drawn from the Croton River, a clear, pure stream of remarkable quality, in Westchester County, which is conducted to the city through a covered way of solid masonry 40½ miles in length. It has a capacity of 60,000,000 gallons a day. It crosses the Harlem River on the High Bridge, a granite structure 1,450 feet long, 21 feet wide, 114 feet high ; is received in two great basins in Central Park, and distributed from two reservoirs through 350 miles of pipes.

The utility of gas was first demonstrated to the citizens in 1817, and in 1825 mains were laid on Broadway. Five chartered companies now supply the city. Of these the Manhattan has two works, which deliver gas through about 170 miles of street mains to 30,000 private consumers and 7,000 street lamps.

The markets are 11 in number, but with hardly an exception are utterly unworthy of a great city, yet the enormous business transacted in them deserves notice. The sales of food for cash were reported by the worthy and efficient superintendent, who lacks neither the will, energy, nor intelligence to make the market system an honor instead of a disgrace to the city, as amounting to $130,000,000 in the year 1874, of which Washington Market alone received $108,000,000. In the height of the season miles of country wagons from Long Island, Westchester County, and the Jerseys line the streets leading to this great country mart, and form as busy a scene, from daylight until late in the forenoon, as can well be imagined. Mr. Devoe, the Superintendent, is authority for the statement that 1,350,000 persons, of both sexes and all ages —1,000,000 residents and 350,000 daily visitors—are fed, every business day, in the city. The Superintendent of Public Buildings estimates the average daily number of guests at the hotels at 200,000.

In 1783, and for many years after the beginning of the present century, travel was still in the old-fashioned primitive manner, and communication from State to State, though more frequent than before the Revolution, did not greatly differ in kind until a much later period. The first land route to Boston was opened in 1732, and stages ran to and fro, starting from each point once each month, and made the single trip in fourteen days. In 1787 the Boston stages set out from Hall's Tavern in Cortlandt street (No. 49) every Monday and Thursday morning, arriving in Boston in six days. In the summer months a third trip was made in each week; the fare four cents per mile. In 1827 a stage left each city daily, and reached its destination in thirty-six hours. To-day the Express trains on the railroads make an easy communication within eight hours. In 1785 the first stages began their trips between New York and Albany, on the east side of the river, with four horses, at the rate of four cents per mile. In 1787 two stages set out for Philadelphia every evening from Powles Hook, Jersey City, at four o'clock, going by the way of Newark, where they stopped for the night, and reached Philadelphia the next day. Another line went by way of Communipaw (Bergen Point), stopped at Elizabethtown at night, and arrived at Philadelphia the next evening. Besides these a stage-boat, leaving the Albany pier twice each week, connected with a stage wagon at South Amboy, which took passengers to Philadelphia by the way of Burlington ; and in addition a boat left Coenties slip every Saturday, if the wind was fair, reached New Brunswick the same evening, and returned to New York the next Tuesday. To-day the trip is made by railroad in three hours.

The first steamboat on the Hudson was the Clermont, built by Robert Fulton in 1807, which moved at the rate of five miles the hour. In 1828 the arrivals and departures of steamboats at New York reached 6,400. They transported 320,000 passengers. To-day the fast summer boats run to West Point, fifty miles distant, in $2\frac{1}{2}$ hours, a rate of twenty miles the hour.

Steam was first practically applied to railroads in the year 1830, when the Mohawk and Hudson, connecting Albany with Schenectady, was opened. The first railroad out of the city of New York was the Harlem, completed October, 1837. This road began at the City Hall, and in 1841 extended to Fordham in Westchester County. There are now (1875) three great railroads having their terminus at the Grand Central Depot, a fine and convenient structure at the corner of Forty-second street and the upper end of Fourth avenue. All these are now under the management and control of the great capitalist and railroad king, Cornelius Vanderbilt. These are the Hudson River, New York Central, and the Harlem, which connect the metropolis with the interior of this State and the Western States. The New York and New Haven carries passengers and freight to the Eastern States, and starts from the same depot, below which steam is not allowed on the city streets. Five railroads connect the city with the interior of Long Island, all having their terminus on the Long Island side of the East River. These are the Long Island Railroad to Greenport at the eastern extremity of the island, the South Side to Patchogue, the Flushing and North Side to Great Neck, the Central to Babylon, the late construction of A. T. Stewart. From the Jersey shore the Erie Railway runs through the State to Buffalo, thence to the Western States, and communications are maintained by an endless network of roads which centre at Jersey City, with the Middle and Southern States. The average speed on these roads is about thirty miles an hour.

The travel was for a long period confined to stages, which, under the name of omnibuses, reached their height in 1851, when there were twenty-four lines. A few lines still remain, but they are gradually disappearing. Our older inhabitants remember the palmy days of the famous lines of Kipp and Brown, the Chelsea and Knickerbocker. The first city railroad for horse-cars was the Sixth Avenue, established in 1852. The Harlem R. R. Company had used this mode of conveyance at an earlier day, but rather as an adjunct to their steam line than as a convenience for city travel. The last report of the State Engineer for 1872 gives the number of passengers carried as 134,588,877, at fares varying from five to eight cents. The steam elevated road, the pioneer of rapid transit, carried the same year 167,153 passengers, at a fare of ten cents. The ingenuity of the best engineers is now tested to devise some mode of rapid transit which may keep pace with the increase of travel, already outrunning all present accommodation.

The first use of steam on ferries was on the Jersey City Ferry, in July, 1812. To-day there are twenty-three ferries, all steam, connecting NewYork with the west shore of the Hudson, Hoboken and Jersey City, Staten Island and Long Island. The boats to Brooklyn and Hoboken run every five to ten minutes by day, and every fifteen to twenty minutes by night, at fares ranging from two to four cents each passenger. The official returns made to the city authorities in 1865 reported the number of passengers carried at 82,321,274. The system of leasing the ferries has taken this valuable franchise from city supervision, but the natural increase of the city and suburbs would carry this number to 100,000,000 as the lowest estimate for the present year. It has been stated that the estimate of the persons who enter and leave the city every day for purposes of business is not less than 300,000. These facts seem to indicate that the centre of the travel of the city and suburbs, of which the cities on the opposite shores are, practically, part, is not far distant from the City Hall Park.

In 1790 the Hackney Coach stand was at the Coffee-House, and the charge one shilling per mile. In 1875 there were 1,800 licensed coaches in the city. Yet the city is in great need of some improvement in the present cab system, for which Paris and London offer such admirable models.

The mails were carried in the early days by men on horseback. In 1673 the post rider began his trips to and from Boston once in three weeks.

During the exciting period which preceded the Revolution, the famous Paul Revere, about whose name, as the Express Rider of the Sons of Liberty, cluster memories as sacred as those which attach to the Grecian runner who brought the holy fire from the Delphic altar, kept the communication between Boston and New York, and Cornelius Bradford between New York and Philadelphia. As an instance of the speed of these journeys, it is recorded in the journals of 1789 that John Adams, then at Braintree, received despatches from Congress in fifty hours. In 1775 the mails were made up in New York twice each week for Boston, once for Albany and Quebec, and three times for Philadelphia and southward. In the winter the Albany post was carried on foot. In 1783 the post-office was kept in a private house, at No. 38 Smith street, where the postmaster dated his notices and made up his mails. In 1810 the amount received for postages in New York was $60,000; in 1826, $113,893.71, and twenty-five persons, including clerks, letter-carriers, etc., were employed in the post-office. To-day the mammoth structure at the southern angle of the City Park is one of the chief ornaments of the city. Besides this great building there are twenty branch stations; the total force employed, including carriers, who make seven daily deliveries, numbers 1,193. In the year 1874 there were delivered by carriers 33,689,117 letters and postal cards, and 16,634,475 city letters; the postage received amounting to $2,589,384.94.

More remarkable is the wonderful growth of the system of telegraphic communication. The Western Union Company, in addition to its large and convenient structure, has 90 branch offices in the city alone, employing 371 operators, 214 messengers, and 238 clerks and other employés. In the year 1875, messages passed over its wires in the city to the number of 242,316, and from the city to other points 1,543,878, in all 1,786,914, or more than ten per cent. of the total messages, numbering 17,153,710, which passed over the lines of this mammoth company in the year mentioned.

Of hardly less interest to the citizen is the American District Telegraph Company, one of the most useful adjuncts of modern city life; valuable also in that it employs boys in its service, and trains them to habits of promptness and fidelity, which will in time show good results in efficient public labor of more important kinds. This company, organized in 1871, has now 3,700 instruments in houses, public and private, throughout the city, and a staff of 500 messenger boys. In the past year they delivered 1,107,454 calls, of which 580,886 were their own district business, the remainder deliveries for the Western Union, with whose local offices they are connected. In addition to this service they delivered 1,890,600 circulars and cards of various kinds.

It only remains to show the progress in the value of taxable property in the city to complete the showing of its growth and establish its progress in the century, 1776 to 1876, which has been under consideration. In 1801, the total valuation of the real and personal estate of the City and County of New York was $21,964,037. The official valuation in 1875 was, of real estate, $883,643,845, and of personal property at $217,300,154—a grand total of $1,100,943,699. To this must be added the large amount of personal property exempt from taxation held by individuals and associations, certainly not less than $300,000,000 and the sum of property will be found to reach $1,500,000,000. Great complaint is made at this time of the depression of business, but allowance must be made for the extreme expectations of our business men, accustomed as they are to the rapid successes of the past. Surely, when the foreign trade alone of New York reached the sum of $735,000,000 in the year 1874, there is still some hope left for the future. Evidently the grass is not to grow in the streets this decade, and the glory of the city is not wholly departed! It is peculiar to the life of great cities that depression in one branch of trade is the cause of increase and thriving in other ways, and that there is a constant compensating balance between the richer and poorer classes of society. Economy and extravagance follow each other in alternate rise and fall, and with its injuries, each metes out its benefits to the community as well as to individuals, while stimulated in turn by each alternately, the life of the city itself maintains its health and vigor, all the better perhaps because of the change.

The marvels we have witnessed in the present century in the use of steam, and the development of the electric and magnetic forces, which now seem destined to supersede it as motors, are reasonable grounds for hope of new applications and new discoveries as marvellous. What changes they are to make in the life of mankind none may prophesy, but it is not unsafe to predict that New York will continue to grow and prosper, to become greater and wealthier in the same increasing ratio as in the past, and that the values of 1885 will show as wondrous an advance over those of 1875 as those of 1875 over those of 1865. What its progress may be in another century no intelligence can measure, no imagination conceive.

In the rapid summary of New York progress a large field of interest has been left wholly untouched—perhaps the most important field of all, that of political government. Nowhere in the history of modern civilization has the experiment of popular government been more severely tried than in this city, where so large a proportion of the foreign immigration which has built up the national prosperity has been received, and so small a proportion of the better element of that immigration been retained. The best minds of the community have been turned, and are still turned, to that serious question in popular government, the harmonizing of strong local government with the principle of universal suffrage. The history of our city charters is that of a series of experiments to this end.

Probably its solution will be found in the results of the constant, unremitting, and noble efforts in which thousands of our citizens of both sexes are daily engaged to raise the moral and physical standard of our population, and fit them for the blessings which the experience of history has shown that no other form of government than the republican is capable of bestowing with equal hand upon the rich and the poor. The coming century will resolve this difficult question. If history provide the element of prophecy, it is safe to assume that the solution will be in favor of individual liberty and popular government.

In thanking you for your kind attention, I beg to urge the necessity of a warm and generous support to this institution, in which alone the materials of a history of our great city are to be found, and to note my own deep obligation to the efficient assistant librarian, Mr. William Kelby, who is himself an accurate living compendium of knowledge on every subject of historical interest concerning New York.

THE WIG AND THE JIMMY:

OR,

A LEAF IN THE

POLITICAL HISTORY OF NEW YORK.

"Alitur vitium vivitque legendo."

PRICE, TWENTY-FIVE CENTS.

NEW YORK:
PUBLISHED BY THE AUTHOR.
1869.

THE WIG AND THE JIMMY:

OR,

A LEAF IN THE

POLITICAL HISTORY OF NEW YORK.

"Alitur vitium vivitque legendo."

Entered according to Act of Congress in the year 1869, by
EUGENE J. POST,
In the Clerk's office of the District Court of the United States for the District of New Jersey.

NEW YORK:
PUBLISHED BY THE AUTHOR.
1869.

PREFACE.

At the instance of the UNION LEAGUE CLUB of New York the House of Representatives, on the 14th day of December, 1868, appointed a Committee of seven to investigate alleged frauds in the Presidential Election of 1868 in the State of New York. Such Committee entered at once upon the discharge of its onerous duties and held sessions in New York City, Peekskill, Kingston, Rondout, Troy, Rochester, Middletown, Port Jervis, Montgomery, Hamptonburg, Newburg and Goshen in the State of New York, and Washington, D. C. The testimony taken by it while very voluminous in extent, covering nearly nine hundred printed pages, was of a directness and importance rarely obtained in similar investigations and necessitated a report of great length and explicitness. Owing to these and other causes it was not until about a week prior to the expiration of the term of the Fortieth Congress that the Committee was able to submit the result of its labors to the House, which at so late a period in the session could take no action upon the bills reported or recommendations made. The large expense attending the printing and binding of the report and testimony led the House Committee on Printing to deem it unwise to publish more than two thousand copies, a number so small as to allow each Member of Congress but four volumes. Unfortunately, the press was unable, owing to the length of the report, to give little more than a hastily prepared telegraphic abstract of the Committee's conclusions. Thus, from causes inherent in the very nature and extent of the work, the circulation and publicity which its importance demanded were estopped, and the legislation which the necessities of the case required was delayed. Knowing that no correct, true or intelligent idea of the facts is prevalent, and believing that only through a general and wide spread knowledge of the illegal and partially successful attempt of the Democracy of New York to thrust minority candidates — both State and National—into places of power and trust, can the American peopl become acquainted with the dangers through which they have passed, or be prepared to protect themselves in the future against the machinations of evil and designing men, the following pages, narrating in a brief and comprehensive form the more important facts sworn to before the Committee, have been prepared.

Without malice, with no motive other than a desire to see perpetuated the institutions of our country, and in the full realization of Bacon's charge that "men's reputations are tender things and ought to be like Christ's coat, without seam," has this pamphlet been written, in good faith, believing the statements contained therein to be true. Confident that the interests of society, good order and puregovernment will beadvanced by its publication, it is respectfully submitted for the earnest consideration of a thoughtful public in every portion of our national domain.

THE AUTHOR.

CHAPTER I.

INTRODUCTORY.

An incident which transpired during the Spring of 1864 in one of the Southern cities convinced the writer, who was an eye witness, that the fear of exposure and the dread of public opinion were the most wholesome and effective means of punishing and preventing evil.

A woman of some thirty years of age was captured one evening shortly after dark, endeavoring to run the lines of the army. A careful search of her person being made, four large bags were found beneath her under garments, suspended from her waist. The contents were mixed—being letters, shoes, thread, needles and quinine.

A young officer on the staff of the Commanding General of the Department, to whom the captured property was forwarded for examination, succeeded the same night in finding and arresting a young woman of high social standing and personal accomplishments as the author of a most unwomanly letter found among this intercepted mail, containing information sought to be conveyed to the enemy, of certain movements about to be made by the Federal forces. The letter was addressed to a lover in the Rebel army, and written in the closest possible manner upon eight pages of French note paper. The sojourn in the neighborhood of the "cursed Yankees" was deplored and regretted, in that Southern girls had been found quite willing to flirt and coquette with the "vandals," and in instances had so far degraded themselves as to form life partnerships. Miscegenation was discussed with much gusto as purely of Northern origin. Four pages were devoted to a minute and detailed rehearsal of private gossip and scandal respecting her more conservative or politic neighbors, who so far recognized the situation as to act under the belief that a Union soldier *might* be a gentleman. Details, so far as she had been able to gather, respecting an expedition about to move upon the rebel capitol, were added as her mite to aid the cause of secession. The information imparted that a letter, which would not have been taken from the Post Office save for the belief that it came from the South under flag of truce, had been recently received from her aunt in Cincinnati, who wrote that two cousins had both served in the Union army, and one had "died fighting bravely for his country at Chattanooga." And finally, as calculated to specially commend her to the affections of her lover, was added, "and I am glad he is dead, fighting in such a cause;" while a closing prayer was uttered that he whom the Almighty had for some unknown reason seen fit to afflict the South with, in the person of General Butler, "may never die a natural death, or be gathered home to his fathers, but may suffer all the torture possible for mortal man to endure."

The facts being reported to the Commander of the Department, that officer directed the immediate release of the author of the letter and return to her home; and, as a punishment for her offense and a warning to others, ordered that the communication be published in the official papers, signed with her full name and address, and an appendatory statement that all future transgressors of the law requiring messages across the lines to be sent under flag of truce would be similarly dealt with. Mark the result. A spontaneous and universal outburst of popular indignation followed, which but for the firm yet merciful hand of military rule, would, regardless of the sex of the offender, have visited her with condign and summary punishment, while the innocent members of the families of a mother and brother were openly insulted and threatened with personal violence. Indeed, so lasting and deep was the popular feeling that total social ostracism and seclusion became obligatory upon the transgressor, and from that hour until the close of the war no communication of any character was known to clandestinely leave the city, while the flag of truce mail for the South from that locality increased the following week to more than two-thirds its former proportions, and so continued.

So that it is seen that what danger of capture, trial by military commission, long imprisonment and risk of life itself had theretofore been unable to prevent, was at once brought to an end by mere dread of publicity and fear of the scorn and contempt of society.

In the belief that known facts are oftentimes the most powerful weapons of offense or defense; that rogues and villains fear exposure; that the arousing of public opinion against any species of crime is the most effective means of thwarting, if not preventing it; and that quick, decisive, yet unremitting warfare should be waged until desired results are attained, we enter upon the work of detailing the history of the election frauds in New York in 1868, the character of the leaders and more active participants therein, and their connection therewith.

During the month of October, 1868, and within a few hours of the State election in Pennsylvania, when both of the great political parties in that commonwealth were bending all their energies to win success, there left the City of New York in the interests of the Democratic party a large number of gamblers, roughs and professional scoundrels of every description, prominent among whom was a member of the Common Council. These gentry on arriving in Philadelphia at once took an active interest in the struggle, and on the day of election were found voting illegally in the several wards and precincts. Subsequently, many of them were indicted by the Grand Jury of Philadelphia for their offences, but before warrants were issued they had hied to their respective homes in the more hospitable City of New York. Believing "an ounce of prevention worth a pound of cure," the Quaker City authorities did not follow the matter vigorously, preferring to hold over them the indictments as security for future good conduct than to risk their trial by jury during the exciting hours of a Presidential election then close at hand.

The experiment on behalf of the Democracy had been far from unsuccessful, and emboldened and encouraged thereby it was determined to carry it out on a larger scale in November in their own strongholds of political power where Grand Juries, Courts and Judges would not or dared not interfere therewith. The programme as accomplished was as shrewd, comprehensive and bold as wicked, illegal and villainous.

The main features were the employment of repeaters and the wholesale issue of fraudulent certificates of naturalization. The details embodied,

First—A wicked, confessedly untrue and libellous proclamation from the Mayor of the City of New York, the Democratic candidate for Governor.

Second—A secret circular issued from the rooms of the Democratic State Committee requesting telegraphic estimates of the majorities in the several towns and cities in the State, to be sent to Wm. M. Tweed, at Tammany Hall, at the minute of closing the polls.

Third—Instructions from A. Oakey Hall, then District Attorney and Secretary of the Democratic Executive Committee, now Mayor of the City of New York, to all Democratic canvassers in the city, to "prolong the count as far as possible," whereby the leaders, knowing the estimated majorities against them in the "State," had it within their power, by means of fraudulent canvassing, altered returns and ballot-box stuffing—most if not all of which were employed—to override and defeat the popular will; and

Fourth—The swearing in by James O'Brien, Sheriff of the County of New York, himself an ex-inmate of the Penitentiary, of some two thousand special deputies—an unusual and unnecessary proceeding—most of whom, judging from the history, antecedents and behaviour of those known to us, were thieves, and other disreputable characters, whose principal occupation appears to have been to protect, aid and abet fraudulent voting, and annoy, threaten and arrest honest and faithful election officers and peaceable law-abiding citizens.

It is not proposed, however, to here consider these details, but to confine ourselves to the two prominent and distinctive measures previously mentioned.

CHAPTER II.

REPEATING.

This form of fraud is first referred to in the annals of our National politics, in a report of the Judiciary Committee of the United States Senate appointed to investigate the frauds in the Presidential election of 1844, when it was proven to have been practiced, although to a limited extent. Since then it has been comparatively unknown. The followers of St. Tammany, after nearly a quarter of a century, revived it in 1868, when its novelty, nature and *modus operandi* seem to have peculiarly attracted the attention of both rank and file.

A repeater is one, who, without right and against law, makes a business of registering or voting, or both. As in bounty jumping and desertion, occupations quite familiar to most repeaters, the number of times a registry or vote may be repeated in a single day depends largely upon the nerve of the man engaged. And a moment's reflection upon the fact that during the War hundreds of men, with the knowledge that an ignominious death would follow detection, hesitated not to enlist, receive bounty and desert more than a half score of times, must convince the most doubting mind that the same class would from innate depravity, if no other reason was found, engage in a work so full of excitement and adventure as "repeating," especially when practically informed by an honorable Justice of the Supreme Court, as will be hereafter seen, that although arrested in the very commission of the crime neither conviction nor punishment would follow. The proof of repeating is sufficiently abundant to fully justify the report of the Congressional Committee which thoroughly investigated the facts, that if it had devoted its entire time for three months to this matter alone, "it would not have been possible to ascertain or take testimony to prove the *number of persons who voted more than once*" in the City of New York, and that the character of the evidence fully proved the fact that "an organized system was perfected and carried into effect by members of the Democratic party to register many thousands of names, fictitious or assumed, and then to vote on them by hundreds of persons voting from two to forty times each day for the Democratic candidates."

The instances given below, while convincing the reader of the accuracy of these opinions, will illustrate the manner in which the work was carried on and the character of the men and means employed therein.

William H. Greene, a patrolman, attached to the Seventh Precinct Police, was one of the officers on duty at the place of registry of the Sixth District of the Seventh Ward during the first two days of registration. On one of those days he observed a gang of men, several of whom were known to him by name, and all of whom he knew had no residence in the district, register themselves from the houses of Wm. M. Tweed (Grand Sachem of Tammany Hall, State Senator, Deputy Street Commissioner and Supervisor), Patrick H. Keenan Coroner of the City and County of New York), and Edward J. Shandley (Police Justice). Most of them were registered without objection on the part of any one, but some few being challenged promptly took the statutory oaths and compelled the registration of their names. The character of these repeaters may be learned from Greene, who has stated under oath that most of them were "thieves who have several aliases," while "the leader of the gang who registered from Coroner Keenan's house, as Henry J. Lawrence, is an Englishman, known by the name of Charles Wilson, alias 'Nibbs' or 'Nibbsey,' a celebrated pickpocket who has stolen fortunes, but somehow or other always slips through and is never prosecuted." On the opposite page may be seen a copy of the likeness of this favorite of the judicial and political ring as it appears in the Rogues' Gallery at Police Headquarters. An unwillingness to leave his counterpart exhibited itself to such an extent when sitting for his photograph, that two stalwart members of the force were compelled to steady his head and control his facial expression.

Another of this gang, by name Patsey Nolan, alias John Reilly, was a notorious thief, since arrested for stealing a diamond pin. Fortunately we are able to trace these worthy Democrats still further. Late at night on Friday the 30th of October, when but a day of registry remained, Inspector George W. Walling, one of the most earnest and

CHAS. WILSON, ALIAS HENRY J. LAWRENCE, ALIAS "NIBSEY,"
Pickpocket and Repeater.

faithful officers of the Metropolitan force, learned that a gang of repeaters under the leadership of William Varley, alias "Reddy the Blacksmith" (so called from the color of his hair and his former occupation), well-known as the proprietor of a low drinking saloon on Chatham Street, the headquarters of one of the worst gangs of thieves and cut throats known to the police, had been engaged in registering from a house on Catherine Street, and proposed the following day changing its rendezvous to No. 29 East Broadway, and resuming operations. For the purpose of verifying his information, Walling, early on Saturday morning, the 31st, accompanied by six officers in citizens dress, proceeded to the locality named and spent several hours in patiently watching the suspected house. Shortly before two o'clock, P. M., signs of activity were manifest and the detectives observed a number of men leave the house and proceed to the place of registry of the First district of the Seventh Ward. From there they returned to East Broadway, and shortly reappearing proceeded to another place of registry in an adjoining district. Satisfied now of the work these men were engaged in, Walling allowed them to return to their rendezvous, when he at once made a descent, drove in and captured a posted watcher before he could give an alarm, arrested the entire gang—eight in all—and seized their book. The men were taken at once to Police Headquarters and incarcerated, and the book turned over to the Superintendent.

An examination and comparison of this book with the original registers for the 1st, 3d, 4th, 6th and 7th districts of the Seventh Ward, established the startling fact that these eight men had registered one hundred and sixty-one fictitious or assumed names, assigning as residences fifty-five different houses in East Broadway, Henry, Market, Monroe and Division Streets, and that they were a part of the same gang of repeaters observed by Officer Greene on the first or second day of registration, registering from the houses of Tweed, Keenan and Shandley. Convinced that "Reddy the Blacksmith," although not with these repeaters when arrested, was one of their number, Walling went at once to his saloon. Not finding him in, he searched the place and seized another book similar in size and appearance to the one previously obtained, containing some sixty additional names with the number of a house and street opposite each, which names were subsequently ascertained to be mainly registered in the 8th District of the Sixth and 4th District of the Seventh Wards. The similarity existing in the assumed names found in the two books thus obtained, and other strong circumstantial evidence renders it quite certain that the latter book was also the property of the arrested eight, thus making *two hundred and twenty* fraudulent and illegal registrations accomplished by this gang.

Of the character of these repeaters, Walling confirmed Officer Greene, in that one of them he "knew very well by reputation as a pickpocket," while Detective Irving stated that another was a deputy of Sheriff O'Brien, from whom was taken at headquarters "his shield, and also some orders of arrest found on his person."

And now reader, mark well how faithfully Tammany protects its supporters and adherents at the expense of law, justice and good order. Between six and seven o'clock in the evening of the day of arrest, Wm. F. Howe, well-known as a criminal lawyer and Democrat, appeared at

Headquarters and served upon Detective Irving, the officer in charge, a writ of *habeas corpus* directing the bodies of the eight to be brought before the Honorable George G. Barnard, Justice of our Supreme Court, at the office of said Justice Barnard, No. 23 West Twenty-first Street, in the City of New York, this 31st day of October, 1868, at 7 o'clock in the evening."

In compliance with the requirements of the writ, no time being allowed for a return thereto *and none being made*, the men were forthwith taken by Detectives Irving and Coyle to Judge Barnard's residence. Arriving there at about 9 o'clock, Coyle remained on the sidewalk with the prisoners, while Irving went into the house where he found Mr. Howe, who took from him the writ, endorsed thereon "The prisoners being charged with no offence *on the annexed return*, I order them discharged, October 31st, 1868," and handed it to a servant girl who took it up stairs to Judge Barnard's room, and soon came down with the Judge's signature attached to it, obtained as she stated from the Judge, *who had gone to bed.* Thereupon the prisoners were discharged.

It is worthy of note that no notice of the issue or hearing of the writ was served upon the District Attorney as the representative of the people, which notice so distinguished a Democrat as Judge McCunn has testified he thought a Judge " bound by law to give to the District Attorney of his county; the statute requires it," and which the then District Attorney, A. Oakey Hall, has sworn, " should be *preliminary* to the hearing, and it is a *misdemeanor* for a judge to hear a writ without notice to the party interested."

The arrest of these repeaters was serviceable in that it prevented them from continuing operations during the afternoon and evening, while the discharge was instructive in affording definite information as to the precise locality of " the office of said Justice Barnard, No. 23 West Twenty-first Street," where as we are informed in " The Ermine in the Ring," the judicial robes of this eminent and high minded magistrate are at times " endued for the occasion when at his utmost altitudes." The prisoners in the custody of an officer were *on the sidewalk*, their counsel and the officer served with the writ, were *in the hallway*, the writ itself with no return thereon was *in the hands of a servant girl*, and the Chief " Justice of our Supreme Court" was transacting chamber business *in his bed*.

The result was, *First* : Discharge of the prisoners and some *sixty* fraudulent and illegal votes polled on the names by them registered. *Second*: A feeling of security on the part of thousands of employed repeaters whereby, to obtain for themselves the promised pecuniary or other reward, their exertions were redoubled to illegally swell the Democratic majority in the City.

But lest it be charged that an extreme case has been instanced, let us examine another.

During the sittings of the Congressional Committee in New York, in January last, an Attorney of the Supreme Court, who at the time of election was an Inspector in the 5th District of the 18th Ward, testified before it, that very late in the evenings of the days for registration, there came to the Board of which he was a member, in groups of four

WILLIAM VARLEY, ALIAS "REDDY THE BLACKSMITH."
Pickpocket, Thief and Democratic "Regulator." (See Appendix.)

or five, as applicants for registration, a large number of young men of from 21 to 25 years of age. These groups were usually led by one Florence Scannell, an ex-member of the Common Council, and a somewhat notorious character. Each of these men being challenged, sworn and examined, stated that he resided at the Compton House, a combination of rum hole, restaurant and cheap lodging house on the corner of Third Avenue and Twenty-fourth Street, of which Fagin and Scannell, both of whom were Deputy Sheriffs, and the latter a brother of Florence, were the proprietors. Further questioning elicited from several the information that "they slept there (the Compton House) two or three nights out of the week, and the rest of the time slept with their mistresses." Deeming this matter worthy of investigation, Florence Scannell was brought before the Committee and sworn.

Being examined, he admitted having employed some thirty men to register names, but stated that he could not tell where they registered for the reason that they had registered *from 150 to 200 names*, and from "*almost every house in the district.*" That on the day of election he had engaged some twenty men who had voted on about *one hundred* of those registered names. Believing he was stating only so much of his operations as he chose and concealing the rest, the original registry book of his district was obtained, when the Compton House *alone* was found to have 152 *names registered therefrom*, while the poll book showed that *ninety-four* votes had been cast from that house, *twenty-seven of which were never registered.*

The registry book being exhibited to Scannell, and also to one Mc-Glade, bar tender of the Compton House, the two swore that they only knew thirty-nine of the one hundred and seventy-nine names registered and voted therefrom, and some of this small number were not residents of the house.

Of the thirty-nine known to them, but twenty-seven voted, and seven of these illegally—six not being registered. So that under Democratic manipulation there were registered from this single house *one hundred and fourteen fraudulent names* and *seventy-four fraudulent and illegal votes polled.*

How an endeavor to so alter the present registry law as to render it easy in the future to discover, thwart and almost wholly prevent any similar attempt was opposed by the Democratic members of the last Legislature, and after the passage of the bill by the Republicans, was strangled by the veto of a Democratic Governor who held his seat solely by means of these and similar fraudulent votes will be seen hereafter.

Yet still another instance, for the field is large and profitable.

A young man, addicted for years to the dangerous yet fascinating and fashionable sin of gambling, but otherwise of good character, was engaged during the latter part of October by Peter Norton, brother of the notorious Michael Norton, State Senator from the Fifth Senatorial District and Alderman from the Eighth Ward, to join a gang of repeaters operating in the Fourteenth, Eighth and Sixth Wards.

The instructions given were "to register as often as possible on the two last registry days." Having served his country well and faithfully for some eight years in the marine corps and regular army, and being "inclined to the side of order and good government," our young friend failed reporting to Norton during the day of the 30th of October. In the evening he repaired to the liquor store of Peter Mitchell, present Democratic Member of Assembly, then a candidate, on the corner of Bleecker and Greene Streets, where he found congregated some forty repeaters. Excusing himself for absence during the day, he was ordered to report the next morning at 7 o'clock, whereupon he left and related the facts to the Superintendent of Police and several prominent citizens. The result was the receipt from them of instructions to join the repeaters, and in the character of a detective learn all possible of their operations. Accordingly on the morning of the 31st he reported at Mitchell's, but found only one of the gang, David Sommers by name, present, who claimed to be Peter Norton's lieutenant. Taking a drink with Sommers who stated that Peter had been up all night with the boys, and was then sleeping, the two visited Peter Burns at his saloon, No. 69 East Houston Street, who gave them each slips of paper bearing a name and residence written thereon. Under these names they registered in the Second District of the Fourteenth Ward, Sommers swearing in his registry. Shortly after three others of the gang joined them, and the five registered in the Second and Third Districts of the Eighth Ward. At the latter place the party was still further augmented in number and visited the First District of the Eighth Ward where they registered as from 84 Greene Street, the residence of Peter Mitchell. Sommers and our detective then called at Peter Norton's, and arousing him, the three joined the others at Mitchell's saloon where they found Senator Norton and Mitchell. Some 25 or 30 slips with names and residences on which to register were then furnished by the two Nortons and Mitchell, and the information imparted that the occupants of the houses from which they were to register understood the matter, and would answer satisfactorily any inquiries which might be made by the police or others. The strength of the gang constantly increasing, they were then divided into parties numbering from four to twelve each, and dismissed in different directions. Attached to a party of five was our detective, and after registering in Varick Street they returned to Mitchell's where Peter Norton transferred the detective to a party of twelve, bound for the Sixth Ward. Walking rapidly, this crowd soon arrived at No. 44 Bowery, known as "Cuddy's Hotel," where they found Edward Cuddy, present member of the Board of Aldermen from the Sixth Ward. This worthy at once produced a book containing some hundreds of names and residences, and from behind his bar handed, or passed over his shoulder to each man a small card or slip bearing a name and residence taken from his book. Thus supplied, the party left and registered in the Ninth District of the Sixth Ward as from 60 and 70 Mott Street and 62 Bayard Street, some being compelled to swear in their registry. This completed the day's work, and our detective returned to Mitchell's where he was directed by Peter Norton to call upon him for his reward, and not fail to be on hand on the day of election. It may be added, for statements made by confederates to each other are good and admissible evidence, that it was stated to our detective that they had done better than is here set forth on the previous day, and since election several of them have boasted of registering and voting from twenty to twenty-five times each. All the facts just stated were fully established under oath by this amateur detective who produced before the

Congressional Committee as coroborative evidence, original notes secretly made by him at the time of the occurrences and some of the identical slips furnished him. An examination of the original registers for the districts mentioned, not only showed every name given by him to be registered as he stated, thus completely confirming him, but also evidenced the fact that from every house of which this crowd of repeaters represented themselves residents, there was a large registration, while from inquiries at the several places and other proof it was established that such registration was in excess of the actual number of legal voters resident, from 6 to 27 names in the different houses.

These are but samples of hundreds of instances which might be given. We could readily detail how men repeatedly registered in the same Election District with no other or further attempt at disguise than the changing of their hats, caps and coats on the public street, and almost within sight of the registrars: how in some districts an examination of the registry was made and the names of the persons legally registered who had not voted were copied and passed to outside parties, whereupon repeaters assuming such names voted thereon; and how inspectors, challengers and others who endeavored to prevent these and similar scenes were threatened, assaulted and arrested; but neither the fact that repeating was practiced by the Democratic party on a most gigantic scale, nor the intricate, subtle or varied means employed to accomplish its illegal purposes would be more clearly comprehended. The cases narrated must suffice.

Yet, we cannot refrain from anticipating the question each reader will undoubtedly ask. Was there no repeating in the interests of the Republican party in the City of New York? The answer is, that while there were doubtless individual instances, there was no attempt made in that direction, either organized and general or by any of its leaders or candidates so far as is known. And while the Congressional Committee, two of whom were Democrats—and one, the Hon. M. C. Kerr, of Indiana, the candidate of his party for the Speakership of the House of Representatives—was in being from the 14th of December, 1868, to the 4th of March, 1869, and held sessions in New York for one third of that time, it is a remarkable and honorable fact in the language of the Committee's supplemental report "*that there is no evidence of any kind that any republican was engaged in false registering in the interest of the republican party, and without false registering there could be no repeating.*"

CHAPTER III.

THE ISSUE AND USE OF FRAUDULENT CERTIFICATES OF NATURALIZATION.

In treating of this subject, but two matters seem essentially worthy of consideration, viz : the extent of the issue, and the men and means employed in the work. And as Courts in a number of the river and central counties of the State were parties to this form of fraud to quite as great an extent comparatively as some of those in the City of New York, we propose in our examination to divide the subject, discussing first

The Naturalization Frauds in New York City.

That we may judge of the number of fraudulent certificates issued in the City of New York, let us glance for a moment at the statistics of former years and the preparations made for naturalization in 1868. Judge Daly of the Court of Common Pleas, in his exhaustive and able article upon naturalization in Vol. xii of the New American Cyclopædia, states that in ten years from 1850 to 1859 inclusive, there were naturalized in the City of New York over 60,000 aliens.

For the eight years from 1860 to 1867, inclusive, the total number was 70,604. The total number of Naturalizations in New York City for each year from 1856 to 1867, inclusive—a period of twelve years, was:—

Year.	No.	Year.	No.
1856, Presidential	16,493	1862	2,414
1857	8,991	1863	2,633
1858	6,769	1864, Presidential	12,171
1859	7,636	1865	7,428
1860, Presidential	13,556	1866	13,023
1861	3,903	1867	15,476

a total average of 9,207 per annum. This was the work of two Courts, viz: the Superior and Court of Common Pleas. The Supreme Court in the First Judicial District had never to this time in the history of the State naturalized a person. Notwithstanding the fact that the yearly average of naturalizations had been but about 9,000; that the greatest number naturalized in a single year never reached 16,500; that three years had elapsed since the close of the war in which 35,927 aliens had been made citizens, a yearly average of 11,975, or an excess of 3,000 per year above the annual average for twelve years; that the addition of such excess to the diminished numbers naturalized in 1862, 1863 and 1864 would preserve the ratio, and account for those who from fear of being drafted had refrained from applying during those years of the war; that the rebellion had reduced the alien population of New York City, many of whom enlisted, were killed, died from disease, or after the war found homes elsewhere; and, finally, that the yearly average of emigration from and including 1847 to 1860—a period of thirteen years—had been 197,435, while for the four years from 1860 to 1863 inclusive—and none who arrived subsequently could be legally naturalized in 1868—the yearly average of alien arrivals had been but 100,962, or an annual loss of one-half, yet orders were early in September passed along the Democratic line to prepare on a gigantic scale for the naturalization of aliens during the coming month. The Supreme Court also determined for the first time to engage in the work of making citizens. In accordance with this known determination, there were printed for the use of the Courts on the days below named the following number of blanks:

	Superior Court.			Supreme Court.	
Date.	No. applications.	No. certificates.	Date.	No. applications.	No. certificates.
Oct. 2	.....	10,000	Sept. 16	10,000	9,000
" 3	10,000	.....	" 19	10,000	.....
" 8	.....	10,000	Oct. 6	25,000	5,000
" 15	.....	10,000	" 12	5,000	5,000
" 16	20,000	.....	" 13	10,000	.....
			" 15	.....	10,000
			" 16	5,000	.....
			" 19	5,000	.....
			" 20	.....	10,000
			" 22	5,000	.....

or a total of 30,000 applications and 30,000 certificates for the Superior Court, and 75,000 applications and 39,000 certificates for the amateur Court (Supreme).

The Court of Common Pleas, which save for a year or two previous had done the larger share of the work of naturalization, did but little in 1868, its total number for the year being 3,145, of which 1,645 were in October. Justice requires the further statement that there was no evidence whatever of any fraud in this Court, although all its Judges were elected as Democrats, while proof was abundant that the duty entrusted to it of making citizens of the United States was discharged throughout with marked propriety and dignity.

In the Supreme and Superior Courts only were frauds proven. To what extent we will now consider. The following table was sworn to as being the daily number of applications for naturalization on file in the Supreme Court Clerk's office for 1868.

1868—October 6	.....	6	1868—October 16	.....	721
" October 7	.....	8	" October 17	.....	633
" October 8	.....	379	" October 19	.....	955
" October 9	.....	668	" October 20	.....	944
" October 10	.....	717	" October 21	.....	773
" October 12	.....	723	" October 22	.....	675
" October 13	.....	901	" October 23	.....	587
" October 14	.....	523			
" October 15	.....	857	Total	.....	10,070

But these applications do *not* show the number of naturalizations granted by this Court, although they should so do. They simply show that for 10,070 certificates issued there are a corresponding number of papers purporting to be applications, on file. Let us examine a moment in detail. The 10,070 certificates admittedly issued (there are known to be 10,093 applications, pretended or otherwise, on file), is but 1,070 in excess of the number of blank certificates printed for use by this Court on the 16th of September—three weeks before it naturalized a man—and is 4,000 *less* than the number on hand on the 6th day of October when it begun operations, although (25,000) *twenty-five thousand* additional were subsequently printed by order of the Clerk, and 10,000 of these within forty-eight hours of the time when the Court ceased to naturalize.

As Charles E. Loew, Clerk of the County and ex-officio Clerk of the Supreme Court, testified that these blanks were "never given out," and that certificates of naturalization were "to be given out *only by the Clerk on the order of the Court,*" the inquiry as to whether the remaining 28,930 blank certificates shown to be printed were in the custody of the Clerk of the Court to whom they were delivered was deemed important and pertinent.

An actual count of the number on hand was therefore required, when the Assistant Deputy Clerk who made the count certified that 1,862 only remained, leaving the large number of 27,068 blanks missing and unaccounted for in any way.

We find, then, an admitted issue by this Court of 10,070 certificates of naturalization in sixteen days, or 10,054 in fourteen days—work not really beginning until October 8th—a daily average of 718. Beyond this is a clearly proven, but on the part of the Court, a concealed, issue of what extent it is impossible to precisely state. Evidence abounds to sustain the position taken by the Congressional Committee that 27,068, the whole number of missing blanks, is the correct amount.

In the Superior Court a singular state of affairs was found to exist. Being required to furnish the committee with the number of naturalizations in that Court in the year 1868, and the daily issue for the month of October, Owen E. Westlake, a clerk, on the 28th of December, swore to the following statement:

1868—January	84	1868—October 9th	1,760
" February	100	" October 10th	1,653
" March	105	" October 12th	1,856
" April	140	" October 13th	1,868
" May	108	" October 14th	2,109
" June	102	" October 15th	1,420
" July	140	" October 16th	1,112
" August	195	" October 17th	840
" September	632	" October 19th	1,026
" October 1st	580	" October 20th	1,004
" October 2d	745	" October 21st	861
" October 3d	840	" October 22d	911
" October 5th	1,425	" October 23d	1,024
" October 6th	1,721	" November	41
" October 7th	1,630	" December	94
" October 8th	1,842		

a total of 27,897 for the year, or 26,226 in twenty days in the month of October, a daily average of 1,311. On the 2d of January, 1869, Joseph Meeks, the Deputy Clerk, swore " that the figures of Westlake were derived from an actual count;" and on the 14th of the same month officially certified the total for the year 1868 to be as above stated, which certificate was presented the Committee, under oath, by Adam Gillespie, assistant naturalization clerk. If evidence is worth anything, surely this should be sufficient to establish the facts testified to. The Committee having meanwhile appointed a clerk—an attorney of the Supreme Court—to count and examine the applications on file in the Clerk's office for the month of October, was not a little surprised to learn from him, under oath, on the 25th of January, 1869, that but about 18,000 papers had been produced for his inspection, and he was informed that these were all there were. Here was a discrepancy of *eight thousand* for a single month, and the loss apparently made since the number was so positively sworn to from "an actual count." Fearing the result of this exposure, Adam Gillespie, aforementioned, and others, were hastened to Washington to explain away this startling exhibit. Quite naturally their statements then made, that the first exhibit submitted and so positively testified to was a mere estimate and not the "actual count" required and sworn to be, were far from satisfactory, as testimony obtained from other sources concerning the manner in which most of the naturalizations in this Court were made, strongly corroborated the accuracy of the original figures.

As then stated the daily naturalizations for the month of October were—

1868—October	1	426	1868—October	13	1,384
" October	2	723	" October	14	1,569
" October	3	785	" October	15	934
" October	5	1,363	" October	16	581
" October	6	1,272	" October	17	418
" October	7	1,415	" October	19	709
" October	8	1,133	" October	20	517
" October	9	877	" October	21	428
" October	10	804	" October	22	459
" October	12	2,017	" October	23	618

a total of 18,432, a daily average of 921, or 7,794 less than previously sworn to, while the Committee's Clerk between the time of these two "counts" by the Court officers could find but 17,915 applications, or 8,311 less than appeared by the first exhibit of the Court Clerks, and 517 less than was shown by the second. But supposing true this last "count" of the Court officials, the *admitted* naturalizations in the several Courts in New York city alone for the year 1868 were—

Common Pleas	3,145	In October alone	1,645
Superior Court	20,103	" "	18,432
Supreme "	10,070	" "	10,070

or a total of 33,318, nearly four times the average of former years, and more than twice as many as ever before, while two courts, in an average of eighteen days sittings each, in addition to discharging their ordinary duties, granted 28,502 certificates, or more than eighty-two per cent. of the whole yearly number. Adding the 27,068 missing blanks as the concealed issue of the Supreme Court, we have a total naturalization for 1868 in New York city of 60,386, which the evidence taken, and much not obtained but readily to be had, shows to be the more accurate and probable amount. And even this, it should be remembered, is without taking into account the 8,311 additional certificates sworn and certified to by three officers of the Superior Court as granted by that Court in October.

Fortunately there is no question as to who were the leaders in this bold and illegal work, for pre-eminently at its head and front must necessarily be the Judges who took part therein. In the Supreme Court no member of the bench but George G. Barnard naturalized a single individual. His position is consequently easily determined. In the Superior Court five Judges at times naturalized, viz.: John H. McCunn, Samuel B. Garvin, Samuel Jones, John M. Barbour and Anthony L. Robertson, now deceased. All the evidence agrees that far the greater portion of the work was done by Judge McCunn, while the gentleman who examined nearly 18,000 of the applications on file in that Court testified, "I should think about eight-ninths," *or more than* (15,000) *fifteen thousand*, "bore his initials." We cheerfully add, that of all the Superior Court Judges he alone is impeached by the testimony taken. These two then, George G. Barnard of the Supreme and John H. McCunn of the Superior Court, are originally the guilty parties. The story is credited and credible, though from its nature difficult to substantiate, that the exertions of both in this matter were demanded by Tammany as the price of renomination to their respective positions. Certain it is that Judge Barnard was at the time a candidate of his party for re-election, while it is well understood that Judge McCunn, nominated to his present seat on the bench by Mozart Hall, is pledged a renomination this fall by Tammany.

The Supreme Court was for naturalization purposes open solely at night, generally from 7 to 10 o'clock, but occcasionally somewhat later. The Superior Court, save upon two or three occasions, was open for this work only during the day, while as a rule Judge McCunn naturalized but in the afternoon. In less than four hours in the Supreme Court and six in the Superior most of this illegal work was done, certificates of naturalization being admittedly granted at a daily average of 718 in the former and 921 in the latter, while as many as 955 were confessedly issued upon one occasion in the Supreme in about four hours, and 2,017 in the Superior in a portion of one day and evening, mainly by Judge McCunn. How strangely in view of these facts does it sound to read from a report made to the House of Representatives in 1844, of the circumstances attending the impeachment and removal of Benjamin C. Elliot, Judge of the City Court of Lafayette, by the Senate of Louisiana sitting as a high Court of impeachment, that "it further appeared that *nearly four hundred* of these certificates (of naturalization) were issued in one day. It seems to your committee impossible that this could have been legally done." If the granting of "nearly four hundred" certificates of naturalization in 1844 brought impeachment and removal upon the offending Judge, it is an easy matter to determine the least punishment demanded for those who in 1868, in a few hours, admittedly granted twice and thrice—aye, nearly four times that number. As time is an important element in determining the character of this work, it should not be lightly passed over. We have said that in the Court of Common Pleas naturalization was honestly conducted. Let us now ascertain the time required to make a citizen and the manner of procedure in that Court, that the contrast between it and the Supreme and Superior may be more apparent. Judge John R. Brady, who for thirteen years has served honorably and faithfully upon the Common Pleas' bench, has testified, "the process has been to have parties appear before the Judge in open Court," and the time required to naturalize a man "depends very much upon the intelligence of the witness. Sometimes it has been done in from three to five minutes; sometimes it has taken more; sometimes I have held cases for reflection for half an hour, or an hour, or an hour and a half." Mr. Jarvis, Clerk of this Court, testifying on this subject, said, "*The action of the Court alone would take probably about five minutes.* There were many cases where I knew the Court to be twenty minutes

JAMES MYERS, ALIAS MULLEN.
Till Tapper and Special Deputy Sheriff. (See Appendix.)

in the examination of a witness, and then to reject the applicant." In response to the direct question as to why more naturalizations were granted in the other Courts and less in his in 1868, the same witness replied, "I cannot state any reason; I may have an impression. I don't think we naturalized them *rapidly enough*." At the rate stated from twelve to fifteen certificates were granted per hour in the Common Pleas. Who can doubt the correctness of Mr. Jarvis' impression on reflecting that in the Supreme Court admittance was not only refused citizens, attorneys and reporters, but that when present they were at times forcibly ejected; that in the same Court the admitted naturalizations must at times have been granted at an average *of more than three per minute;* and that Judge McCunn, of the Superior Court, has himself testified he could naturalize *two persons a minute;* while in practice he must have done even better than that? The Congressional Committee, a majority of whom were lawyers, and some of whom had served upon the bench, thought as a rule "a Judge could not actually and properly naturalize over twelve in an hour"—the average in the Court of Common Pleas. He who taking into consideration these facts does not clearly comprehend why for the first time the Supreme Court was compelled to take part in naturalization; who does not fully understand the extensive preparations early made by the Supreme and Superior Courts for this work; and finally, who does not in the subsequent illegal and fraudulent practices of these Courts perceive the strongest evidences of a preconceived plan and conspiracy on the part of the Democracy to issue, circulate and employ for purposes of illegal registration and voting thousands of fraudulent certificates of naturalization, is either a knave or a fool. Such as he would not be convinced were "one to rise from the dead." Yet another fact, and one which conclusively establishes the fraudulent nature of a large number of the certificates admittedly granted, is the great proportion of "minor applications." By law if an alien arrives in this country before the age of eighteen he is entitled, if a resident for five years, to be naturalized upon reaching twenty-one, without having two years prior to application declared his "intentions." Of the 10,070 certificates admittedly issued by the Supreme Court, all but 382, or *more than ninety-six per cent.* were issued upon these "minor applications," while of the 18,000 papers examined in the Superior Court 14,000, or *eighty per cent.*, were of the same character. In the Court of Common Pleas about fifty per cent. only of those naturalized were "minors." The efficient aid which the use of these "minor applications" would render in dispensing with the production of a certificate of previously declared intentions was never lost sight of by the conspirators, while the astounding number of *baby* applicants seems in no wise to have disturbed the equanimity of our immaculate, disinterested and honest Judges—McCunn and Barnard.

But the essential aid rendered by these Judges need not be further detailed. It was mainly comprised in one or more of the following criminal derelictions of duty:

I. Hasty and incomplete examination of applicants and witnesses.

II. Total neglect at times to examine the one class or the other.

III. Through negligence, imposition which might easily have been guarded against, or direct complicity, the issue of certificates in the names of persons who never appeared in Court, applied therefor, produced a witness or took an oath.

IV. Similar issue of certificates to applicants, persons of assumed or fictitious names and others, upon the oath of residence and moral character of persons of assumed and fictitious names, or of known criminals and persons of immoral character.

V. Similar issue of certificates based upon "minor applications" when the persons to whom such certificates issued were known or could readily have been ascertained to be unentitled thereto on such applications.

VI. Total neglect or refusal to commit known disreputable persons and others whose business it was for a pecuniary or other consideration to act as witnesses and who in such capacity repeatedly appeared before them.

VII. The conducting of naturalization proceedings in a secret manner, by causing citizens and others to be denied admission to the Court-room, or ejected therefrom when observed.

As auxiliaries in the plot of procuring and furnishing fraudulent certificates were numerous offices under the control of Tammany Hall, or its Committees, and the several Democratic Ward organizations. Also an improvised office in the basement of the City Hall. In most if not in all these places applications were given out and filled up, professional witnesses employed or permitted, and illegal and fraudulent certificates procured from the Courts and distributed, given away or sold. Some of the Democratic candidates and many then office holders, either secretly or openly countenanced and aided these or similar establishments or engaged in outside operations of a like character on their own responsibility. Without attempting to detail the many methods adopted to secure naturalization certificates on the part of speculators, politicians, thieves and repeaters, we shall instance a case or two illustrative of hundreds which might be recited, and in the appendix name the more prominent characters with a statement of their efforts.

A young man, whom for obvious reasons we shall designate as Henry, formerly an attache of the city press, being out of employment during the month of September and observing signs of activity in the neighborhood of the City Hall, determined to engage for himself in the work of procuring naturalization certificates. Having a large acquaintance in the 20th Ward, he made arrangements that the names of persons for whom certificates were desired should be left at a liquor store in 32d Street. Establishing himself at a lager beer saloon in Chatham Street, in close proximity to the Courts, with a stock in trade consisting of an ink bottle, a few pens and a number of blank applications obtained from the offices of the County Clerk and Democratic Committee, this was briefly his mode of doing business.

Receiving each night at his up town headquarters such names as had been left for him during the day, he would on the following morning fill up his blank applications, sign them as witness with his own or a fictitious or assumed name, or procure others to so sign, and when necessary, would in a similar manner sign both as applicant and witness.

During the day or evening he would present these papers to the Courts, sometimes with and sometimes without the company of the applicant. In this manner appearing on occasions as witness, at other times as applicant, and when necessary, as both applicant and witness, Henry has testified he procured *more than six hundred certificates*. These he furnished to different parties, receiving for his services from one to five dollars from each.

It may be added that Henry has further testified to seeing "as many as one hundred" men "called up by Judge Barnard," and sworn in a batch, while other witnesses swore before the Congressional Committee to the same effect, one stating that he saw oaths administered by Judge Barnard to batches of men numbering "from one hundred to about two hundred, and I remember one occasion when I counted over one hundred and eighty in a batch. There would be four or five batches varying from one hundred and ten to two hundred in number, averaging about one hundred and forty or one hundred and fifty, *got through by Judge Barnard in each hour*."

A man somewhat actively connected with the Democratic party and for years an office holder under Democratic Judges, through a simple desire to do his best to swell the Democratic vote, procured the assistance of two young friends and together the trio prepared and filled up mainly with fictitious or assumed names, some seventy-five applications. These were handed to John B. McKean, Clerk in Judge Barnard's Court, on two occasions and certificates in the names of such parties received on the following days, no person having appeared in Court therefor, or been sworn either as applicant or witness. Most of these papers were subsequently furnished repeaters and others to aid them in registering and voting. The writer sometime since had placed in his hands several of these particular certificates, together with a number of others issued by the Supreme and Superior Courts in the various modes related herein. In instances he has the affidavits of those whose names they bear, detailing the facts relative to their obtaining possession thereof.

A single other fact and we pass to the consideration of affairs in the State. It was sworn to before the Congressional Committee, that contracts were made by two brothers, whose sole business was appearing as professional witnesses, for the delivery of certificates in Kings and Orange Counties, N. Y., and the States of Connecticut and New Jersey, for fifty cents each. Some of these certificates were obtained by employing eight or ten men who under assumed names repeatedly appeared in court and swore themselves through. Others were received direct from the hands of the court clerk, no one appearing either as applicant or witness. Under these circumstances it behooves all in the Counties and States named (and elsewhere, for the writer believes many were sent to Pennsylvania), who would protect the purity of the ballot box, to closely scan in the future all certificates presented and purporting to have been issued by these Courts in 1868. No one should be allowed to register or vote thereon without at least being challenged, sworn and thoroughly examined.

Naturalization Frauds in the State outside of New York City.

The Committee, while not having time to make an extended tour through the State, visited every county where they had information naturalization frauds had been perpetrated. These embraced Westchester, Orange, Dutchess, Rensselaer, Livingston and Monroe. In all of these gross frauds were proven but generally of a character different from those committed in New York City. In almost every case the certificates issued in these counties, amounting in the aggregate to about six thousand are totally null and void, having been issued without authority or warrant of law in any respect. As a rule no court was held, and no Judge was present. The pretended natralizations were made by County Clerks, their assistants, deputies, and in instances, acting assistants. Not a single certificate so granted is worth the paper it is written upon, and no person should be allowed to register or vote thereon. In Westchester, Orange and Dutchess, a large number of certificates were found, purporting to have been obtained from the Supreme and Superior Courts of New York City. In the main these were sent to some prominent democrat who delivered them to the parties whose names they bore or placed them where they could be readily obtained by such persons. Very few of those who thus received certificates applied therefor, appeared in court or were sworn.

The great length of this chapter precludes any further or more elaborate statement, while the points given, if carefully noted, may prove of service in future elections. A single copy of the evidence taken by the Committee, can at least, be obtained by some wide-awake and energetic citizen, from his member of Congress, the details and extent of the frauds learned therefrom, and a plan devised to prevent the injurious use of these certificates.

But our history would be incomplete were we to omit to state the stricking fact that in every county where frauds in naturalization were found to have prevailed, the Judges and County Clerks or those who granted the certificates were Democrats. Not a single illegal or fraudulent certificate was proven to have been issued in a county where the Judges and Clerks were Republicans or by an officer of that political faith. The writer has no comments to make.

The facts are stated, the record is made and the truth alone has been written. The reader must draw his own conclusions, and in the future when called upon to exercise the right of suffrage, let him with the light before him act conscientiously upon his own convictions of right, and justice, and his duty to himself and his country.

CHAPTER IV.

CONSIDERATIONS FOR THE FUTURE AMD REMEDIES PROPOSED.

No candid reader of the foregoing chapters can fail to comprehend that unless measures of the most positive character be taken to prevent in the future a repetition of scenes so disgraceful, illegal and criminal, as are there recited, the days of a Republican form of government in our country are already numbered. Based as our government is upon the fundamental idea of popular suffrage and the rule of majorities, if a few men, or a party, with the intent to defeat and subvert the will of the people and aggrandize office and power to themselves, can secretly concoct, boldly plan, and successfully execute on the grandest scale the most dangerous and criminal schemes of fraud; can escape all punishment for their offences, and whenever, and as often as the occasion shall in their opinion seem to demand it, can perpetrate anew their nefarious operations with the aid derivable from the fraudulent instruments previously obtained, then, indeed, are American institutions a failure, and revolution, anarchy and ruin sure to follow.

We have no desire to be considered an alarmist. But no sane man, in view of what has been shown to have transpired in New York, and with the knowledge that courts in California and Pennsylvania also engaged in issuing fraudulent certificates of naturalization to no inconsiderable extent, can doubt that the effort was seriously made by or on behalf of the Democratic party to carry the last Presidential election by fraud.

And if the certificates so issued cannot, or are not to be treated as other than legal and valid, what is to prevent in the future one or more courts in each State, or county if deemed necessary, engaging in similar attempts? Or again, if two courts in New York can, in an average period of less than three weeks, issue some 60,000 certificates of citizenship upon which votes may be cast, what is to hinder those courts in a period of a few short months from granting such a number of naturalizations as would make the attempt to elect national officers of a political faith other than Democratic as futile and useless as it now is in the metropolis of the nation to endeavor to place a Republican in the Mayor's chair?

Let none be deceived by the thought that such certificates could not be used on the day of election. From 1845 to 1865 the average per centum of votes cast in the State of New York, as compared with the actual number of voters, was less than 77 per cent. The average in Presidential years, from 1848 to 1864 inclusive, was 87.19 per cent. In 1868 this average in the State, owing to frauds, was *ninety-two* (92) *per cent.*, while in the city of New York the per centage was *one hundred and eight* (108). In other words, the number of votes cast in the city of New York at the Presidential election of 1868 was, as compared with the actual number of voters therein, more than twenty per cent. in excess of the average in the State at any previous Presidential election, sixteen per cent. more than the average in the State at the same election—although, as a rule, more votes proportionately are polled in the country than in the city— and *eight per cent. more than the whole number of voters in the city,* supposing every such person to have voted.*

The frauds we have shown lost the Republican party New York and New Jersey with their forty electoral votes, nearly one seventh of the whole number of the electoral college and one-half of the official strength of the Democracy in that body. What then is to be done? It is idle to talk of punishing repeaters and others when Judges of our highest courts are themselves the most wilful and flagrant violators of the law. Not a man has been placed on trial in New York city by the State officials for a violation of the election laws at the election of 1868,

---

* Calculations based upon census of 1865.

though hundreds of such criminals are well known to the authorities. But this is the rule, thoroughly established and well understood, with hardly an exception known. The probabilities of conviction or punishment we are wholly relieved from considering. Indeed, a Grand Jury mainly composed of prominent Tammany politicians, evidently selected for the purpose, and which assembled shortly after the election, with the cry of frauds on the elective franchise ringing in their ears upon every side, could find nothing in that direction worthy of injury, but devoted their time to a Paul Pry endeavor to ascertain what, if any amounts of money Republicans had contributed towards the expenses of the canvass. And when, as has been testified to by a gentleman summoned before them, the direct offer to furnish proof of frauds in the election was made them by him, one of the jurymen "replied that I (he) was not called for that purpose: that if they needed me (him) they would let me (him) know." The advantages and privileges enjoyed by, and the protection afforded to the adherents of Tammany, who for the benefit of the Democratic party engage in any form of illegal work which depraved ingenuity can devise, or wicked and abandoned characters perpetrate, could not be more forcibly shown. But one remedy remains—legislation. Congress can and must enact such laws as will prevent the recurrence of extensive frauds in repeating canvassing, etc., at future elections for President and Members of Congress. The present naturalization laws, embraced as they are in a number of statutes, should be repealed, and a general act, with every section carefully considered and explicitly expressed, should be passed. But nowhere is this more fully appreciated than at Washington. The only troublesome question has been as to what courts and officers shall exercise the power of making citizens. Probably not less than twenty bills on the subject of naturalization were introduced in the two houses at the last Session of the Fortieth Congress. That the matter was not acted upon at that time was solely because it was thought the wisest and safest course to await the report of the Committee investigating the frauds in New York. When that was received, as stated in the preface, no time remained. There will be, however, no unnecessary delay at the coming session, and one of the plans below mentioned will certainly be adopted.

I. The power to naturalize will be confined to the Circuit Court and District Courts of the United States, and the highest court of record in each State, or

II. Such power will be conferred only upon the United States Courts, Commissioners in Bankruptcy, and where necessary officers to be appointed by the President, or Chief Justice of the Supreme Court of the United States, to hold office during life or good behavior, and be known as Commissioners of Naturalization.

In either case the illegal action of judges, officers and clerks will be more closely guarded against than heretofore, and all derelictions of duty will be made punishable in the United States Courts. In the opinion of the writer the second method would be preferable, and the only objection which has ever, so far as his information extends, been made thereto, viz.: that it creates new officers, should weigh but little against the advantages and results derivable from its adoption. It is known to more nearly meet the views of the members of Congress from the Eastern and Middle States than any other. As originally proposed the measure restricted the right to naturalize to the United States Courts and the Commissioners in Bankruptcy. In this shape the Southern and Western members were strongly opposed thereto, such courts and officers being less numerous in their section of country than with us. The addition of the section providing for the appointment of Commissioners of Naturalization, who should hold court for the purpose of naturalizing in each county in their districts in each month, obviated this otherwise serious objection.

Among other measures tending to prevent and punish frauds upon the elective franchise which will be strongly urged, are bills drawn by the Hon. Wm. Lawrence, of Ohio, Chairman of the Committee which investigated the New York frauds, providing methods of punishing repeating, false registering, illegal voting, and fraudulent canvassing at elections for President and Members of Congress; requiring Congressional Elections to be held on the same day throughout the Union; and providing measures whereby a Presidential election may be contested. Thus much we are promised from the National legislature.

Let us now consider what, if anything, has been done or remains to be done by the State of New York. The last Legislature passed and the Governor signed a bill affixing penalties for any attempt to register or vote upon naturalization certificates known to be illegally issued or fraudulently procured. Beyond this the State could not go so far as preventing the future use of such certificates is concerned.

A bill to provide and punish frauds in canvassing was unfortunately not passed. The fact may be partially attributed to the resignation of the Hon. J. C. Bancroft Davis—now Assistant Secretary of State at Washington—who had the bill in charge. This bill should receive early attention from the next Legislature.

But the most important measure remains to be considered. Early in April, 1869, the attorneys who had represented the Election Committees of the Union League Club of New York in the Congressional investigation, and whose attention had been specially directed to every detail of the frauds, reported that if a few simple yet important amendments were made to the existing registry laws the opportunities for illegal conduct and action would be greatly lessened.

They were instructed at once to prepare and submit a bill embodying the proposed changes, to have it speedily presented in both branches of the State Legislature, and to urge its passage.

Acting under such orders a bill was drawn, and on the 10th of April introduced in the Senate by the Hon. A. W. Palmer, and on the 16th of the same month offered in the Assembly by the Hon. N. B. La Bau.

By hard work this bill was got through the latter body on the 4th of May, and passed the Senate two days later, and within a few hours of the final adjournment of the Legislature. Every Democrat in both houses strenuously opposed it for no apparent reason, save that it was what it purported to be, a bill "to ascertain by proper proofs the citizens who shall be entitled to the right of suffrage." By the State Constitution, all bills which having passed the Legislature shall not be returned by the Governor within ten days after presentation, become laws without his signature, unless the Legislature by adjourning shall have prevented such return: in such case they are dead. As the Legislature adjourned so soon after the passage of the act under discussion, it was feared by the advocates of the measure that the Governor, who it was never supposed would sign the bill, would carefully refrain from making public his objections thereto.

Most happily were they disappointed. On the 16th of May, Governor Hoffman sent the bill to the office of the Secretary of State without his signature, and with a singular lack of political sagacity accompanied the same with the following statement of his reasons for disapproving the measure.

> In my annual message I took the ground that "there should be one Registry law for the whole State, imposing equal conditions and restrictions everywhere, and it should be the aim thereof to secure to every citizen his right of suffrage free from intimidation, corruption, or onerous exactions."
>
> This bill not only makes regulations for the cities of New York and Brooklyn, differing from those which it applies to the other parts of the State, but it contains provisions likely to deprive honest voters of their rights, and to impede the free exercise of the suffrage.
>
> Section 3 of the original Registry law, as amended by chapter 812 of the laws of 1866, provides that the meeting of the inspectors for final revision of the registry lists shall be held on Friday preceding the election, and that they shall, "on that day add to said lists the name of any voter who would on the first Tuesday of November be entitled to vote."
>
> Section 3 of this bill abolishes the Friday meeting, and substitutes another day as the day of final revision, and does not re-enact, as applicable to the substituted day, or any other, this provision for adding the names of those who, not then entitled to vote, would nevertheless be so entitled on the day of election, by having meantime come of age. The law as it would stand, if this bill were approved, would exclude this class of persons from a constitutional right
>
> Section 4 of the bill provides that if one inspector choose not to declare a man's name to be on the list, his voice shall not be received, or, if received by the Board of Inspectors, such vote shall not be counted in any subsequent "legislative or judicial scrutiny" of the election. The bill provides only that a special list be kept of the persons whose votes shall be received under such circumstances, but it is obvious that to make the the provision that the vote shall not be afterward counted effectual, not only the voter but his ballot must be identified.
>
> This could only be done by marking the ballot, and although the law does not authorize this to be done, yet the practice of doing so would be apt to grow up. To do this would violate the secrecy of the ballot. As the existing election law requires that all ballots for any officer by whomsoever cast, shall be deposited in the one box provided for such ballots, it is plain there is no other way of carrying the provision into effect, except by marking the ballot or compelling the voter, in the subsequent scrutiny to reveal how he voted. Both these methods would be in violation of every elector's right to vote by secret ballot. JOHN T. HOFFMAN.

With the Governor's objections before us, let us examine the provisions of the bill and review the statements of the veto.

In considering the bill we shall note the changes which it would have made in the existing laws and the occasion therefor. The first section simply substituted Tuesday four weeks for Tuesday three weeks before the day of election as the time for the first meeting of the Boards of Registry. The second section provided a new method of registering which, while simple and easy of execution, could but prove of incalculable benefit in the prevention of fraud. Under the existing law the inspectors register the names of the voters alphabetically, according to their respective surnames, so as to show in one column the names in full, and in another column the residences. By the plan proposed, the names of the voters in each house would be registered under the number of the house and street in which they reside.

(ALIAS LAWRENCE) FARRELL, ALIAS WM. PIERCE.
Burglar, etc., etc. (See Appendix.)

As now conducted, it is evident that it is beyond the power of the inspector, without a long and tedious search through every letter of the alphabet and on every page of his register, to ascertain who or what number of persons have registered from any given house. Yet this is information he should be able to obtain at a glance. The election districts in New York city seldom, if ever, exceed three or four blocks in extent—some are but two—and there is rarely a district of which at least one of the inspectors is not a resident, or personally acquainted with most of the legal voters; nevertheless, the fact is notorious that from the very necessities of the case and the occasion, men are often times illegally registered, frequently a large number, from the residences of persons well known to the inspectors, whose attention is first drawn to the fact after the close of registration, when the evil is done and the remedy substantially gone. If, however, the mode suggested had been adopted, the moment an address was given, as the inspectors turned to place on the registry the electors name, the house by street and number would he brought prominently to the attention of at least some one of the Board, who would remember its precise locality, who owned, who resided there, and whether it was a private residence, boarding house, hotel or tenement. In short, an opportunity for the detection of fraud would be presented, which under the present law does not exist.

The third section provided that registration should close on the second Monday preceding the day of the general election. This would allow six working days to intervene, whereas under the existing law there is but one. The justice and propriety of this change must be evident to all when it is remembered that in most of the cities of our State, especially in New York where were registered last fall over one hundred and seventy thousand names, nearly one-half of the entire registry is made up on the last day or days, while under the existing law no opportunity is afforded for scrutinizing and verifying the lists, canvassing the several districts, preparing challenge books, and otherwise endeavoring to secure a fair and honest expression of the public will, prevent the polling of illegal votes, and provide for the arrest of those who would violate the laws and usurp or destroy the rights and liberties of the people. Bad and designing men have simply to refrain from registering until late in the afternoon or evening of the Saturday preceding the day of election (Tuesday) when within sixty hours thereafter—forty of which are either sacred to religion or devoted to rest—they are able to vote without fear of detection, and against the will of the lawful electors to place in positions of honor, trust and profit, executive, legislative and judicial officers.

The more important features of the fourth section provided that two inspectors of different political faith, should each have sole charge of the registry on the day of election, for the purpose of checking the names of those who voted, and that a uniform mark should be used as such check. Also prohibited the receiving of any vote until the said two inspectors should have found and declared the elector's name to be on the register. The objects aimed at by these provisions were all attempted to be covered by section six of the act of 1865, but the more thorough detail of this bill and the addition of a clause requiring any violation thereof to be noted in writing in the inspectors' books, and making such violation a misdemeanor punishable by heavy fine or long imprisonment, or both, would, it was believed, secure a more perfect compliance with the law on the part of its officers. It is well known that a large number of votes have been received at every election without time being allowed the single inspector, who, under the present law, is placed in charge of the check copy of the register, to ascertain if the parties offering to vote were registered, while it is equally notorious that hundreds of votes were polled in the city of New York at the election last November—and this must have been with the aid and connivance of said check inspector—who were *never registered*.

By the change proposed no *one* inspector or clerk could connive at the commission of fraud so deliberate and destructive as this, and the honor of the State as well as the general welfare would seem to demand that the opportunity should not be afforded. It will be observed, that, by the system of checking proposed, the check registers would show not only the number registered but the number of votes polled and the names of the voters, thus uniting in one book a registry and poll list, and affording a means of detecting fraud on the part of poll clerks or canvassers. To illustrate; it was testified to before the Congressional Committee that at the November election in the third district of the Fourth Ward of New York, during the absence of one of the poll clerks, his associate copied fom the register list in the hands of an inspector eighty-five (85) names which he added to both of the poll lists without the knowledge of the other clerk. When the canvassers took possession this number of votes was dropped among the ballots as they were turned from the boxes upon the table and counted in the return made, yet under the existing law no means are provided for the detection of so skillful a fraud.

The fifth and last section provided for the inspection of all registers and poll lists without charge, by any elector. This is substantially the present law, the amendment being merely adding the poll lists not now open to examination.

Let us now examine the Governor's objections to this seemingly just and necessary bill. They may be briefly stated:

I. Because the bill made "regulations for the cities of New York and Brooklyn, differing from those which it applied to the other parts of the State."

II. Because it contained "provisions likely to deprive honest voters of their rights, and to impede the free exercise of the suffrage."

There is a reference by the Governor to a portion of his Annual Message, in which he advocated a registry law for the whole State, but it is evidently not spoken of as a reason for declining to sign this bill, so that the two heads given cover his objections. The first is a statement of fact. The second of opinion solely. The former is true; the latter, as we shall show, is without foundation. But while admitting the charge of differing regulations for the Cities of New York and Brooklyn —and such differences have always existed, and must necessarily continue to exist—we are at a loss to know which of such differences the Governor disapproved of, for he utterly fails to designate it. Possibly all were distasteful, and so his language would imply, yet it is difficult to se why he sh ould disapprove of an additional day being allowed residents of New York and Brooklyn in which to register, or object to the Boards of Registry in those cities being compelled to hold sessions an hour earlier and two hours later than in the other portions of the State. Nor does it seem possible that he could have objected to a single additional copy of the registry being made in the City of New York, for the purpose of being filed in the office of the Bureau of Elections, or the requirement that the mark which inspectors must make in their check registers opposite the name of every person voting, should in New York and Brooklyn be similar to a letter V.

Indeed, we are confident no one will for a moment pretend to believe that the Chief Magistrate of the State of New York refused to sign this bill in consequence of these differences- Yet every provision making regulations for the cities of New York and Brooklyn differing from those applicable to the remainder of the State which are not specially included by the Governor as falling under his second objection has been mentioned save one.

The exception consists in the requirement that in every district in New York and Brooklyn, two inspectors, one of each political faith, shall each have on the day of election the sole charge of a copy of the registry for the purpose of checking the names of such persons as vote. No change in this respect was made in the remaining districts of the State, the existing law directing one inspector to keep such copy, but not preventing two from so doing if they chose. It would hardly seem that this simple provision could have caused the Governor to withhold his signature, but doubtless it did, and a reason for such belief can be readily given. Prior to the year 1828, acting under the existing law, the Democratic Board of Supervisors of Kings County, who had the appointment of all election officers, had uniformly followed the practice of the Republican Board of Police Commissioners in New York, and divided such appointments equally between the two political parties. At the election in 1868, when Hoffman was the candidate of his party for Governor, the Democratic majority in this Board of Supervisors, acting if we may judge from its proceedings under a preconceived and fixed plan, held a quasi secret session, and appointed the election officers. Their selections being made known, it was found that with hardly an exception, every inspector of registry and elections was a Democrat. The same condition of affairs would have existed in New York had the Democracy had a majority of the Board of Police Commissioners. The section of the bill last noticed, in providing for the checking of the registry by two inspectors, and requiring each to be of different political faith, would have prevented the repetition in the future of any such proceeding, and always secured the minority one out of the four inspectors.

The honest and fair minded of all parties will not only believe the provision eminently wise and proper, but somewhat less than just. The Governor, grateful to his party for their conduct and course, could only regard it as an objection to the bill and a hindrance to future partisan action on behalf of himself and his political friends.

But we pass to the consideration of the second and last objection. The bill, says the Governor, "contains provisions likely to deprive honest voters of their right, and to impede the free exercise of the suffrage." Fortunately, these provisions are designated by the Governor, and his views thereof expressed at length, wherefore we may examine them both and see not only if the fact be so, but if his arguments are correct. He first says that by chapter 812 of the laws of 1866, the Friday preceeding the election was designated for the meeting of the inspectors to finally revise the registry lists, and that said inspectors were by that law required " on that day to add to said lists the name of any voter who would on the first Tuesday of November be entitled to vote." That the words are correctly quoted by the Governor no one will dispute. He adds that section 3 of the bill under discussion amends so much of chapter 812 as fixes the Friday before election for final revision by substituting the " Tuesday, one week preceding the day of the general election" as the time for such revision. This is true, and the Governor makes no objection to the change. Proceeding, he says this bill " does not re-enact as applicable to the substituted day, or any other, this provision for adding the names of those who not then entitled to vote, would, nevertheless, be so entitled on the day of election by having meantime come of age." Again correct. But adds the Governor: " the law as it would stand, if this bill were approved, would exclude this class of persons from a constitutional right." Here we beg. leave to differ with our Chief Magistrate. Only so much of the law of 1866 would have been changed by this bill as was expressly amended. All that was not altered would have remained in force. Now, as this bill only changed " the Friday preceding the election," as the day of final revision, to the " Tuesday, one week before the election," the remainder of the section providing for the registration of the class referred to by the Governor would have remained as operative as before. It is painful to think that the Governor allowed his party zeal to so affect both his mind and his official action as to cause him to wholly overlook so apparent a fact. But again. The law of 1866 seems to have been worded with the very change proposed in this bill in view. After fixing a day for the revision of the registry, it reads: " And they (the inspectors) shall *then* revise the said lists and shall on *that day* add the names of those who would be legal voters on the day of election." Whether the words " then" and " that day" refer only to the day named, " Friday," or are to be considered more general and to mean *the day of revision*, may be somewhat questioned. The writer believes the latter is the true application. But grant that the Governor's assumption is correct, and the Friday before the election is the day indicated. Immediately following in the same section we read: " But in making such addition on that day, (Friday the Governor says, and for argument's sake we admit it,) *or any prior day*," the inspectors shall conform to the requirements of the other provisions of the registry laws prescribing their duties. If the interpretation of the Chief Magistrate is correct, we should be pleased to know what the words " or any prior day were inserted for."

Do they not clearly imply that another day prior to Friday preceding the election, may be named for the revision of the list, and that " then," and " on " that day—the day of revision—the names of certain persons shall be added? We so think, and with the knowledge that the bill objected to by the Governor designated a " prior day" for such revision, and the well known rule of law and parliamentary usage that whatever of a law is not repealed by a subsequent act remains alive and of legal effect, it is exceedingly difficult to believe the class of persons spoken of by the Governor would or could be excluded " from a constitutional right."

The next provision, which the Governor thinks "likely to impede the free exercise of the suffrage" is contained in section four of this bill. He states it as follows: "That if one inspector choose not to declare a man's name to be on the list, his vote shall not be received, or if received by the Board of inspectors, such vote shall not be counted in any subsequent legislative or judicial scrutiny of the election." The Governor is here a little unfortunate in his language. What the section under discussion did require may be learned by referring back to the foot of page 25, where it is fully set forth. The existing law declares, "Nor shall the name of any person be placed or retained on such register without the concurrence of three of the four inspectors." It also provides that no vote shall be received save from a person found to be previously registered, wherefore it follows that no person can vote unless three of the inspectors consent thereto. As well might the Governor say that under that law "the free exercise of the suffrage" is impeded, because if two inspectors choose not to place a man's name on the list, his vote can not be received. Yet no difficulty was found in 1868 in registering 170,222 names, and polling 156,060 votes in New York city. The necessity for the objectionable provision has been fully shown, and it is only needed to direct attention to the heavy penalties attached to the refusal or neglect of any officer of election to properly discharge his duties, and which were never before a part of any registry act, for all to understand how trifling and untenable is the Governor's position. To that portion of the section requiring a list to be kept of all votes received contrary to the provisions of the bill, and forbidding that any such votes should be counted in any "legislative or judicial scrutiny," the Governor also objects, and quite naturally. For while the existing and all prior laws have contained in the very words of this bill the prohibitory portion of the clause, the requiring of a list of such illegal votes to be kept, would greatly aid a contestant who believed himself wrongfully kept from his rights, and prove beneficial in preventing fraudulent voting and connivance thereat on the part of election officers. The Governor attempts, at the close of "his objections," to argue for a secret ballot, apparently forgetful that by the State Constitution and the decision of the Court of Appeals, all voting is and must be by secret ballot. The pretense, that in order to throw out any illegal vote in the event of a "legislative or judicial scrutiny," it would be necessary (although the bill "does not authorize this to be done," the Governor says) to mark the ballot is so foolish, shallow and untrue, as to be unworthy of notice. With hardly an exception, not a legislative session, state or national, has been held for the last quarter of a century, without seats therein being contested, committees appointed, evidence taken, and the knowledge as to *how*, when and where an elector voted, obtained with comparatively little difficulty. But the Governor, having never served in a legislative body, and being still in the hands of his party trainers may have been ignorant of such fact, and innocently unaware of the rule of such bodies governing testimony and witnesses. We must, therefore, forbear all further discussion of the subject, for "where ignorance is bliss 'tis folly to be wise" was truthfully written long years ago.

APPENDIX.

"REDDY THE BLACKSMITH."

William Varley, *alias* "Reddy the Blacksmith," now an inmate of the Tombs, awaiting trial for the robbery of one Lawrence Graham, of New Jersey, who was enticed into his saloon in the cellar of No. 7 Chatham Square, is a villain of the deepest dye. He is 35 years of age, 5 feet 7 3-4 inches high—light complexion, with red hair and known to the police as a pickpocket, and a thief, large sandy moustache. Although very well he has always managed to escape punishment, for the reason that his valuable political services during the time of elections in manipulating votes and voters in the 4th and 7th Wards, could not be dispensed with by Tammany. Whether he will be similarly fortunate this time is a question, the settlement of which is anxiously awaited by the public. The cut presented on a preceding page is from a picture for which "Reddy" sat a short time since.

Following the example of many illustrious predecessors "Reddy" rejoices in being the chief or leader of a gang or tribe which does him honor by bearing his name. It seems hardly necessary to add that "Reddy's" followers possess a name and character similar to their leader, although generally less widely known. The writer not long since came into possession of an authentic list of members of "The William Varley Association," and takes pleasure in being able to make their names public. They are:

William Varley, *alias* "Reddy the Blacksmith."
William Johnson,
Allen Martin, (?)
Charles Taylor,
William Manning,
Mathew Bannan,
James Moore,
Patrick Nolan, *alias* "John Reilly,"
James Walker,
John Finn,
Michael Cobey, *alias* Henry Williams, *alias* Charles Grant,
Richard Hayes,
William Brown,
Wall Walsh,
David Callahan,
Thomas Osborn,
William Burton.
Thomas Varley, brother of "Reddy,"
George Knowles,
Charles Wilson, *alias* Henry J. Lawrence, *alias* "Nibbs,"
Lawrence Fitzgerald.
Michael Varley, brother of "Reddy," *alias* Chas. Anderson.

The following is a literal copy of an original letter received by "Reddy" from a confederate incarcerated in the Tombs for theft. The original is now in the possession of the writer. As illustrative of the nature of the transactions of "Reddy" and his gang it is inserted.

December 28th.

friend Wm. Varley, will you Be so kind to send me Borack By some one if you cant come to see me yourself one Dollar and a bit of chuck for I am starving and perishing with cold. friend general it his not much I ask and you know if I get away you would have it—I geus you no that. Tom Davis was in here to see some one. I geus Dan Noble But passing my cell I called Tom and they stopt talking to me what I was in for and I told them and then ask me do go to down Reddys and I sayed yes. he then asked me how you was getting on and I told him you was Doing good and then Dan and him ask Did send me anything. I told I Did no Dout you would if you knew where i was. old general this fust i ever ask and I hope you wont Deny me it will not Break you nor make you. Give best wishes to your Wife Emma my Best friend. my respects to tom and Mickey.

tell Emma if I get away she would have the pleasure wearing one. she knows that.

I am in my own name Michael Sullivan, cell 99 third tier. old general you do that for me and it will be luck to you for you and Emma his the only tow friends i have. I geus sing sing this time. But never mind, ash for Breakfast and a shower Bath for supper. But they cant served me worst than I have Been. so no more at present from your well wisher. Borack for god sake Do it for I shall croak here with cold.

PATRICK H. KEENAN.

This gentleman is a Coroner of the City and County of New York. We have on page six referred to a gang of repeaters registering from his residence and given the portrait of the leader of the gang. Coroner Keenan being examined under oath by the Congressional Committee testified that but "three males" over 21 years of age resided in his house, himself, James Ryan and Denis O'Neil. The names of ten other persons, among which was that of Robert A. Jones, who had illegally registered therefrom, were then read to him and the question put him, if he knew men of those names. The reply was, "I do not." The officer who saw the registrations made testified that he knew Robert A. Jones, and that said Jones "goes (went) to Keenan's house a good deal, but he does (did) not live there." When the writer first noticed this discrepancy in the testimony he endeavored to believe that it was possible for Jones to visit Keenan's house considerably and Keenan not know him, as it might be that Jones visited Ryan or O'Neil, though the latter is Keenan's brother-in-law. Since then the author has received certain evidence which convinces him that the Coroner *did know* Robert A. Jones when he swore on the 31st of December, 1868, he did not. That each reader may judge for himself whether the fact is not so, the following paper, a copy of the original in the possession of the writer is appended.

NEW YORK, Oct. 27, 1868.

SIR:—A meeting of the P. H. KEENAN ASSOCIATION will be held at No. 29 East Broadway, on Saturday evening, the 31st inst., at eight o'clock. Your punctual attendance is requested.

R. A. JONES, President.
E. N. LAFFEY, Secretary.

It should be remembered that 29 East Broadway, where this meeting of the Keenan Association was called for, was where Walling arrested the repeaters and seized their book. (See page six.) The evening, October 31st., was the night Judge Barnard discharged said repeaters. (See page seven,) and the hour for the meeting eight o'clock, was one hour after the time mentioned in the writ of *habeas corpus* procured by Counsellor Howe for the appearance of the repeaters at Judge Barnard's house. (See page eight.) A singular state of affairs certainly, but it must not be assumed that the arrested eight were anxious to attend the meeting of the P. H. Keenan Association. The writer has, however, an opinion upon the subject. Each reader will form his own.

JOSEPH FARRELL.

The portrait of this man as it appears in the Rogue's Gallery at Police Headquarters has been heretofore given. He is also known by the *aliases* of Lawrence Farrell and William Peirce. He is about 19 years of age, 5 feet 11 1-2 inches in height, of light complexion, and a burgiar by occupation. Under the name of Lawrence Farrell he was brought before the Congressional Committee by one of the Democratic members. His direct examination was very brief, and elicited no information. but upon being subjected to a severe cross-questioning he testified that he could furnish "a thousand persons" who had repeated at the Presidential election. His statement unsupported would be utterly worthless, but taken in connection with his admission that on the night before the election he was at the Jackson Club rooms, where Sheriff O'Brien was present, and a "lot of men" were congregated renders it probable that in this matter Farrell told the truth.

JAMES AND PATRICK GOFF.

These two brothers are the men referred to on another page as being engaged before the courts in obtaining fraudulent naturalization certificates. It was testified to before the Congressional Committee that an examination of the records on file in the Clerk's office of the Supreme and Superior Courts showed that these two individuals were accepted as witnesses to the residence and "good moral character" of *six hundred and sixty-six* (666) applicants. Of this number they appeared in the Supreme Court *five hundred and twenty-two* times and in the Superior *one hundred and forty-four*. Of the 27,068 certificates in the Supreme Court unaccounted for there is no method of ascertaining how many were obtained by these men. That it was a very large number there can be no doubt as it was sworn before the Committee that one of them was seen to have in his possession last Fall, in the opinion of the witness, "over *four thousand*" naturalization papers.

That the public may fully comprehend the character of the witnesses which satisfied Judges Barnard and McCunn as to the qualifications and "good moral character" of applicants for citizenship it is only necessary to add that the brothers Goff are well known disreputable and criminal characters. A member of the police force testified before the Committee that he had arrested both of them; that James was "*a professional thief*;" and that within forty-eight hours of the close of naturalization proceedings in the courts "James was arrested for stealing a gold watch and chain and two diamond rings." Of course they escape punishment.

JAMES O'BRIEN.

This individual is the Sheriff of the County of New York. He is about 29 years of age, some 5 feet 7 inches in height, of light complexion, smooth face and stout build. His early life was passed in the employ of a stonecutter. When about 18 he was arrested, indicted and convicted "of riot and assault and battery." Judge Barnard, then Recorder, sentenced him to "six months" imprisonment "in the Penitentiary of the City of New York," but he was pardoned by the Governor before the expiration of his term. He has since served as a member of the Common Council and for some two years past as Sheriff. We have heretofore referred to the characters of those who surrounded him and enjoy his confidence, and shall hereafter notice others of his more promising and trusted satellites. It was established before the Congressional Committee that on the night before the election there assembled at the rooms of the Jackson Club—an association of which the Sheriff is a prominent and active member—some two or three hundred men. That a large number of those men remained there all night, and before daybreak on the following morning were piloted to what they were informed and believed was the Sheriff's residence where breakfast was furnished them. Their hunger being satisfied they were shortly started out, and furnished from the Club House and elsewhere with names and residences upon which they voted throughout the day in the most reckless and extravagant manner. The Sheriff being examined as to these matters admitted his connection with the Jackson Club; that he was present at the Club rooms the night before election; that a large number of men were there at that time; and that on election morning he kept "open house from five to six o'clock" and breakfasted a considerable number of men.

DAVID MYERS,

alias David Mullen, is a Till Tapper, about 25 years of age and 5 feet 6 1-2 inches high. The cut we have published is engraved from a photograph in the Rogue's Gallery. He was arrested on the 28th of November, 1868, together with two other disreputable characters, on suspicion of Grand larceny, but on examination before a magistrate was discharged. On the person of one of the men was found a warrant appointing David Mullen a special Deputy Sheriff to assist in preserving the public peace at the time of the election.

PATRICK McCAFFREY.

This man was formerly a special Deputy Sheriff. Quite naturally he was found largely engaged in procuring fraudulent naturalization certificates. It has been testified that his name appears as a witness two hundred and fifty-one times in the Supreme Court, and upon two hundred and fifty-two applications in the Superior. A total of *five hundred and two* persons known to him to be of "good moral character" and entitled to naturalization.

JOHN MORAN.

During the time when the Supreme and Superior Courts were engaged in naturalization this man was one of the most active and earnest participants in the work of obtaining fraudulent certificates. It was testified to before the Committee that in the Supreme Court he appeared by the records to have been a witness for *four hundred and fifty-five* (455) applicants, and in the Superior for *two hundred and ninety-nine* (299), or a total of *seven hundred and fifty four* (754) persons. Of these *one hundred and twelve in a single day* in the Supreme Court. A most excellent witness as to qualifications and "good moral character." For some reason shortly after the election he entered the employ of the Sheriff, and for conniving at the escape of a noted bond robber placed in his custody for delivery at the State Prison, was subsequently convicted and sentenced to imprisonment in Sing Sing, where he is supposed now to be.

FLORENCE SCANNEL

is a man of about 5 feet 6 in height, light complexion and stout build, with a chestal and muscular development such as the writer never saw equalled. He is about 23 years of age, a butcher by trade, and the owner of one or more valuable stands in West Washington Market. His ostensible business is styled by him as "horse trading," though the police, who are thoroughly acquainted with the details, designate it by a name more in accord with its real nature. During the war Scannel was largely interested in faro banks in Washington and Alexandria, and, as we are informed and believe, now "runs a small game" in Fourth avenue, near Twenty-seventh street, which nets him a monthly income of some $1,600. His education is somewhat limited, but enables him to read print quite readily and write his name in a very fair hand, but it is with difficulty he can read the most ordinary words when written. He is exceedingly popular with the "b'hoys," and prides himself on a reputation of being a teetotaller. In politics Scannel is an unadulterated Democrat of unbounded pluck and rare political strength. He was chosen to a seat in the Board of Councilmen in 1866. As will be seen on page nine, Scannel was examined as a witness before the Congressional Committee. His appearance and manner were striking and peculiar.

At the close of the examination being informed that he might go he turned to the Committee and in his blandest tones said: "Well gentlemen, I bid you good day. I have no doubt we shall meet again, for I'm coming down there to Congress some day. You may just bet your lives I am." His belief and prediction were speedily verified, although not in the manner threatened, for having in response to a question of the Committee refused to answer, adding "I would rather go to the Tombs all my life than do it," he was arrested, brought before the bar of the House of Representatives and directed to answer the question. Still refusing, claiming that he had forgotten the desired facts, he was fined the cost of his arrest (some $75) and incarcerated in default of payment. Preferring to enact the role of a martyr to paying the fine he was furnished quarters in the basement of the Capitol for some five weeks, and until the adjournment of Congress.

JOHN T. HOFFMAN.

On the 3 st of October, the day on which Inspector Walling arrested the repeaters and seized their books, and the day on which Judge Barnard illegally released those repeaters, the then Mayor of the city of New York, now Governor, and prospective Democratic candidate for the Presidency issued a proclamation. He charged I. that "gross and unfounded charges of fraud are being made * * against those high in authority." II. That "threats are made against naturalized citizens, and the authority of the judges and the seal of the Supreme Court is defied." III. "A grand jury of the United States Court summoned through the agency of those who are in this scheme has, as I have been informed, been induced without that preliminary examination which is usual, and which is afforded by law for the protection of character to find in great haste and secrecy bills of indictment against divers persons f r the purpose openly avowed of intimidating them in the discharge of their public duties." IV. "The United States Marshal * * has assumed to himself the power and duty of appointing swarms of special deputies to take their place at the polls to threaten and awe the electors of the State of New York in the exercise of their high privilege of casting their votes for the chief officers of the nation and the State." These several acts the Mayor proceeded to say were done "for two purposes."

"First. To conceal and cover their own schemes of fraud which they hope to consummate by the aid of untried or unpardoned criminals.

Second. So to excite the masses of people in this city who are opposed to them as to lead them into acts of disorder and violent resistance."

Mr. Hoffman was called before the Congressional Committee and being sworn was very severely examined upon each of these points. The writer never saw a more pitiable spectacle than the Mayor presented at that time. But our readers may judge thereof for themselves. Not a single charge contained in the proclamation could the Mayor sustain in any way. He swore that it "was common report based on the statements of many individuals," &c., that threats were made against naturalized citizens, but stated that he could not mention the names of a single person who made such a statement. He swore that "it was announced in many of the papers," &c., "that the registrars * * * had a right to go behind the certificates of naturalization * * * to deny the validity of them, to examine into their genuineness or irregularity, and to refuse to register, if in their judgment they thought proper so to do," but that he could not furnish a reference to any such newspaper. He swore that he "had no knowledge" of the issue of fraudulent naturalization papers, although "such charges were made in the papers," and that he took no steps to ascertain the correctness of such charges. In reference to the third charge of his proclamation he swore that it was so "generally understood in the city," although he could not give the name of "any person" who so stated, and he did not believe the United States grand jury "had been summoned or procured to be summoned in any other than the legal and usual way," or that the indictments found by it "were found without the examination that is usual by grand juries in that court." He swore in reference to his fourth charge that it was so "generally understood," but that he took no steps to ascertain from any official source whether it was true or not. Marshal Murray testified that *he did not* appoint a single deputy. In reference to the first purpose for which he charged these things were attempted the Mayor swore that he had "merely the statements made to me (him) by confidential friends and the District Attorney in reference to Theodore Allen for whose arrest a bench warrant had been issued which the police "would not execute." There were others he believed mentioned by the District Attorney, but their names were not given him, and he took no steps to ascertain their number. He swore that he supposed he had evidence that republicans were engaged in schemes of fraud, because they held certain secret meetings, and for the reason that "it was very well understood that immense sums of money were being contributed by very wealthy men, candidates for office and others." This and this only was the purport of the Mayor's justification for his wicked and lying proclamation.

It speaks for itself in every particular, save the reference to Theodore Allen. Let us therefore ascertain the facts in that matter.

Mr. A. Oakey Hall, then District Attorney being examined as to the information given Mayor Hoffman by him in this matter, testified that he knew of *but a single case*. That it was not Theodore Allen but one Wesley Allen for whose arrest the bench warrant had issued. That said warrant "was out three weeks before the election, and was never executed until after the election, although the man was in the city, and I, (Dist. Attorney Hall) could have arrested him at any moment."

It would seem therefore that the "untried or pardoned criminals" charged by the Mayor as about to be used by the Republicans to conceal and cover their own schemes of fraud, consisted of *one individual*, Wesley Allen who was in no manner charged to be or ever to have been a Republican to any extent or in any measure whatsoever. Capt, Mills to whom the bench warrant was delivered, and who in the language of the District Attorney is "a high minded, incorruptible, splendid police captain" was next examined. He testified that late in October he received from the District Attorney a bench warrant for the arrest of Wesley Allen, with positive instructions to let no one know that he had such warrant. That acting under such orders he made every possible exertion to find Allen, even visiting Brooklyn "and other places where he frequented" for that purpose. That he communicated the fact of his having the warrant to no "living soul," not even to his own sergeants or the police superintendent, but that it was not until the 16th of November that he was able to find Wesley Allen, when he at once arrested him. Thus it will be seen that in every respect Capt. Mills performed his whole duty. It may not be uninteresting to our readers to add that Capt. Mills further stated, and this will show the force of Mayor Hoffman's charge as to *pardoned criminals*, "that Wesley Allen was a notorious thief," who had twice been to State's Prison, but that his second term had been shortened by a pardon granted by Governor Fenton. *upon the application of District Attorney Hall* and others. And that Mr. Hall had himself stated to him this was the fact, and that he (Hall) was "satisfied Allen was not" guilty of the crime for which he was sentenced – and still further – upon arresting Allen he was turned over to the District Attorney and incarcerated in the Tombs for about a month, "when he was set at liberty."

THE WIG AND THE JIMMY:
OR,
A LEAF IN THE
POLITICAL HISTORY OF NEW YORK.

This work is a concise and accurate statement of the gross frauds on the elective franchise perpetrated by or on behalf of the Democratic party in the State of New York at the Presidential election of 1868 as the same were ascertained by a Committee of the House of Representatives of the Congress of the United States. As its title would imply the wicked and illegal conduct of the JUDGES and THIEVES who aided, abetted or participated in the conspiracy is fully considered. The reasons which prevented action by the Fortieth Congress upon the report of the Committee, the remedies proposed and bills sure to become laws at the coming session of the Forty-first Congress, the amended registry bill passed by the last State Legislature, and the reasons of the Governor for refusing to sign such bill are each and all fully detailed and carefully discussed.

A short appendix descriptive of some of the more active conspirators abounds in interesting and startling facts.

The following extracts from letters received by the author from the members of the Congressional Committee who investigated the facts, establish the accuracy of the work and its value as a means of affording reliable information upon the subjects treated of:

[*From the Hon. Wm. Lawrence of Ohio, Chairman.*]

"Your work is much needed to enable the American people to become acquainted with the dangers through which they have passed, and to provide adequate remedies to prevent their recurrence in the future. * * * The certainty of exposure of men guilty of frauds is one of the great auxillaries by which the public indignation may be aroused. Your work supplies the needed expose to call into useful exercise the law-making power and the force of public opinion."

[*From the Hon. Henry L. Dawes of Mass.*]

"As far as I have been able to examine the advance sheets of your work, they seem to be very full and accurate. Unless the nation awakes to the magnitude and enormity of the gigantic frauds by which it was attempted to deluge the ballot box in New York in 1868, and has the courage to apply the remedy in season, the forms of an election will soon be of little or no use. I bid you God speed in disseminating this information."

[*From the Hon. Austin Blair of Mich.*]

"I think your work cannot fail to do good. In fact I am glad to see any effort to arouse the people to a sense of the great enormity of the frauds upon the elective franchise which seem to have grown into an organized system in New York, and to be spreading into other cities."

FOR SALE EVERY WHERE.

PRICE.

SINGLE COPIES - - - - - 25 CENTS

On all orders for Fifty Copies and upwards to one address, a liberal discount will be allowed. Address Box 4924, New York Post Office.

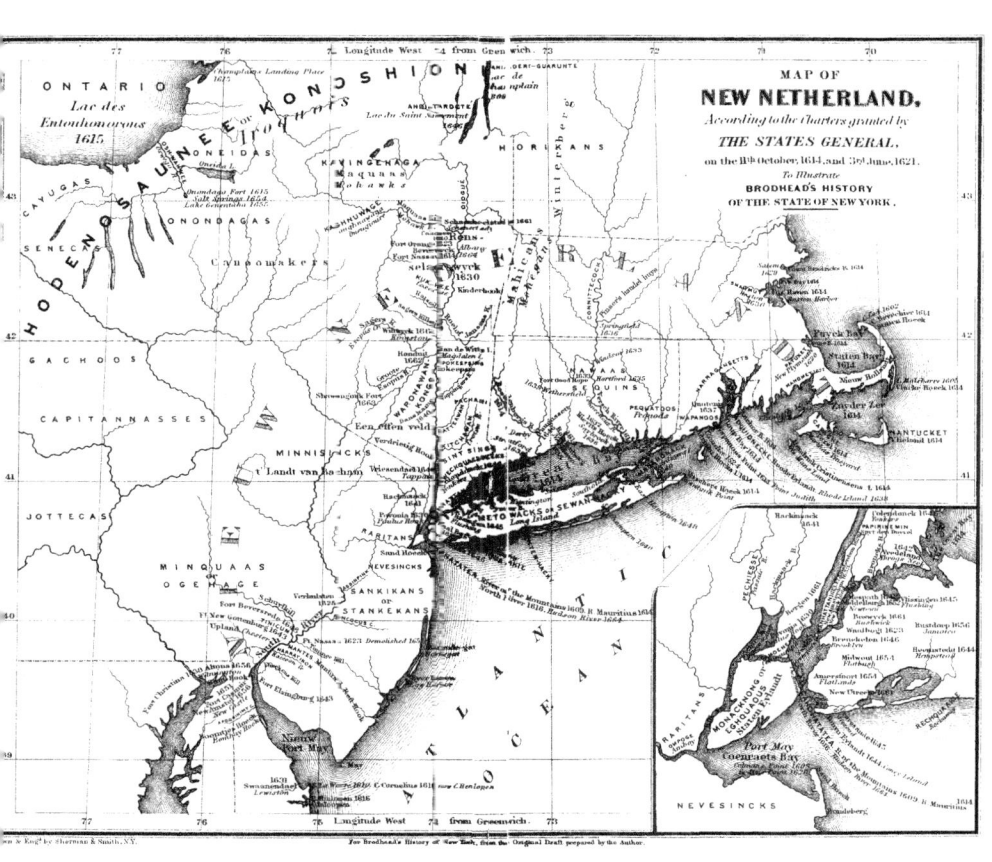

COMMEMORATION

OF THE

CONQUEST OF NEW NETHERLAND,

ON ITS

TWO HUNDREDTH ANNIVERSARY.

BY THE

NEW YORK HISTORICAL SOCIETY.

NEW YORK:
PUBLISHED BY THE SOCIETY.
M DCCC LXIV.

COMMEMORATION

OF THE

CONQUEST OF NEW NETHERLAND,

ON ITS

TWO HUNDREDTH ANNIVERSARY.

BY THE

NEW YORK HISTORICAL SOCIETY.

NEW YORK:
PUBLISHED BY THE SOCIETY.
M DCCC LXIV.

C. A. ALVORD, PRINTER.

COMMITTEE OF ARRANGEMENTS

FOR

THE COMMEMORATION.

1864.

GULIAN C. VERPLANCK,
GEORGE BANCROFT,
HAMILTON FISH,
JAMES W. BEEKMAN,
EVERT A. DUYCKINCK,
FREDERIC DE PEYSTER,
AUGUSTUS SCHELL,
GEORGE FOLSOM,
CHARLES P. KIRKLAND,
ANDREW WARNER,
GEORGE H. MOORE.

ORATION

ON THE

CONQUEST OF NEW NETHERLAND,

DELIVERED BEFORE THE

NEW YORK HISTORICAL SOCIETY,

On Wednesday, the Twelfth of October, 1864.

BY

JOHN ROMEYN BRODHEAD.

NEW YORK:
PUBLISHED BY THE SOCIETY.
M DCCC LXIV.

AT a Meeting of the New York Historical Society, held at the Hall of the Union, Cooper Institute, on Wednesday Evening, October 12th, 1864, to commemorate the Two Hundredth Anniversary of the Conquest of New Netherland,

"GULIAN C. VERPLANCK, LL.D., submitted the following Resolution, which was seconded by GEORGE BANCROFT, LL.D., and adopted unanimously:

"RESOLVED, That the thanks of this Society are eminently due and are hereby tendered to JOHN ROMEYN BRODHEAD, LL.D., for his eloquent Oration, delivered this evening, in commemoration of the Conquest of New Netherland, and that a copy be requested for the Archives of the Society, and for publication."

Extract from the Minutes:

ANDREW WARNER,
RECORDING SECRETARY.

Entered according to Act of Congress, in the year 1864, by
JOHN ROMEYN BRODHEAD,
In the Clerk's Office of the District Court of the United States for the Southern District of New York.

COMMEMORATIVE ORATION.

BROTHERS OF THE NEW YORK HISTORICAL SOCIETY:

Two hundred years ago, an English squadron, filled with armed men, came up our Bay, and anchored near what is now our Battery. Its presence foreboded and produced results of momentous interest to our city, our State, and our nation. You have directed that the anniversary of this event should be fitly observed; and, in obedience to your call, I venture to review the circumstances and consider the consequences of the transaction which we are this day assembled to commemorate.

In the summer of the year sixteen hundred and sixty-four, the eastern coast of North America was occupied by various separate Colonies, which had been founded by several European nations. For nearly half a century, England, France, and the United Netherlands had each been endeavoring to appropriate territory there, and rear dependent Plantations. France, the pioneer in successful colonization, had first pushed her adventurous way through the valley of the Saint Lawrence, and set up the cross of her faith with the lilies of her king, among the savages who dwelt on its borders. Thus began her dominion over New France, or Canada and Acadia. Farther south, England had kept closer to the sea-coast, the clear waters of which abounded with fish, and where safe harbors invited the emigrant to linger near those crystal waves which could roll unbroken to Land's End. Yet England had not occupied the whole of that more southern coast. Midway between Virginia and New England, colonists from Holland, following their countrymen who had explored the unknown wild, planted themselves quietly among the natives from whom they bought the soil, and sought to add a NEW NETHERLAND to the Batavian Republic.*

All these various colonies were settled under the authority of the respective countries in Europe whence they came. In the earlier period of adventure, those countries had adopted the principle that the savage territories which each might discover should become the absolute property of the explorer. As Columbus had discovered the New World—which ought to have borne his illustrious name—in the service of Spain, Pope Alexander the Sixth decreed that the Spanish sovereign should hold forever nearly the whole of that vast region which the Atlantic washed on the west.† A few years afterwards, the Cabots, under commissions from Henry the Seventh of England, discovered Newfoundland, and sailed, at a distance along the coast, as far south as Albemarle Sound. By virtue of these discoveries, the successors of Henry claimed sovereignty over all that part of the North American continent along the shores of which the Cabots had sailed.‡ But, as the previous sweeping title of Spain

---

* Tacitus describes the Batavians, who dwelt at the mouths of the Rhine, as "the bravest" of all the Germanic tribes—"*virtute præcipui Batavi;*" De Mor. Ger., 29. These Batavians were the forefathers of the founders of that Republic, the early history of which Mr. Motley has so worthily written. I use the word "Batavian" as synonymous with "Dutch." In its proper English sense the term "Dutch" is exclusively applied to the people of Holland, or the Netherlands, or Low Lands. It is a common blunder to call the people of Germany "Dutchmen," instead of "Germans," which is their correct national name in English.

† Chalmers's Political Annals, 6, 10; Hazard's Collections, I. 3–6; Irving's Columbus, I. 185–200; Holmes's Annals, I. 7, 559; Brodhead's History of New York, I. 2.

‡ Chalmers, 4, 8, 9; Bancroft, I. 10–14; Brodhead, I. 2; Palfrey's New England, I. 62, 63.

cut off any English claim, Queen Elizabeth declared that "*prescription without possession is of no avail;*" or, in other words, that actual occupation must follow discovery, in order to confer a valid right to savage territory.* This principle, which echoed the old Roman law, was first asserted by the Queen of England in 1580, because it was convenient for her to assert it against Spain; and it was deliberately confirmed by Parliament in 1621.† It established a most important rule in regard to European colonization in America.

Accordingly, France, with the quiet assent of Spain and England, explored the Saint Lawrence and occupied Canada and Acadia. A Florentine mariner in her service had, as early as 1524, discovered the Bay of New York, and praised its lake-like beauty. But as the voyage of Verazzano did not lead to colonization, France claimed no title to these regions which he had visited. Neither did the explorations of Gomez, in the following year, induce the Spaniards to occupy our coast.‡

---

* The doctrine maintained by Queen Elizabeth was, "*Præscriptio sine possessione haud valeat;*" Camden, Annales Eliz., 1580 (Ed. Hearne), 360; Brodhead I. 4, *note*. The translation of Camden in Kennett's England, II. 481 (Lond., 1706), renders the passage as follows: "Moreover, she understood not why her or any other Prince's subjects should be debarred from the *Indies*, which she could not persuade herself the Spaniard had any just title to by the Bishop of *Rome's* Donation (in whom she acknowledged no Prerogative, much less authority, in such cases, so as to lay any tie upon Princes which owed him no obedience or observance, or, as it were, to infeoffe the Spaniard in that New World, and invest him with the possession thereof), nor yet by any other claim than as they had touched here and there upon the coasts, built cottages, and given names to a River or a Cape; which things cannot entitle them to a Propriety. So that this donation of that which is another man's, which is of no validity in law, and this imaginary propriety, cannot hinder other princes from trading into those countries, and without breach of the Law of Nations, from transporting colonies into those parts thereof where the Spaniards inhabit not, forasmuch as Prescription without Possession is little worth." This very sound doctrine annihilates the English claim by "Prescription," derived from the voyages of the Cabots, who, unlike the Spaniards, do not appear to have "touched here and there upon the coasts, built cottages, and given names to a River or a Cape; which things cannot entitle them to a Propriety."

† Commons' Debates, I. 250, 251; Chalmers, 6 Grotius, II. 2; Brodhead, I. 143; New York Colonial Documents, IX. 265, 378, 913.

‡ Holmes, I. 54, 56; Bancroft, I. 17, 38; Brodhead, I. 2, 3; Palfrey, I. 64, 65; New York Historical Society's Collections, (II.) I. 37–57.

In the reign of Elizabeth, the first English colonists were sent to Virginia. But the adventure failed; and the name which Raleigh gave to the savage lands he had attempted to occupy alone survived. A few years afterwards, the enterprising English mariners, Gosnold, Pring, and Weymouth, visited the rivers of Maine, and explored the coast as far south as Buzzard's Bay. No European emigrants, however, came to take possession of one acre of the wild territory between Acadia and Virginia. To promote such occupation, by which alone, according to the English rule, a valid title could be secured, King James the First, in April, 1606, granted to two different companies the privilege of planting and governing two distinct and separate colonies in that part of North America lying between the thirty-fourth and the forty-fifth degrees of latitude, or between Cape Fear and Acadia, not "actually possessed by any Christian prince or people." Two English settlements were accordingly begun in the following year. The first of these, within the Chesapeake Bay, became the prosperous colony of Virginia. The second, at the mouth of the Sagadahoc, or Kennebec, was abandoned in 1608. But no attempt was made to occupy any part of the intermediate region, nor had any English mariner yet searched the shore between Buzzard's Bay and the Chesapeake.*

In this situation of affairs, another Englishman, Henry Hudson,† sailing from Amsterdam in the service of the Dutch East India Company, explored, in the autumn of 1609, "THE GREAT RIVER OF THE MOUNTAINS," the

---

* Hazard, I. 50–58; Smith's Virginia; Pinkerton, XIII. 211; Brodhead, I. 5–15.

† It is a vulgar error to substitute "Hendrick" Hudson for "Henry" Hudson. De Laet probably originated it, by writing, in Dutch, Hendrick for Henry, in his "New World," cap. VII. p. 83, Ed. 1625. Van der Donck does the same, although he speaks of Hudson as an Englishman. Lambrechtsen names him correctly. Purchas of course calls him "Henry;" see N. Y. Historical Society's Collections, I. 61, 81, 102, 146, 173. Mr. H. C. Murphy, in his recent interesting monograph on Hudson, p. 36, gives a copy of the contract of the 8th of January, 1609, to which the name signed is "HENRY HUDSON."

mouth of which Verazzano had discovered and Gomez had revisited nearly a century before. This memorable event was duly commemorated by our predecessors and associates fifty-five years ago, when the Reverend Doctor Miller delivered the first anniversary discourse before the New York Historical Society.* The track of the yacht HALF-MOON was soon followed by emigrants from Holland; and, in 1613, Dutch trading establishments were formed at Manhattan, and at the present city of Albany. The islands, coasts, and rivers between Sandy Hook and Buzzard's Bay were now for the first time explored by Adriaen Block, who sailed in the "Restless," or "Unrest," through Hell-Gate; and other Holland mariners pushed their examinations eastward, as far as Acadia. In October, 1614, the General Government of the Dutch Republic granted a Charter to the owners of the vessels which had thus been employed in American adventure, authorizing them exclusively for three years from January, 1615, to visit the "newly discovered lands" they had explored between New France and Virginia, extending from the fortieth to the forty-fifth degree of latitude, which region was now formally named "NEW NETHERLAND."†

The title which Holland thus acquired to New Netherland—as far east, at any rate, as Buzzard's Bay—was as just and valid as any of which the history of the world contains a record. According to the English rule, it undoubtedly belonged to the Dutch. Unquestionable discovery had been followed by the actual occupation of

---

* See New York Historical Society's Collections, I. 17-60.

† See Appendix, Note A; N. Y. Colonial Documents, I. 10, 11; Brodhead, I. 25-65. Another vulgar error which must be noticed, is the absurd use of the term "*the New Netherlands*," instead of "NEW NETHERLAND." In this respect, the translations of Lambrechtsen, Van der Donck, De Vries, and De Laet, in N. Y. Hist. Soc. Coll. (II.) I. 79, 129, 250, 291, are gratuitously faulty. The original Dutch in every case is "Nieuw Nederlandt," and not "*de Nieuw Nederlanden*." Even Smith, in his History of New York, I. 5, gives the name correctly, as "Nova Belgia, or New Netherland."

savage territory by a Christian people.* Still further to maintain their rights, the Dutch Government, in June, 1621, after the expiration of the original New Netherland Charter, incorporated a West India Company, with power to colonize and govern the "fruitful and unsettled" regions in Africa and America which it might occupy.†

Under this charter New Netherland grew into a Province, invested by the States-General with the arms of a Count, and deriving its laws, its habits, and its religion from its Batavian Fatherland. Manhattan Island was honestly purchased from the aborigines, and made the emporium of the fur-trade, which produced the chief provincial revenue. Fort Amsterdam was built on its southern point, as a refuge in case of an attack by the savages. Posts were also established at Fort Orange, now Albany, on the North River; at Fort Nassau, near Philadelphia, on the South, or Delaware; and at Good Hope, now Hartford, on the Fresh, or Connecticut. Agricultural colonies, subordinate to the general Provincial Government, were likewise settled, under Patroons, at several points on the North and South Rivers.‡

Six years after the Dutch Federal Government had fixed the name of New Netherland on the map of the world, King James the First, adopting the term originally proposed by John Smith, sealed a patent in November, 1620, for the colonization of "New England in America." In this he included all the territory between the fortieth and the forty-eighth degrees of latitude, and from the Atlantic to the Pacific. But the patent candidly provided that no territory was intended to be granted which was "actually possessed or inhabited by any other Christian prince or

---

* See Note B, in the Appendix.
† Hazard, I. 120-131; Brodhead, I. 134-137.
‡ N. Y. Col. Doc., I. 37, 139, 181, 262, 283-290; Brodhead, I. 148, 151, 153, 164, 200-203, 235. An engraving of the Provincial Seal of New Netherland embellishes the title-page of this publication.

estate." This proviso clearly excepted New France and New Netherland.*

The same year, a second and more successful experiment was made in colonizing a part of titular New England. This adventure was undertaken, however, before the patent of King James was sealed. The emigrants were English Puritans, most of whom had enjoyed an asylum for several years in Holland, and were so well satisfied with its liberal government, that they desired to settle themselves in America under its flag. Their minister at Leyden, John Robinson, who was versed in the Dutch language, accordingly offered to accompany four hundred families from Holland and England to New Netherland, and plant there a new commonwealth, under the jurisdiction of the Prince of Orange and the States-General. But the authorities of the Republic, preferring that their American Province should be first colonized by their own citizens, and unwilling to excite the jealousy of the King of England, by transplanting and protecting there his refractory subjects, who wished to emigrate, declined to encourage Robinson's proposition.† The Puritan refugees, having obtained a large patent from the English Virginia Company, which authorized them to settle themselves south of the fortieth degree of latitude—in what now forms part of New Jersey, Delaware, and Maryland—therefore set sail in the Mayflower, intending to make their first land at Sandy Hook, which was the best known point.‡

---

* Hazard, I. 103–118; Trumbull's Connecticut, I. 546–567; Smith's Virginia; Pinkerton, XIII. 208; Chalmers, 81, 83; Brodhead, I. 90–96, 252. It is to be remarked that while the first Patent of April, 1606, only reached to the forty-fifth degree (*ante*, p. 10), this second Patent, of November, 1620, grasped three degrees farther north. At the time of its grant, the French occupation of Canada was notorious, and the Dutch possession of New Netherland must have been known to the English authorities; Brodhead, I. 95, 96, 144; Note B, Appendix.

† N. Y. Col. Doc., I. 22–24; Brodhead, I. 115–128; Bradford's Plymouth, 42, 43.

‡ The northern boundary of Virginia, according to its second Charter of 1609, was two hundred miles north of Point Comfort, or about the fortieth parallel of latitude, which intersects the neighborhood of Barnegat and Philadelphia;

But, after a boisterous voyage, they were driven northward to Cape Cod; and, having vainly attempted to sail around the shoals of Cape Malebarre, they at length, in December, 1620, accidentally landed on the sandy beach of New Plymouth.*

This first Puritan colony in New England was followed, after a few years, by a larger emigration to Massachusetts Bay. Before long, other English settlements were begun on the Fresh or Connecticut River, and at New Haven, which regions Adriaen Block had discovered, and from which it was thought profitable to "crowd the Dutch out."† Rhode Island was also founded, in a spirit of catholic magnanimity, by fugitives from the sectarian despotism of Massachusetts. The eastern end of Long Island (around the whole of which Block had been the first to sail, and which was first laid down on a Dutch map)‡ was soon afterwards adversely occupied by emigrants from Massachusetts and Connecticut. All these settlements, except the first one at New Plymouth, were made under the general authority of the New England Patent; and, in the case of Long Island, under special grants from the Earl of Stirling, to whom it had been conveyed by the Patentees of James the First.§

Chalmers, 25; Hazard, I. 58–72; Holmes, I. 133; Brodhead, I. 15, 122, 129, 252. It has been stated (*ante*, p. 12), that the New England Patent of November, 1620, extended from the fortieth degree (or the northern boundary of Virginia), north to the forty-eighth. The Mayflower "Pilgrims," therefore, intended to settle themselves *south of the fortieth degree of latitude*, where only their Patent from the Virginia Company could advantage them. Mr. J. S. Barry, however, in his recent History of Massachusetts, I. 70, conjectures that if that Patent should ever be discovered, it would "*be found to cover territory now included in New York.*"

* Bradford's Plymouth, 44–88; Brodhead, I. 128–133.

† J. H. Trumbull's Colonial Records of Connecticut, I. 565.

‡ See the "Figurative Map," in N. Y. Col. Doc., I. 13, referred to in Note A, in Appendix. I do not find sufficient evidence that Gomez sailed through Long Island Sound, or that it is represented in Ribero's Planisphere of 1529; see Palfrey, I. 65, 66; Asher's Introduction to "Henry Hudson, the Navigator," lxxxviii., xci.—xciii., cli. The curious copper globe which Mr. Buckingham Smith recently deposited with the New York Historical Society does not exhibit Long Island.

§ Brodhead, I. 189, 208, 234, 240, 241, 259, 260, 293–300, 324, 331, 332.

While these colonies were thus growing on the north and east of New Netherland, another English settlement was established on her southern frontier. Lord Baltimore, a Roman Catholic peer of Ireland, obtained from Charles the First, in 1632, a patent for that part of the territory of Virginia lying between the north bank of the Potomac and the fortieth degree of latitude, which, in honor of the Queen, was named Maryland. Emigrants, chiefly of the Roman faith, soon came over to occupy the Province, which was founded on more liberal principles than any that British subjects had yet planted in America.*

In the mean time, New Netherland flourished apace. Churches were built; Dutch clergymen, educated and ordained in Holland, were established; schoolmasters were employed, and schools opened; and laws, based on the jurisprudence of the Batavian Republic, were enacted. Names familiar in the Fatherland replaced, with more affection than good taste, the sonorous and descriptive nomenclature of the aborigines. The young metropolis on Manhattan became New Amsterdam, and hope whispered that the glory of the latter city might, in time, eclipse the greatness of the old.†

The Provincial government of New Netherland was vested in a Director and Council, and a Fiscal or Attorney-General, appointed by the West India Company. The supreme laws of the Province were the ordinances of the Director and Council, the instructions of the Company, and the statutes and customs of the Fatherland. To administer this government and execute these laws, the Company appointed Cornelis Jacobsen May to be the first Director of New Netherland, in 1624. May was suc-

---

* Bancroft, I. 241–248; Brodhead, I. 251–253.
† Brodhead, I. 183, 196, 223, 313, 337, 343, 374, 467. The population of Amsterdam, in 1857, was 259,873; that of New York, in 1860, was 813,669.

ceeded, the next year, by William Verhulst. In 1626, Peter Minuit, a man of sagacity, was made Director; and in 1633 he was replaced by the more stolid Wouter van Twiller. From 1638 until 1647, William Kieft, a person of more activity but less prudence than any of his predecessors, struggled through a turbulent administration. In the summer of 1647, Peter Stuyvesant began a service as Director-General, which lasted for seventeen years, and ended only with the downfall of the Dutch dominion.*

Stuyvesant was one of those remarkable men who stamp their names worthily on history. The son of a Dutch clergyman in Friesland, he was educated at the famous High School at Franeker, where he acquired that familiarity with the Latin tongue, which he was always rather fond of displaying. Having entered the military service of the West India Company, he was sent to Curaçoa as their Director. While in that office he lost a leg in a venturesome attack on Saint Martin, and was obliged to return to Holland. Before long he was promoted to the Directorship of New Netherland, whither he sailed, after having taken his oath in the presence of the States-General.† With many of the nobler characteristics, Stuyvesant oftentimes exhibited some of the weaker and more frivolous qualities of mankind. He delighted in pomp, and the ostentation of despotic command. Imperious and irascible, he was honest and faithful. Obeying the orders of his superiors with scrupulous zeal, he insisted on the implicit obedience of his subordinates. If he was arbitrary, he was generally just. He loved his Fatherland, her laws, and her religion, with hearty devotion; and if, at times, his earnestness carried him beyond the bounds of discretion, none can impeach the sincerity of his pur-

---

* Brodhead, I. 154, 159, 162–164, 222, 223, 275, 413, 414, 465.

† N. Y. H. S. Coll. (II.) III. 263, 264; Col. Doc., I. 164, 173, 175–178; Brodhead, I. 413, 414, 432, 433. A translation of Stuyvesant's Commission is in the Appendix, Note C.

poses, or fail to admire the energetic firmness with which he enforced his own convictions.

Under such administration, in spite of much selfish mismanagement on the part of the West India Company, New Netherland increased abundantly. Emigrants constantly came over from Holland, while French and English subjects flocked in from the neighboring colonies. From Massachusetts, especially, several persecuted Protestants were attracted by the freedom of conscience which was the well-known characteristic of the Dutch Province. Others came from afar, to share the substantial prosperity which its comprehensive system, no less than its physical advantages, insured. "Promote commerce," wrote the West India Company to Stuyvesant, in the winter of 1652, "whereby Manhattan must prosper, her population increase, her trade and navigation flourish. For when these once become permanently established—when the ships of New Netherland ride on every part of the ocean—then numbers, now looking to that coast with eager eyes, will be allured to embark for your island."* The prophecy was splendidly fulfilled. New Amsterdam rapidly grew in importance, and was allowed a municipal magistracy of her own, consisting of Schout, Burgomasters, and Schepens, in imitation of her imperial namesake on the Zuyder Zee. Her foreign commerce soon began to rival her domestic trade. The first vessel ever built by Europeans in North America—after the "Virginia of Sagadahoc," in 1607—was Block's significantly named "Restless of Manhattan," in 1614. One of the largest merchantmen in Christendom was launched by her shipwrights in 1631. Strangers eagerly sought burghership in the rising metropolis, and the tongues of many nations resounded through her ancient winding streets.† Like her pro-

---

* Albany Records, IV. 91; Brodhead, I. 547; Bancroft, II. 294.
† Col. Doc., I. 296, III. 17; Brodhead, I. 14, 55, 212, 215, 219, 374, 548; *ante*, p. 11.

totype, New Amsterdam was always a city of the world.

The Province of New Netherland was, indeed, the most advantageously situated region in North America. Its original limits included all the Atlantic coast between Cape Henlopen and Montauk Point, and even farther east and north, and all the inland territory bounded by the Connecticut Valley on the east, the Saint Lawrence and Lake Ontario on the north, and the affluents of the Ohio, the Susquehanna, and the Delaware, on the west and south. Within those bounds is the only spot on the continent whence issue divergent streams which find their outlets in the Gulf of Saint Lawrence, the Atlantic Ocean, and the Gulf of Mexico.* Across the surface of the Province runs a chain of the Alleghanies, through which, in two remarkable chasms, the waters of the Delaware and the Hudson flow southward to the sea. At the head of its tides, the Hudson, which its explorers appropriately called "the Great River of the Mountains," receives the current of the Mohawk, rushing in from the west. Through the valleys of these rivers, and across the neighboring lakes, the savage natives of the country tracked those pathways of travel and commerce which civilized science only adopted and improved.† Along their banks soon grew up flourishing villages, contributing to the prosperity of the chief town, which, with unerring judgment, had been planted on the ocean-washed island of Manhattan. In addition to these superb geographical peculiarities, every variety of soil; abundant mineral wealth; nature, grand, beautiful, and picturesque, and teeming with vegetable and animal life; and a climate as healthful as it is delicious, made New Netherland the most

---

* The water-shed of Central New York was the seat of the Iroquois Confederation, long before European discovery.

† The Erie Canal and the Delaware and Hudson Canal follow the old Indian trails.

attractive of all the European colonies in America. From the first it was always the chosen seat of empire.

It was the wise decree of Providence that this magnificent region should first be occupied by the Batavian race. There was expanded the germ of a mighty cosmopolitan State, destined to exert a moral influence as happy as the physical peculiarities of its temperate territory were alluring. Yet the growth and prosperity of the Dutch Province were fatal to its political life. The envy of its neighbors was aroused. Covetousness produced an irrepressible desire of possession, which could be appeased only by its violent seizure by unscrupulous foes.

If at this time Englishmen had any one national characteristic more strongly developed than another, it was jealousy of the Dutch. Strangely, too, this sentiment seemed to have grown with the growth of Puritanism. It was enough for the British islander that the continental Hollander spoke a language different from his own. It mattered not that Coster, of Haerlem, invented the art of arts; or that Grotius, Erasmus, Hooft, and Vondel, among scholars, and Boerhaave and Huygens, among philosophers, and Rembrandt, and Cuyp, and Wouverman, among painters, were illustrious sons of the liberal Republic. Even William the Silent and Barneveldt were of little account among insular Britons—" divided from all the rest of the world."* Coarse wit and flippant ridicule were continually employed in educating the Englishman to undervalue and dislike the Hollander. On the other hand, Holland, at the zenith of her power, was not jealous of England. The Dutch maxim was "*Live and let live.*" Both nations were fairly matched in military and naval

---

* "*Toto divisos orbe Britannos,*" Virg. Ec., I. 67. Dryden, in his translation of Virgil, describes his early countrymen as—

"A race of men from all the world disjoined."

strength. During the period of the English Commonwealth, the only opportunity had occurred of testing against each other the skill of their admirals and the valor of their seamen. If Blake and Ayscue maintained the honor of their flag, De Ruyter won equal glory, and Tromp placed a broom at his mast-head, in token that he had swept the channel clear of English ships. Both nations were Protestant, and each had learned to respect the proverbial courage of the other. But the commerce of the Dutch Republic was now the vastest in the world.

> "The Sun but seemed the labourer of the year:
> Each waxing Moon supplied her watery store,
> To swell those tides which from the line did bear
> Their brim-full vessels to the Belgian shore."*

Such splendid prosperity of a rival, the selfishness of England could not brook; and Dryden took care to stimulate the envy of his countrymen when he wrote of the Hollanders:

> "As Cato fruits of Afric did display,
> Let us before our eyes their Indies lay:
> All loyal English will like him conclude—
> Let Cæsar live, and Carthage be subdued."†

This sentiment of jealousy accompanied the English colonists to America, and even burned more fiercely in some parts of the wilderness. The motives to their emigration were various. The communities which they founded were dissimilar. Virginia was occupied by Royalists, who admired the hierarchy; New England by Puritans, who abhorred prelacy; Maryland by larger-minded Roman Catholics. But all these were Britons—naturally selfish, exclusive, and overbearing—who, with marked differences in creeds and fashions, were still the subjects of a common sovereignty, and, as such, felt a

---

* Dryden's Annus Mirabilis, 1666.
† Satire on the Dutch, 1662.

common enmity against the colonists of that nation which was the successful rival of their own.

This antipathy, however, was not equally strong in all the English colonies. It was slight in Virginia; it waxed hotter in Maryland; while it blazed into malignant envy in New England. Between Virginia and New Netherland, the relations had almost always been friendly, because neither had injured, while each had benefited the other. With Maryland, embarrassing questions had arisen respecting the occupation of the Delaware by the Dutch and the Swedes. But from the time of the first intercourse between Manhattan and New Plymouth, the Puritan emigrants pertinaciously insisted that the Dutch colonists of New Netherland were "intruders" into New England. With inconsistent reasoning, but characteristic assurance, they maintained their own title under the patent of 1620, while they denied that of the Hollanders, which was recognized in its proviso.* Gradually they crowded on westward of the Connecticut River, until, in 1650, it was agreed between Stuyvesant and the New England authorities that the eastern boundary of New Netherland should be Oyster Bay on Long Island, and a line running northerly from Greenwich on the continent. Mainly through their representations, Cromwell directed an expedition to wrest from the Dutch Republic its American Territory. But, by the treaty of 1654, the Protector virtually conceded New Netherland to Holland. The States-General, in 1656, ratified the colonial boundary agreement of 1650; but the British Government avoided any action on the subject, and the Dutch Province continued, for a while longer, to be what New England writers have pertly called "a thorn in the side."†

---

*See *ante*, p. 13; Appendix, Note B.
† N. Y. Col. Doc., I. 283–293, 364, 451, 458, 463, 464, 471, 475, 486, 487, 541, 548, 556–575, 610–612; Brodhead, I. 519, 520, 544, 545, 586, 601, 602; Palfrey, II. 372.

in the history of States, might generally overbears right. Of this fate New Netherland was a conspicuous example. While Maryland threatened on the South, Connecticut, which had constantly encroached westward along the Sound, procured, in 1662, from the heedless King of England, a patent which covered a large part of the Dutch Province, the inhabitants of which she did not scruple to describe as her "noxious neighbours." Under this patent, Connecticut extended her jurisdiction as far as Westchester on the mainland, and over nearly the whole of Long Island. Attempts were even made, under the lead of Captain John Scott, to reduce the suburban Dutch villages of Brooklyn, Midwout or Flatbush, Amersfoort, New Utrecht, and Bushwick. To these bold encroachments Stuyvesant could offer only a feeble resistance. Justice and weight of argument were on his side, but his adversaries had the decisive advantage of superior numbers. The most that could be done was to put the Dutch capital in a condition of defence against any attack of a colonial enemy. The danger which menaced the Province induced the Director to resort to the people, as he and his predecessor had been obliged to call on them before. A LANDTDAG, or Assembly of deputies from the several towns, was accordingly convened at New Amsterdam, in the spring of 1664. It was there determined that, without aid from the home government, it would be impossible to regain the towns on Long Island which the English, who were six to one, had usurped from the Dutch. Repeated appeals had been sent to the West India Company for re-enforcements, by which alone could the rest of New Netherland be preserved to Holland. Its population was now full ten thousand, and that of New Amsterdam about fifteen hundred. In spite of the clouds which lowered around the narrowing horizon of the Province, Stuyvesant hopefully looked forward to its becoming still more profitable to the Fatherland, and urged upon the company that its waste lands, which could feed a hundred thousand inhabitants, should be peopled at once by the oppressed Protestants of France, Savoy, and Germany.*

Yet the perilous condition of New Netherland was not rightly appreciated in Holland. It had been unwisely intrusted to the government of a great commercial monopoly, which thought more of its failing corporate interests than of those of the nation, or of its colonists in America. When, at length, the danger which threatened the Province could not be disregarded, the States-General took insufficient measures to confirm their power there. In January, 1664, they desired the British Government to order the restitution of all places which the King's subjects had usurped from the Hollanders in New Netherland, and the cessation of further aggressions.† But Sir George Downing, the English ambassador at the Hague, who was one of the earliest, ablest, and most disreputable graduates from Harvard College in Massachusetts, could not forget the prejudices he had imbibed, and startled the Grand Pensionary De Witt by claiming that the inhabitants of the Dutch Province were "the incroachers" upon New England.‡

Downing's words were full of ominous import. The Restoration of King Charles the Second was the prognostic of the fate of New Netherland. One of the first acts of his reign was to appoint a Council for Foreign Plantations, with orders to render "those dominions useful to England, and England helpful to them." This was the key to the British colonial policy. A new Navigation Law was passed, more effectually to cripple Dutch com-

---

* N. Y. Col. Doc., II., 234, 248, 368, 374, 389–409, 512; Valentine's Manual, 1860, 592; Trumbull's Connecticut, I. 249, 252, 265, 513; Brodhead, I. 317, 325, 474, 475, 559, 695, 702, 703, 719, 722, 723, 726, 728, 729, 733, 734; Appendix, note G.

† Col. Doc., II. 227; Brodhead, I. 730.

‡ Lister's Clarendon, III. 276; Col. Doc., II. 416–418, *note.*

merce by excluding all foreign vessels from trading with any of the English colonies in Asia, Africa, or America. Soon afterwards, Lord Stirling complained that the Dutch had intruded into Long Island, which had been conveyed to his grandfather, and prayed that they might be subdued or expelled. While this subject was under the consideration of the Plantation Council, it was found that the Navigation Act was disregarded or evaded in the English-American colonies. The trade carried on between New Netherland and Virginia, Maryland, and New England, was reported to be a loss to the King of many thousand pounds a year. A more stringent Navigation Law was therefore enacted. Still the forbidden intercolonial traffic was continued. The statute could not be enforced as long as New Netherland remained a Dutch Province. It was necessary to the success of that most intensely selfish law that New Netherland should be under the government of England, and it was determined that it should be reduced to subjection.*

The easiest way to sustain this characteristic logic was to insist that the Dutch Province was the true inheritance of the English King. Under this pretence, the means to obtain its possession could be mildly called a Resumption rather than a Usurpation. The Dutch title to their Province, although, in the judgment of Louis the Fourteenth himself, it was "the best founded,"† was as little regarded by Charles the Second as the injunctions of the Decalogue. Notwithstanding the rule asserted by Queen Elizabeth, and confirmed by Parliament; the proviso in the Patent of James the First, and the continuous occupation of New Netherland by Hollanders, Lord Chancellor Clarendon, under the instigation of Downing, was not ashamed to pronounce that they had "no colour of right" to its pos-

---

* Col. Doc., III. 35, 40–50; Brodhead, I. 686, 702, 725, 735.
† D'Estrades's Letters, &c., III. 340.

session.* Clarendon then purchased for his son-in-law, James, Duke of York and Albany, Lord Stirling's claim to Pemaquid and Long Island, and advised the King to grant a new Patent to the Duke, including those regions, together with all the Dutch territory on the mainland.†

Accordingly, on the Twelfth of March, 1664, Charles granted, under the Great Seal, to his brother James, a part of Maine, the whole of Long Island, Martha's Vineyard and Nantucket, and the Hudson River, with all the mainland from the west side of the Connecticut to the east side of Delaware Bay. The Grant included all those portions of the present States of Connecticut and Massachusetts lying west of the Connecticut River, as well as the whole of Vermont and New Jersey. His Patent invested the Duke with "full and absolute power" to govern all English subjects, inhabiting this territory, according to English law, and authorized him or his agents to expel by force all persons who might dwell there without his special license. It was the most impudent, as it was the most despotic instrument ever recorded in the Colonial Archives of Great Britain.‡

This action of Charles the Second was not, however,

* Lister's Clarendon, III. 347.

† Col. Doc., III. 225, 606, 607, V. 330, VII. 431; Duer's Life of Stirling, 37, 38.

‡ See Patent at length in the State Library at Albany; in Book of Patents in Secretary's Office, I. 109-115; in Leaming and Spicer's Grants and Concessions, 3-8; and in N. Y. Colonial Documents, II. 295-298. See also Col. Doc., VII. 597, and VIII. 107, 436, for description of the territory granted. If this Patent was good as far as it related to the territory in Maine, Long Island, Martha's Vineyard, and Nantucket, which the English already possessed, it was certainly invalid in regard to the Dutch Province, of which the grantor never had possession. Even Chalmers, in his Political Annals, p. 579, says, that "As the validity of the grant to the Duke of York, while the Dutch were in quiet possession of the country, had been very justly questioned, he thought it prudent to obtain a new one, in June, 1674." See also Col. Doc., V. 596, VII. 596, 597. It is worthy of remark that by his first Patent, of 12 March, 1664, the Duke was authorized to govern *only English subjects* inhabiting his territory; and that in his second Patent, of 29 June, 1674, the words, "*or any other person or persons*," were added; see Col. Doc., II. 296, and Leaming and Spicer, 5 and 42. After obtaining possession of New Netherland, therefore, the Duke could not govern its Dutch inhabitants unless as British subjects; but he could expel them if they remained there without his permission.

influenced by any sympathy with the likes or the dislikes of his New England subjects. They had received the tidings of his Restoration with distrust, and had proclaimed him King with peevish austerity. If he had been induced to grant a part of New Netherland to Connecticut, he took pains to avoid his careless bounty by a more unscrupulous appropriation to his own brother. The age of Chartered Oligarchies had passed away. Royal or Proprietary Governments were thenceforth to enforce the British Colonial policy. New England was now in disfavor at Whitehall; and the Duke of York was desired by the Privy Council to name Commissioners, whom the King determined to send thither, to see how the several Colonies observed their Charters, and to settle their differences about boundaries. James accordingly selected four persons, whom history has honored with an unequal notoriety. The first was Colonel Richard Nicolls; a university scholar, a brave soldier, and a prudent officer, who had been the Duke's companion in exile, and was one of the Grooms of his bedchamber. The other three were Sir Robert Carr and Colonel George Cartwright, of the Royal Army, and Samuel Maverick, a former resident in Massachusetts. These Commissioners were furnished with full instructions to guide their conduct in America. One of these instructions was, to obtain the active assistance of the New England Colonies in reducing the Dutch in New Netherland to subjection.*

The Duke of York also commissioned Nicolls, on the second of April, to be his Deputy-Governor in the territory which the King had given him, and execute all the powers which his Patent authorized.† To gain possession, by force if necessary, was the next step. As Lord

---

* Col. Doc., III. 51-65; Mass. H. S. Coll., XXXII. 284; Notes and Queries (II.), III. 214-216.
† A copy of the Duke of York's commission to Nicolls is in the Appendix, Note D.

High Admiral of England, James assigned for the reduction of New Netherland the frigate Guinea, of thirty-six guns, Captain Hugh Hyde; the Elias, of thirty, Captain William Hill; the Martin, of sixteen, Captain Edward Grove; and a chartered transport, the William and Nicholas, of ten, Captain Thomas Morley. Early in May the Royal Commissioners embarked in these vessels, with about four hundred and fifty veteran soldiers, forming three full companies, commanded by Colonels Nicolls, Carr, and Cartwright, under whom were several other commissioned officers in the British Army. Among these were Captains Mathias Nicolls, Robert Needham, Harry Norwood, and Daniel Brodhead. some of whom, intending to settle themselves permanently in New Netherland, after its acquisition, were accompanied by their families. The expedition, which was well provided with all necessaries for war, set sail from Portsmouth in the middle of May, with orders to make its first anchorage in Gardiner's Bay at the eastern end of Long Island.*

These portentous movements did not escape the attention of the Dutch Government at the Hague. As early as February, 1664, Stuyvesant had distinctly warned the West India Company of the King's intended grant to the Duke of York, and that not only Long Island, but the whole Province, would be lost to Holland unless speedy re-enforcements should be sent. The Company, however, now on the verge of bankruptcy, replied with marvellous infatuation, in the following April, that the Royal Commissioners were only going to install Bishops in New England, the inhabitants of which, who had gone there to escape Prelacy, would rather live under Dutch authority, with freedom of conscience, than risk that in order to fall

* Patents, III. 43; Col. Doc., II. 243, 445, 501, III. 70, 104, 117, 149; Smith's New York, I. 16; Clarke's James the Second, I. 400; Hazard's Annals of Penn., IV. 31; Coll. Ulster Hist. Soc., I. 51; Brodhead, I. 736, 737.

under a government from which they had formerly fled. This absurd letter had scarcely been dispatched before the real object of Nicolls's expedition was better understood. Downing bluntly told De Witt that New Netherland existed "only in the maps."* Prompt orders to De Ruyter, who was then on his way to the Mediterranean, might have hurried his fleet to Manhattan in time to aid Stuyvesant in repulsing the treacherous force of England. But a purblind confidence in the honor of Charles the Second, and an unjust estimate of the importance to the Fatherland of its American Province, clouded the Grand Pensionary's judgment. The necessary orders were not sent to De Ruyter, and New Netherland was abandoned to her fate.

A tedious voyage of ten weeks brought the squadron of Nicolls to Boston. The Royal Commissioners immediately demanded the assistance of the New England colonies; which Massachusetts promised, with frugal reluctance, while Connecticut showed more selfish zeal, because she hoped to secure Long Island to herself. Piloted by Boston mariners, the English ships then sailed for the mouth of the Hudson; and, on the sixteenth of August (Old Style), the leading frigate Guinea, with Nicolls and his colleagues on board, anchored just inside of Coney Island, at Nyack, or New Utrecht Bay, where she was joined, two days afterwards, by the other vessels. Here the King's Commissioners were met by John Winthrop, Samuel Willys, and other Connecticut magistrates. Thomas Willett, also, appeared on the part of New Plymouth. John Scott was likewise at hand, with a force "pressed" at New Haven. The train-bands of Southold, and the other English towns at the eastern end of Long Island, under John Younge, soon increased the threatening array. Northern Indians and French rovers were held as re-

---

* Col. Doc., II. 234, 235, 236, 367, 408, 493; Lister's Clarendon, III. 307, 320.

serves. Thomas Clarke and John Pynchon hastened from Massachusetts to the Royal Commissioners; but as there was already gathered an overpowering strength, the services of the auxiliaries promised by that Colony were not required.*

The harbor of New Amsterdam was at once blockaded, and the Long Island farmers were forbidden to furnish supplies to the City. A Proclamation was issued by the Royal Commissioners, on the twentieth of August, promising that all persons, of any nation, who would submit to the King's Government, should peaceably enjoy their estates, "and all other privileges, with His Majesty's English subjects." The inhabitants of Long Island were specially summoned to meet the Commissioners at Gravesend, a few days afterwards. Large numbers accordingly attended, when Nicolls published the Duke of York's Patent and his own Commission, and demanded their submission to his authority. Winthrop, as Governor of Connecticut, declared that, as the King's pleasure was now made known, the claim of that Colony to the Island ceased. Nicolls, on his part, promised to confirm all the then officers in their places, and call an Assembly, where laws should be enacted. This assurance quelled opposition. Long Island, inhabited chiefly by English subjects, submitted at once to the Government of the Duke of York; and the militia from its eastern towns, under Younge, joining with the New England auxiliaries, marched from Amersfoort and Flatbush towards Brooklyn, to assist the Royal expedition in reducing New Amsterdam.†

Lulled into a false security by the unhappy letter of the

* Mass. Rec., IV. (II.) 117–128. 141, 149, 157–168; N. Y. General Entries, I. 2–7, 29; Col. Doc., II. 372, 410, 414, 438, 501, III. 65, 66, 84; New Haven Rec., II. 550; Thompson's Long Island, I. 127; Trumbull's Conn., I. 267; Morton's Memorial, 311, note; Appendix, Note II.

† Col. Doc., II. 410, 414, 434, 438, 443, 501; Oyster Bay Rec., A. 19; N. Y. Gen. Ent., I. 7, 8; Thompson, I. 124, II. 323, 328.

West India Company and certain contradictory statements of Willett, Stuyvesant had meanwhile suspended the measures which he had begun to take for the defence of the Capital, and had gone up to Fort Orange, to repress some hostilities that had broken out among the savages in its neighborhood. On learning the approach of the English forces, the Director hurried back to New Amsterdam, which he reached on the fifteenth of August—or the twenty-fifth, according to the New Style—only one day before the Guinea Frigate anchored at Nyack, in the lower Bay. In concert with the Municipal authorities, every possible measure was taken for the defence of the Metropolis. All the inhabitants, without exception, were ordered to labor in strengthening the " old and rotten palisades," which could hardly be called fortifications; a constant guard was established; the brewers were forbidden to malt any grain; and heavy guns, furnished by the Director, were mounted on the indefensible works. But the condition of the City was hopeless. The Harbor was soon effectually blockaded by the British squadron. No aid could be obtained from Long Island. The regular garrison in Fort Amsterdam did not exceed one hundred and fifty men, and its supply of powder was very short. Its low earthen walls, originally built to resist an attack of the savages, might have been sufficient against any Colonial force, but could not be held against the ships and the veterans of Nicolls. The Director had, long before, expressed his military opinion, that "whoever by water is master of the river, will be, in a short time, master by land of the feeble fortress." The anticipated contingency had now actually happened, and hostile English ships were in full command of the port. The burghers, of whom only two hundred and fifty were able to bear arms, thought more of protecting their own property, and of obtaining favorable terms of capitulation, than of defending their open town against the overwhelming superiority of the invaders. The whole City force, placed man by man, four rods apart, could not guard its hastily-built "little breastwork."*

Nevertheless, Stuyvesant determined to hold out to the last. To the peremptory summons of Nicolls, he opposed as able a vindication of the Dutch title to New Netherland as the most experienced publicist could have drawn. This was conveyed to Gravesend on Tuesday, the twenty-third of August—or the second of September, according to the New Style—by four of the most trusted advisers of the Provincial and the City Governments, who were instructed to "argue the matter" with the English Commander. But reasoning was useless in the absence of De Ruyter. Avoiding discussion, Nicolls answered that the question of right did not concern him, but must be decided by the King of England and the States-General. He was determined to take the place; and if the reasonable terms he had offered were not accepted, he would attack the City, for which purpose, at the end of forty-eight hours, he would bring his forces up nearer. "On Thursday, the fourth," he added, "I will speak with you at the Manhattans." The Dutch deputies replied: "Friends will be welcome if they come in a friendly manner." "I shall come with my ships and soldiers," said Nicolls, "and he will be a bold messenger, indeed, who shall then dare to come on board and solicit terms." To the demand of Stuyvesant's delegates: "What then is to be done?" he answered, "Hoist the white flag of peace at the Fort, and then I may take something into consideration!"†

---

* Col. Doc., II. 248, 372, 410, 432, 434, 438, 439, 440, 441, 443, 446, 475, 494, 505; Val. Man., 1860, 592, 1861, 603–605; New Amsterdam Records, V. 552–554, 567–570; Albany Records, XVIII. 319; Letter of Domine Samuel Drisius, of 15 September, 1664; Appendix, Notes G. and H.

† Col. Doc., II. 411–414; Smith, I. 18–26; Hazard's Reg. Penn., IV. 31, 41, 42;

Nicolls, indeed, had no wish to proceed to extremities. His summons was imperious, but his policy was to obtain a bloodless possession of the Dutch Province. He therefore authorized Winthrop to assure Stuyvesant that, if it should be surrendered to the King, there should be free intercourse with Holland in Dutch vessels, or a virtual suspension of the English navigation laws. This was communicated to Stuyvesant at New Amsterdam, on the same day that his messengers saw Nicolls at Gravesend. But all the persuasions of the Connecticut Governor could not move the patriotic Director. In vain did he tear in pieces Winthrop's friendly letter. The people, who soon learned the liberal offers of the English, became mutinous; work on the fortifications ceased; complaints against the West India Company were freely uttered; and it was pronounced impossible to defend the City, "seeing that to resist so many was nothing else than to gape before an oven."*

Perceiving that Stuyvesant was disposed to hold out, Nicolls ordered the squadron to move up from their anchorage near Gravesend, and reduce the Dutch "under His Majesty's obedience." Again messengers came down from New Amsterdam, proposing a cessation of hostilities, and the appointment of Commissioners to treat about "a good accommodation." The English commander replied that he would willingly appoint Commissioners "to treat upon Articles of Surrender." At the solicitation of the Dutch delegates, orders were given that the ships should not precipitately fire on the city. But Nicolls declined

---

Val. Man., 1860, 592; Albany Records, XVIII. 319, 320, XXII. 317; Appendix, Note G.

* Gen. Ent., I. 12; Mass. H. S. Coll., XXXVI. 527–529; Col. Doc., II. 444, 445, 476. The original draft of Winthrop's letter to Stuyvesant, of 22 August (1 September), 1664, with the autograph approval of the Royal Commissioners, Nicolls, Carr, and Cartwright, is in the possession of Mr. Benjamin Robert Winthrop, one of the Vice-Presidents of the New York Historical Society, who is a lineal descendant of both the Dutch and Connecticut Governors.

their request that the troops should not be brought up nearer. "To-day I shall arrive at the Ferry," he added, —"to-morrow we can agree with one another."*

On Thursday, the twenty-fifth of August (or the fourth of September), the British infantry, consisting of three companies of regular soldiers, eager for loot, were accordingly landed at Gravesend, whence Nicolls marched at their head to "the Ferry," at Brooklyn, where the New England and Long Island militia were already posted. Two of the frigates then sailed up the Bay, and anchored near "Nutten," or Governor's Island. The other two—coming on with full sail, and all their guns, of one battery, ready to pour their broadsides on the "open place," if any hostilities should be begun against them—passed in front of Fort Amsterdam, and anchored above the City. Watching their approach from a parapet of the Fort, Stuyvesant was about to order his gunner to fire on the enemy, when the two Domines Megapolensis, leading him away between them, persuaded him not to begin hostilities. Leaving fifty men in the Fortress, under the command of the Fiscal De Sille, the Director, at the head of one hundred of the garrison, marched out into the City, in order to prevent the English from attempting to land "here and there "†

By this time the Dutch garrison in Fort Amsterdam had become "demoralized." They openly talked of "where booty is to be got, and where the young women live who wear chains of gold." Reports also came from Long Island, that the New England levies declared that "their business was not only with New Netherland, but with the booty and plunder." Their threats caused the burghers

---

* Gen. Ent., I. 13, 14, 15, 21, 22, 27, 28; Alb. Rec., XVIII. 321; Col. Doc., II. 414; Hazard's Reg. Penn., IV. 31, 42, 43; Smith, I. 27; S. Smith's New Jersey, 40, 41, 42; Brodhead, I. 740.

† Col. Doc., II. 414, 422, 444, 445, 501, 502, 503, 508, 509; Val. Man., 1860, 592; Letter of Drisius; Appendix, Notes G. and H.

of New Amsterdam to look upon them as "deadly enemies, who expected nothing else than pillage, plunder, and bloodshed." Moreover, it was understood that six hundred Northern Indians, and one hundred and fifty French privateersmen, with English commissions, had offered their services against the Dutch. Seeing that it was impossible to defend the place, the whole population of which was only fifteen hundred, against a powerful squadron and more than a thousand well-armed foes, the municipal authorities, the clergy, the officers of the burgher-guard, and most of the leading citizens, joined in a Remonstrance, drafted by the elder Domine Megapolensis, urging the Director and Council to accept the terms offered by the English commander. His threats, it stated, "would not have been at all regarded, could your Honors, or we your Petitioners, expect the smallest aid or succour. But, God help us! whether we turn for assistance to the north or to the south, to the east or to the west, it is all vain! On all sides we are encompassed and hemmed in by our enemies." Women and children came in tears, beseeching Stuyvesant to parley. To all their supplications he replied: "I had much rather be carried out dead!"*

At length, almost solitary in his heroism, the Dutch Director was obliged to yield. Further opposition on his part would have been unavailing, and might have deprived the people of the advantages to be gained by a capitulation. It was some solace that the English Commander, now encamped at the Brooklyn Ferry, "before the Manhatans," voluntarily offered to restore the Fort and the City, in case the differences about boundaries in America should be arranged between the King and the States-General. Moreover, Stuyvesant's religion consoled him with the text in Saint Luke, that with ten thousand men

---

* Alb. Rec., XVIII. 320, 321; Col. Doc., II. 248, 249, 369, 423, 476, 503, 508; Val. Man., 1860, 592; Letter of Drisius; Appendix, notes G. and H.

he could not meet him that came against him with twenty thousand.* And if, in that bitter hour, the brave old chief could call to mind the classical learning which he had acquired in his Fatherland, he might well have applied to himself the sad words which the shade of Hector addressed to Æneas:

> "Could any mortal hand prevent our fate,
> This hand, and this alone, had saved the State."†

Six Commissioners were accordingly appointed on each side, on Friday, the twenty-sixth of August, or fifth of September, to settle the terms of surrender. Those on the part of the Dutch were John de Decker, Nicholas Varlett, and Samuel Megapolensis, representing the Director and Council, and Cornelis Steenwyck, Oloff Stevensen van Cortlandt, and Jacques Cousseau, representing the City authorities. Besides his two colleagues, Sir Robert Carr and Colonel George Cartwright, Nicolls chose John Winthrop and Samuel Willys, of Connecticut, and Thomas Clarke and John Pynchon, of Massachusetts, in order to engage those two colonies more firmly with the Royal expedition, "if the Dutch had been over-confident of their strength." The commissioners on both sides met at Stuyvesant's "Bouwery," or farm, on Saturday, the twenty-seventh of August, or sixth of September, and arranged the Articles of Capitulation. All the inhabitants of New Netherland were to continue free denizens, and were guaranteed their property; while the Dutch were to enjoy "their own customs concerning their inheritances," and "the liberty of their consciences in divine worship and church discipline." Free trade with Holland was stipulated. The existing magistrates were to remain in office until their terms expired. The Articles of Capitula-

---

* Gen. Ent., I. 30, 31; Col. Doc., II. 440; Saint Luke's Gospel, xiv. 31; Appendix, note E.
† Pitt's translation of Virgil, Æneid, II.

tion were to be ratified on both sides, and exchanged on the next Monday morning, at the "Old Mill,"* on the East River, near what is now the foot of Roosevelt street, when the City and the Fort were to be surrendered, and the Dutch garrison were to march out, with arms shouldered, drums beating, colors flying, and matches lighted.†

These conciliatory and very advantageous terms were explained to the citizens at the Town Hall, on the following Sunday, at the close of the second service in the afternoon—the last which was expected to be celebrated under the Dutch flag—in Kieft's old church in Fort Amsterdam. It was also quietly agreed between Stuyvesant and Nicolls that the New England and Long Island auxiliaries should be kept at the Ferry, on the Brooklyn side of the East River; because the burghers "were more apprehensive of being plundered by them than by the others."‡

On Monday morning, the twenty-ninth of August, or eighth of September, Stuyvesant, having ratified the Capitulation, placed himself at the head of his garrison, and marched out of Fort Amsterdam with all the honors of war. The Dutch soldiers, who saw no enemy, moved sullenly down Beaver street to the water-side, whence they were quickly embarked on the ship Gideon for Holland. Colonel Cartwright, with his company, now occupied the City gates and the Town Hall. Accompanied by the Burgomasters, who "gave him a welcome reception," Nicolls, at the head of his own and Sir Robert Carr's com-

---

* This "old mill" is distinctly marked on the map which forms one of the illustrations to Valentine's Manual for 1863. It was on the shore of the East River, at the mouth of a brook running out of the "Kolck," or what is now vulgarly called "the Collect," and it was the nearest point to "the Ferry," at Brooklyn. See Valentine's Manuals, 1859, 551, and 1863, 621; Brodhead, I. 167, *note*.

† Alb. Rec., XVIII. 325; Gen. Ent., I. 23–26, 30–33; Col. Doc., II. 250–253, 414, 111. 103; Brodhead, I. 742, 762, 763; Hazard's Reg. Penn., IV. 43, 44; Appendix, note E.

‡ Alb. Rec., XVIII. 323, 324; Col. Doc., II. 445, 446.

panies, marched into the Fort. The English flag was run up; the name of the Fort was changed from Amsterdam to "JAMES," and the City was ordered to be called "NEW YORK." A few weeks afterwards Fort Orange was surrendered, and became "ALBANY," in commemoration of the Scotch title of the Proprietor. The conquered Province was named "NEW YORK." On Sunday, the second or twelfth of October, sixteen hundred and sixty-four, the Dutch Fort at Newcastle on the Delaware was taken by the English, and the entire reduction of New Netherland was accomplished.*

BROTHERS OF THE NEW YORK HISTORICAL SOCIETY: Thus ended, two hundred years ago, the dominion of Holland over the fairest portion of our continent. Nine years afterwards, that dominion was triumphantly reconquered by the Dutch. But they held it only for a short period; and its temporary repossession by them had no important influence on Colonial affairs. The three-colored ensign,† which for half a century had rightfully waved over New Netherland, was replaced by the "meteor flag;" and, from Virginia to New France, all European colonists were obliged to acknowledge Charles the Second as their King. His usurpation of New York decided the fortunes of North America. It prepared the way for our national independence, and our federal Union. The history of our own State centres upon it, as the most important epoch in her colonial existence. Let us now

---

* Alb. Rec., XVIII. 326; Col. Doc., II. 272, 415, 445, 502, 509, III. 67–73, 346; Thompson, II. 165; Brodhead, I. 742–745; Val. Man., 1860, 593; Appendix, Notes F. and G.

† The Dutch national ensign was adopted about the year 1582, just after their Declaration of Independence, at the suggestion of William the Silent, Prince of Orange. It was composed of the Prince's colors — orange, white, and blue — arranged in three equal horizontal stripes. After the death of William the Second of Orange, in 1650, the predominating influence of the Louvestein, or De Witt party caused a *red* stripe to be substituted for the ancient *orange;* and the Dutch flag at this day remains as it was thus modified two centuries ago: Brodhead, I. 19, *note.*

contemplate some of the peculiar features and direct consequences of this momentous event.

The conquest of New Netherland by the British sovereign was an act of almost unparalleled national baseness. It was planned in secret, and was carried out in deliberate treachery towards a friendly government. Because England coveted New Netherland, and not because she had any just claim, she seized it as a prize. It was essential to the success of her colonial policy to secure that prize. The whole transaction was eminently characteristic of a selfish, insolent, and overbearing nation. On no other principle than that which frequently afterwards stimulated the predatory aggressions of Great Britain in India and elsewhere, can her conquest of the Dutch-American Province be defended. In the utterance of this judgment, I trust that a descendant of one of the English conquerors of New York has not been moved by any uncandid sentiments towards the birth-land of his ancestor.

Yet, outrageous as was the deed, the temptation to commit it was irresistible. Its actual execution was only a question of time. Unjustifiable as it was, the usurpation of the English could not have been prevented, unless the Dutch Government were prepared to reverse their previous policy, and hold New Netherland at every hazard, against the might of all enemies. The Province of Holland and the West India Company, alone, could not successfully oppose England. The General Government of the United Netherlands would not take the indispensable action, because they never rightly estimated the importance of their American colony, and felt no sufficient interest in its preservation. It was not until the last years of their rule, that they gave serious attention to the necessity of measures for its security. Even then, they procrastinated when they should have acted. This apparent indifference encouraged the monopolizing purposes of British colonial statesmanship; and the Dutch transatlantic Province became an easy prey to undeclared foes, who skulked, like pirates in time of peace, into her chief harbor. War followed between the Netherlands and England; but the captured prize was never restored. And so, NEW YORK replaced NEW NETHERLAND on the map of the world.

But, even if its importance had been adequately estimated in Holland, our State could not have remained much longer a Dutch Province. Its existence as such would soon have proved inconvenient to all parties. It was not insular, nor easy of defence. Its territory adjoined the colonial possessions of France, as well as of England; and its inland frontier was not defined by natural boundaries. Sufficient measures for its protection against either of these powers would have required larger expenditures, on the part of the West India Company, than commercial thrift might have considered expedient. The States-General were less interested in its preservation than was the impoverished Corporation, which thought more of revenue than of patriotism. Moreover, the Federal Government would soon have found that another European sovereign, besides Charles the Second, viewed with jealousy the existence of a Dutch Province in North America. If England had not seized New Netherland when she did, France would almost certainly have taken and held it, not long afterwards, in the Second Dutch war of 1672; and would thus have accomplished her long-cherished design of extending Canada, from Lake Champlain southward, through the Valley of the Hudson, to the ocean at Manhattan. And had Louis the Fourteenth succeeded in obtaining its possession, the subserviency of Charles and of James would doubtless have so confirmed the French power on this continent, that neither the conquest of Canada by Great Britain, nor the American

Revolution, could have happened. Both these events depended on the fate of New Netherland. Even if the Province, after its reconquest in 1673, instead of being finally ceded to England by the Treaty of Westminster, in 1674, had remained subject to Holland for fifteen years longer, until Englishmen called the Dutch Stadtholder to their throne, the crisis would then have come; and our forefathers, following the fortunes of their chief, would have spontaneously proclaimed William the Third as their King, with acclamations as triumphant as when they first welcomed his short-lived colonial authority with shouts of "ORANJE BOVEN !"*

The terms of capitulation which Nicolls offered, and Stuyvesant accepted, were, perhaps, the most favorable ever granted by a conqueror. In theory, the King "resumed his own." In fact, he gained a foreign Province by a conquest, the effect of which was limited only by the Articles of Surrender. The clear policy of the Duke of York, as Proprietor, was to obtain peaceful possession of New Netherland, and, at the same time, induce its Dutch inhabitants to remain and become loyal British subjects. His defective Patent, indeed, authorized him to govern such subjects only. The Articles of Capitulation accordingly provided that the people of the Dutch Province were to continue free denizens of England. The most

---

* The popular cry, "*Oranje Boven,*" appears to have originated at Dordrecht, in Holland, in 1672. The partisans of the Prince, and soon chosen Stadtholder, William the Third, who were the opponents of the Brothers De Witt, hoisted on the tower of that city an orange flag above a white flag. On the orange flag was the inscription, in Dutch,

"*Oranje boven, de Witten onder;
Die 't anders meend, die slaat den Donder.*"

Or, in English:

"Orange above, the Whites under:
Who thinks not so, be struck by thunder."

The Dutch word *wit* means "white;" hence *de Witten*, or "the De Witts," signifies "the Whites." Basnage, Ann. Prov. Un., II. 284; Wagenaar, Vad. Hist., XIV. 165; Davies's Holland, III. 108.

liberal offers, to conciliate them, were made with ostentatious benevolence. It is not surprising that the Dutch colonists, chagrined at the seeming indifference of the authorities of their Fatherland, and having many causes of complaint against their own Provincial Government, should have generally accepted this change of their rulers at least calmly and hopefully, if not with positive satisfaction.*

There was, at all events, one point on which there was almost universal acquiescence. As a choice of evils, the Dutch inhabitants of New Netherland were far more content with becoming subject directly to the King of England and the Duke of York, than they would have been with the mastery of those Eastern neighbors, who had so long, but so vainly, coveted the possession of their Province. This feeling we have observed strongly exhibited in the very agony of the surrender. It was a natural feeling. The early colonists of our State had but little liking for most of the emigrants to New England, or their characteristics. If they sympathized with any of them, it was chiefly with the people of tolerant Rhode Island. The genial English cavalier was much nearer the Hollander's heart than was the ascetic English Puritan, who would not be comforted in his exile by the calm pleasures of a Leyden Sunday. Across the Atlantic, local circumstances produced deeper repugnance. New York and Massachusetts—rivals and antagonists nearly from the start—were colonized by men not only of different races,

* In October, 1664, a few weeks after the surrender, Governor Nicolls required all the Dutch inhabitants to take an oath of allegiance to the King, and of obedience to the Duke of York and his officers, as long as they should live in any of his Majesty's territories. The leading burghers of New York, however—fearing that the proposed oath might "nullify or render void" the Articles of Capitulation—declined to swear it, until the Governor formally declared "that the Articles of Surrender are not in the least broken, or intended to be broken, by any words or expressions in the said oath." This removed every doubt, and allegiance was cordially sworn.—Gen. Ent., I. 49, 50; New Amst. Rec., V. 614–618; Val. Man. 1861, 605–607; Col. Doc., III. 74–77.

but of essentially opposite ideas. The cardinal principle of the one was comprehensive liberality; the systematic policy of the other was Procrustean rigor. There never was a greater contrast in the civilized peoples of the earth. Thus it happened that there was almost constant enmity between the Dutch Province and her Puritan neighbors. This early antipathy was, doubtless, largely increased by those territorial encroachments which were so offensively pushed on from the East. Yet the contrariety survived long after the question of boundaries was settled. It continued to manifest itself most conspicuously, in what frequently appeared to be a meddlesome and callous obtrusiveness on the one side, which was met, on the other, by the decorous reserve which the rules of good society promote. In the end, it was well that such characteristic differences existed. With more intimate association, each rival race learned to respect and to value the excellencies which distinguished the other. Narrow provincialism grew more magnanimous with larger observation; and while but few were found willing to abandon the valleys of the Hudson and the Mohawk, crowds pressed from New England, in later years, to irresistibly attractive homes in New York—none the less gladly because of the unjealous greeting which welcomed their approach. The acute ingenuity, anxious energy, and austere virtues, which were thus contributed by its immigrants from the East, blended admirably with the steady industry, quiet conservatism, and grand comprehensiveness, which always marked the pioneers of our own State; and the combination has yielded results of magnificent prosperity, which God grant may be perpetual!

It was for the true interest of America that New York was founded by the Batavian race. That founding produced our own magnanimous and cosmopolitan State, the influence of which on our nation has always been so happy and so healthful. Providence never meant our variegated country to be the antitype of a single European sovereignty. There probably never was a population more homogeneous than that of New England in its early days. Of the twenty thousand persons who, at the end of twenty years after the first settlement at New Plymouth, formed its several colonies, nearly all were English emigrants, and most of them were Puritans. For more than a century their descendants lived and multiplied, a distinct people, secluded from other communities in a very remarkable degree. This seclusion generated or stimulated vehemently dogmatic individualism. It helped, very powerfully, to produce what is sometimes called the "intense subjectivity" of the New England mind. The result was legitimate. The British Puritan loved true liberty less than he loved dominion. He wished always to do what pleased himself; but he longed, still more, to compel all others to do as he pleased. He was uneasy unless he could domineer. This tyrannical and unscrupulous, but thoroughly English spirit was not softened by its transplantation in America. It seems, on the contrary, to have grown more rank, and to have developed peculiar social characteristics, in the secluded New England colonies. Of these characteristics, none was more remarkable than the system of "mutual inspection," which, pushed to its extreme limits, would subject all to a discipline as galling as it is unwholesome and dwarfing. "The Inquisition," writes one of Massachusetts' most honored sons, "existed in substance, with a full share of its terrors and its violence."* It is obvious that liberality, magnanimity, and comprehensiveness, could not flourish among a people so isolated, and so incessantly occupied in brooding over, and working out within itself, its own problems. Yet, I would be the last to withhold an expression of sincere

* Story's Miscellanies, 66; Coit's Puritanism, 218; Brodhead, I, 208, 331.

respect, justly due to the many sterling qualities which illustrate that renowned stock, the descendants of which have exerted so wide and so marked an influence throughout our whole country.

When he emigrated, however, the New Englander did not readily lay aside his native peculiarities. He yearned to propagate unmodified his ingrained provincialism. But this he could not do in the cosmopolitan atmosphere of New York. That he could not, was happy for our country. It was not her cramped destiny to perpetuate or reproduce the ideas or the policy of only one of the nationalities of the Old World, or of but one of its plantations in the New. The arrogant claim—so flattering to British pride, so sycophantic in Americans who would flatter England—that the United States of America are of wholly Anglo-Saxon origin, is as fallacious as it is vulgar. "Time's noblest offspring" was not the child of England alone. There was a Fatherland, as fruitful as the Motherland. There were many parents of our multigenerous people. The great modern Republic sprang from a union of races as various and contrasted as the climates from which, and to which, they emigrated. Sweden, Holland, Germany, Savoy, Spain, France, Scotland, and Ireland, all co-operated, no less mightily than England, in peopling our territory, moulding our institutions, and creating our vast and diversified country, "one and indivisible." To its heterogeneousness, and not to its supposed homogeneousness—to its collisions and its comminglings of races—to its compromises and its concessions—does that country owe its grandest moral, social, and political characteristics.

Among these various races, the Batavian founders of New York marked their impress deep upon their State and upon the confederated nation. The motives to their emigration were different from those which led to the colonization of other American territories. They had suffered no persecution in their tolerant Fatherland. They left its shores not as refugees, but as volunteers—not to seek "Freedom to worship God" for themselves, and deny it to others—not to establish inquisitorial dogmatism, but to live, and let others live, in comfort. "Not as the conqueror comes," came the unaggressive forefathers of our State. The plain-spoken and earnest, yet unpresumptuous men who first explored and reclaimed New Netherland, and bore the flag of Holland to the cabins of the Iroquois, crossed the ocean to better their condition, and add another far-off Province to the Dutch Republic. They remembered, with deep affection, the great history of the little country they had left; and with their household gods, they carried

<blockquote>" The wreaths and relics of the immortal fire."*</blockquote>

They hoped, perhaps, that in time they might rear, among the rocks, and the maples, and the pine-trees on the banks of the River of the Mountains, "the Exchange of a wealthier Amsterdam, and the schools of a more learned Leyden."† They gave to their new abodes among the red men of the forest, the names which they had loved in their distant Belgian homes. Born in that "hollow land," rescued from the sea, where the first lessons of childhood taught them self-reliance and industry, they brought over into the wilderness those thrifty national habits which soon made it to bloom and blossom as the rose. Longer lines of barges than ever crowded the Batavian canals, are now drawn through those magnificent channels from the lakes to the ocean, which the experience of Holland suggested, and the enterprise of her sons helped to construct. Distinguished by that modesty which generally accompanies merit, the Dutch pioneers of New York

* Dryden's Æneid, II. † Macaulay, I. 219.

made no loud-sounding pretensions to grandeur in purpose, superiority in character, or eminence in holiness. They were the very opposites of the Pharisees of ancient or of modern times. They were more ready to do than to boast; and their descendants have never been ambitious to arrogate and appropriate excessive praise for what their forefathers did in extending the limits of Christendom, and in stamping on North America its resplendent features of freedom of religion and liberality in political faith. With the magnanimous ideas, and honest maxims, and homely virtues of their Fatherland, they transplanted her national Church and her public Schools, her accomplished "Domines" and her well-educated Schoolmasters. The huge clasped Bibles, issued from her proverbially elegant press, were preserved as venerable heir-looms in their families. The system of free public or common Schools—in which New England takes no less pride than New York—was borrowed, or imitated, from the Dutch Republic, where the exiled Puritans saw it for the first time in successful operation, through the influence of her Calvinistic national Church.* The holidays of the Netherlands, observed by us here to this day, renew the genial and hallowed anniversaries of "Paas" and "Saint Nicholas;" while, year by year, the people of New York are invited to render thanks to God, as their forefathers were invited to keep "Thanksgiving Day" in Holland, long before Manhattan was known, and while New England was yet "a rocky desart."† Those forefathers fearlessly deposed the King of Spain, while they humbly worshipped the King of kings. The children of such ancestors added no weak ingredient to the blended masses of our Union!

Yet while Hollanders formed the chief element in her

---

* Davies's Holland, II. 202, 203; Bor., XX. 672; Brodhead, I. 462, 463.
† Smith's New England; Pinkerton, XIII. 206; Brodhead, I. 41, 64, 443, 747.

population, New Netherland enjoyed the advantage of a happy intermixture of other European races. Her first settlers, imbued with the liberal sentiments of their ancestral land, viewed free navigation and free trade as the solvent of national antipathies. Accordingly, without regarding diversities in doctrine or lineage, they made the hearth-stone the test of citizenship, and residence and loyalty the only obligations of the multifarious nationalities which soon came to nestle among them. Walloons from Flanders, Huguenots and Waldenses from France and Savoy, Swedes, German Lutherans, wandering Israelites, Roman Catholics, Anabaptists, and English Quakers, all planted themselves, more or less quietly, beside the natives of Calvinistic Holland. Marvell's Lines on Old Amsterdam might almost describe her trans-Atlantic child, which with

> "Christian Pagan, Jew,
> Staple of sects and mint of schism grew;
> That bank of conscience. where not one so strange
> Opinion, but finds credit and exchange.
> In vain for Catholics ourselves we bear,
> The universal church is only there."

As early as 1643, the Jesuit Father Jogues—that illustrious apostle who consecrated with his life the "Mission of the Martyrs" among the Mohawks at Caghnawaga*— found that eighteen different languages were spoken in New Amsterdam. There was always popular freedom and public spirit enough in the Dutch Province to attract voluntary emigrants from the neighboring British Colonies. If the Fatherland gave asylum to self-exiled English Puritans, New Netherland as liberally sheltered refugees from the intolerant governments on her eastern

---

* The Indian word "Caghnawaga" means "the Rapids," or "a carrying-place;" Col. Doc., III. 250, *note;* General Index, 282; Shea's Catholic Missions, 304; N. Y. H. S. Coll., III. (II.) 171; Brodhead, I. 423, 659. I cannot refrain from protesting against the hideous want of taste which has belittled this sonorous, significant, and historical name into "Fonda!"

frontier. Her magnificent destiny, foretold in Holland,* began to be accomplished, when numbers, looking to her with eager eyes, were allured to embark for her shore. Far across the sea came crowded ships from Scotland, and France, and Ireland ; while from the upper waters of the Rhine flocked multitudes of a kindred race to those at its mouth, who first chose Manhattan as their home. Here, on our own rocky island—the Tyre of the New World— where Dutch sagacity, integrity, liberality, and industry laid the foundations—Saxon and Celt, Frenchman and German, Jew and Gentile, Northerner and Southerner— men of all races, and tongues, and climes, and creeds, have worked together to build up the golden throne of Commerce. New Amsterdam was but the miniature of New Netherland, and the prototype of cosmopolitan New York. And so, with large and comprehensive spirit, our Dutch forefathers established the grandeur of that imperial State whose

"Far-off coming shone."†

But if it was for the true interest of America that New York should be founded by Holland, it was equally for the greatest good of the greatest number that she should be acquired by England. She could not long have remained an isolated dependency of the Dutch Republic. The time was not yet at hand for her own State Independence. Nor was it the purpose of Providence that New Netherland should ever become a separate American Sovereignty. Her central and commanding position, her picturesqueness, variety, and universality, all foreshadowed her grand destiny—forever to bind together the North and the South, and to unite with the Ocean the Lakes and the Prairies of a future vast and undivided country. To

* *Ante*, page 17.
† The Arms of the State of New York, adopted in 1778, represent the Sun rising over distant mountain-tops, and her significant motto is "EXCELSIOR."

that wise end, her colonial allegiance was determined. If, instead of becoming the connecting link between the British American Plantations, our State had been annexed to Canada by Louis the Fourteenth, the Iroquois would have been rapidly exterminated; the dominion of France on this continent would have grown impregnable; no Wolfe would have scaled the heights of Abraham; and no such Revolution could have happened as that which produced our nation. New France, including the Valleys of the Ohio and the Mississippi, might yet have possessed her "broad-armed ports" at Quebec, Manhattan, and New Orleans; and a Bourbon might still have dated the instructions of his Vice-Roy at Versailles. Instead of Canada and Nova Scotia, New England and Virginia, deprived of the sympathy of New York, might perhaps, at this moment, have been receiving orders from Whitehall. But the confirmation of British supremacy in New Netherland was the augury of our national independence. The Fatherland had done all that the wisdom of the Almighty had given her to do in the work of American colonization. Thenceforward, her trans-Atlantic offspring was to become the ward of a severer guardian, whose fate it was—like that of Spain—to educate a new Republic of United States. This glorious consummation could not have begun, nor have been so wisely accomplished, if New York had not suffered in common with other colonies under the oppression which produced unanimous revolt; and if she had not taught her Confederates some of those exalting principles of political and religious liberality, which, preserving her through long generations untainted by fanaticism, have made her the majestic monument of her Batavian founders.

With the supremacy of England came a necessary change in the language, the laws, and the institutions of

New York. This change, however, was very gradual. The Articles of Capitulation happily restrained what otherwise might have been an insufferable exercise of the conqueror's power. Guaranteed their own religious worship and church discipline, the Dutch, in due time, cordially welcomed the Service of the Church of England.* Freedom of conscience was forever secured by the influence of the ancient Reformed Dutch Church, which effectually prevented the establishment of any one denomination as "The Church" of the Province. The Episcopal communion, although fostered by the servants of the Crown, never became her predominating sect.† This was owing, in a great degree, to the high personal and scholarly standing of the Dutch clergymen, of whom a regular succession, educated and ordained in Holland, continued to be sent over until 1772, when the ecclesiastical authority of the Classis of Amsterdam ceased.‡ The cosmopolitan character of New York was but made more permanent by the bloodless revolution, which, preserving the old, infused fresh elements among the original staples of her greatness. Relieved from the anxiety that for some time had been oppressing them, her people, as they grew in

---

* The Charter of Trinity Church could hardly have passed Fletcher's Council on the 6th of May, 1697, without the friendship of its Dutch members, Phillipse, Van Cortlandt, and Bayard; Council Minutes, VII. 236; Doc. Hist. N. Y., III. 249.

† The Colonial act of 22 September, 1693, was passed by an Assembly in which there was only one Episcopalian, and which never thought of establishing that denomination as the Provincial Church. In point of fact the Episcopal Church never was established, except in some of the Southern counties of the Province. See Col. Doc., V. 321, 322; Doc. Hist., III. 150, 151; Smith's New York, I. 131, 134, 187, 337, 339, II. 234; Sedgwick's Life of Livingston, 78, 88; Force's Tracts, IV. (IV.) 3, 35, 40, 52.

‡ See Verplanck, in N. Y. H. S. Collections, III. 89; Gunn's Memoirs of the Reverend John H. Livingston, D. D., 141, 142 (Ed. 1856.) Demarest, in his "History and Characteristics of the Reformed Protestant Dutch Church," p. 96, remarks that "She, of all Churches in the land, was least able to succeed without an educated ministry, for she had been always taught to consider this as essential. It was required by the Articles of Union, that provision should be made for it. Moreover, the Church in Holland would not consent to the independence of the American Churches until this had been guaranteed."

prosperity, remembered with fading regret the event, which, although it severed them politically from Holland, could never take from them the heritage of her virtues, her teachings, and her historical renown.

By becoming British subjects, the inhabitants of New Netherland did not, however, gain civil freedom. New names, they found, did not secure new liberties. "Amsterdam" was changed to YORK, and "Orange" to ALBANY. But these changes only commemorated the titles of a conqueror. Stuyvesant, and the West India Company, and a republican sovereignty, were exchanged for Nicolls, and a Royal Proprietor, and an hereditary King. The Province was not represented in Parliament; nor could her voice reach the chapel of Saint Stephen at Westminster, as readily as it had penetrated the chambers of the Binnenhof at the Hague. It was nearly twenty years before her Ducal Proprietor allowed, for a short time, to the people of New York even that faint degree of representative government which they had enjoyed when the three-colored ensign of Holland was hauled down from the flag-staff of Fort Amsterdam. Not until the authority of the British Crown was shaken, did New York become again as really free as New Netherland had been.

There was one remarkable feature in which our State differed from every other British-American dependency. A conquest from Holland, she became for twenty-one years a Proprietary Dukedom, and then, for nearly a century, she remained a Royal Province. Without a charter, like those of Maryland or Pennsylvania, New York resembled none of the New England colonies, except, perhaps, New Hampshire. It was not until after the accession of the Dutch Stadtholder to the English throne, that she permanently obtained the privilege of an Assembly elected by her freeholders. Even then, her Governor and her Counsellors were appointed directly by the King.

This circumstance, in connection with others peculiar to her original colonization, fastened upon New York a distinctive quality of social aristocracy, which survived the period of her Independence. It was perhaps owing to these causes, that so few comparatively of her Puritan neighbors came to add to her colonial population. New England and the north of Ireland contributed, at one time, considerable numbers. But her largest accessions of emigrants, during the reigns of William, Anne, and the Georges, besides Englishmen and Hollanders, were French Huguenots and German Calvinists and Lutherans. Most of the latter were refugees from the Palatinate, who settled themselves on the Hudson and the Mohawk Rivers. West of Herkimer, the country was possessed by the Iroquois; and it was not until long after our State Constitution was formed at Kingston, in 1777, that emigrants from New England ventured to push beyond the German Flats, and occupy the rich pastures of Onondaga and the Genesee. North of the north line of Massachusetts, New York remained for many years the true owner of the region west of the Connecticut, and she thus became the mother of the present State of Vermont. Her original territory, as defined by the Dutch Government in 1614, was so partitioned, in the progress of events, as to form the several States of Maine, New Hampshire, Massachusetts, Rhode Island, Connecticut, Vermont, New York, New Jersey, Pennsylvania, and Delaware. Little did the quiet men who, in the Binnenhof at the Hague, first placed the name of NEW NETHERLAND on the map of the world, anticipate that it would become the parent of such a noble progeny of sovereignties!

To all the changes which followed its conquest, the Dutch colonists of our State submitted with characteristic good faith. A few, who could not bear the separation, returned to end their days in their Fatherland. But

Stuyvesant, with the Dutch clergy and most of the colonial officers, honestly swore allegiance to the King and to the Duke, and remained faithful as long as English supremacy lasted.* No more loyal subjects than they were ever brought under the British crown. Yet it was no pleasant thing for them to watch the Red Cross of England waving where the emblems of the Netherlands had floated for fifty years. To Holland they felt a deep, unalterable, hereditary attachment. Nor has the whirligig of time extinguished this sentiment in their descendants. Two centuries have scarcely weakened the veneration which citizens of New York of Dutch lineage proudly cherish towards the birth-land of their ancestors. Year by year, the glorious and the genial memories of Holland are renewed by those whom long generations divide from the country of their forefathers. But it is generally true, that Colonists retain more affection towards their Fatherland than those who remain at home ever feel toward the emigrants who leave its shores. As years roll on, the contrast becomes more marked. Two centuries have almost wiped out of the recollection of Holland the once familiar name of New Netherland. A few of the more curious of her scholars and her statesmen may now and then, by careful search, discover the meagre paragraphs in which her ponderous histories dismiss the story of her ancient trans-Atlantic Province. The most complete separate sketch of it in the Dutch language is the work of a Zealander,† which, though written not many years ago, is already a literary rarity. But the people of the Low Countries scarcely know that New York was once their own New Netherland, or that they have any right to the glory of having laid the foundations of the mightiest State in the American Union, and the metropolis of the Western world!

---

* See *ante*, p. 41, *note*. † N C. Lambrechtsen, of Middelburg.

While it is thus to be regretted that the history of New Netherland should be so little known in Holland, it is still more discreditable that, until recently, it continued to be as little understood, and perhaps even less appreciated, in America. There is no State in our Union which has better reason to be proud of its annals than New York. Yet of no State were the beginnings left for generations in greater obscurity. Official records and original accounts by contemporary writers have never, indeed, been wanting. But these were generally like sealed books, written in the vernacular—almost unknown to Englishmen—of William the Silent, and Grotius, and Barneveldt. The only colonial historian of New York, after its conquest, was a Royalist of English descent.* His meagre outline of its first half-century seems to have encouraged a former Chancellor of our own State incautiously to tell us, thirty-six years ago, that the annals of its Dutch period "are of a tame and pacific character, and generally dry and uninteresting."† The remark might have been somewhat just, if it had been applied—not to their quality, but—to the disgracefully neglected condition in which our earliest archives were formerly suffered to remain.‡ If the sources of history were thus sealed, it is not surprising that History herself should have been silent. Like the many brave men who died before Agamemnon, the modest founders of New York for a long time slept,

"Unwept, unknown:
No bard had they to make all time their own."§

This is doubtless owing, in some degree, to ignorance

---

* William Smith, who died in 1793, Chief-Justice of Canada.
† Chancellor Kent, in N. Y. H. S. Coll., (II.) I. 13.
‡ I avail myself of this opportunity to express gratification that Dr. E. B. O'Callaghan has been, of late years, in charge of the Historical Records of our State at Albany. He is one of the very few who are fitted for the peculiar office of Archivist; and it would be a calamity if the public should be deprived of the advantage of his services.
§ Francis's Translation of Horace's Odes, IV. 9.

of the Dutch language, which few English or American
authors have ever attempted to master. But it is still more
owing to an inherited or imitative spirit of supercilious
depreciation of every thing Dutch, which, with some brilliant exceptions, seems to have infected so many writers
in our own country, especially those of New England.* It
is the good fortune of that section of our land to possess
abundant easily read records of the deeds and virtues of
her founders; and it is greatly to her comfort that so many
of her children have done their best to extol her glory and
spread abroad her fame. Yet, while a monotonous repetition of indiscriminating panegyric may gratify its subjects, it does not always enlarge human knowledge. It
may well be questioned whether zeal has not run into
injustice, and whether, while incessantly magnifying the
praise of one portion of our Union, a candid acknowledgment of the merits of others has not been systematically
shunned. The Tacitus of our country, in the grandeur of
his comprehensive genius, has not failed to do eloquent
justice to the honest memories of New York, his chosen
home. But too many of our approved authorities and
school-books, professing to teach American history, seem
as if they were carefully calculated for a provincial meridian, and cunningly manufactured to inculcate only accounts of New England. The beginnings of the Empire
State are passed ignorantly by; or, if they are alluded to,
it is too often in niggard or reluctant words, unworthy of
any scholar who ventures to relate our country's story.
The patriotic calendar of America has pertinaciously canonized the little company which landed on Plymouth
beach; while it has jealously suppressed a just reference to

---

* Everett and Bancroft are national jewels. Motley has done immortal honor
to New England and to himself by his admirable Dutch histories. Not less
worthily has Tuckerman, in his "Optimist," and his "Biographical Essays,"
shown that just appreciation of New York and her characteristics which a scholar
of his fine taste and cultivation could not help exhibiting.

the progeny of those who, long before they sheltered that Pilgrim band at Leyden, had showed the world how to depose a King and declare a People free and independent.

The retirement of Holland from an unequal strife, left France and Spain to contend with England for colonial supremacy in North America. Mistress of all the Atlantic coast between Nova Scotia and Florida, the power which had conquered New York soon aspired to uncontrolled dominion from sea to sea. The acquisition of New Netherland, which had formerly kept Virginia apart from New England, gave to the British Crown the mastery of the most advantageous position on our Continent, whence it could at pleasure direct movements against any Colony that might attempt a premature independence. With short-sighted triumph, England rejoiced that her authority was dotted on a new spot in the map of the world. But her pride went before her destruction, and her haughty spirit prepared the way for her terrible humiliation. The American Republic was fashioned in the first Congress of 1765, which met at New York. It was a most significant, but only a just decree of Providence, that the retribution of England should begin with the very Province which she had so iniquitously ravished from Holland, to set, as her most splendid jewel, in the diadem of her colonial sovereignty!

Yet for a long time the Plantations which had thus become geographically united were neither homogeneous nor sympathetic ; and they never were actually consolidated. While New England, Maryland, and Virginia were radically Anglo-Saxon Colonies, the mass of the population of New York, New Jersey, Pennsylvania, and Delaware, which had formed the later territory of New Netherland, was, as we have seen, made up of Hollanders, Huguenots, Waldenses, Germans, Frenchmen, Swedes, Scotchmen, and Irishmen. A similar want of homogeneousness characterized some of the more Southern Colonies. Among these manifold nationalities, ideas and motives of action were as various and discordant as the differing dialects which were uttered. In the progress of years, a common allegiance and common dangers produced a greater sympathy among the English Plantations in North America.

Nevertheless, while she formed a part of the British Colonial Empire, New York never lost her original social identity nor her peculiar political influence. Her moral power lasted throughout the whole succession of events which culminated in the American Revolution. It is impossible for me now to attempt a fitting historical review of this demonstrable truth. It is enough to say that, if the legitimate influence of New York has not heretofore been always worthily acknowledged, it has never been openly denied. Nor has her salutary moral power ever ceased. The history of her Fatherland—besides the idea of toleration of opinion—furnished the example of the Confederation of Free and Independent States, and made familiar the most instructive lessons of *Constitutional administration. While that history taught the sacred right of revolt against the tyranny of an hereditary King, it enforced the no less sacred duty of faithfulness to deliberate obligations, and loyalty to the General Government founded by the solemn compact of Sovereign but United States. The patriots who deposed Philip the Second were the great originals of those who in the next century dethroned Charles the First, and in the century following rejected George the Third. From Holland came William, "the Deliverer" of England from the tyrant James. The Declaration of the Independence of the United Provinces of the Netherlands was the glorious model of the English Declaration of Right, and of the grander Declaration of the Independence of the United

Colonies of North America. The Union of Utrecht was the noble exemplar of the Philadelphia Articles of Confederation. The Dutch motto, "EENDRAGT MAAKT MAGT"—*Unity makes might*—suggested our own "E PLURIBUS UNUM."

All these teachings of Dutch history are the peculiar heritage of our own Empire State. It was the proud destiny of New York to temper the narrow and sometimes fanatical characteristics of her English sister Plantations with the larger and more conservative principles which she had herself derived from Holland. It was her lot to sustain more severe trials, and gain a more varied experience, than any other American Colony. Midway between the Saint Lawrence and the Chesapeake, she stood, for almost a century, guarding her long frontier against the enmity and might of New France. And when at last the Conquest of Canada filled the measure of British aggression, and pampered still more the British lust of power, the augury of two hundred years ago was fulfilled, and NEW YORK—worthy to be distinguished as THE NETHERLAND OF AMERICA—became the Pivot Province, on which hinged the most important movements of that sublime revolt against the oppression of England, the only parallel to which was the triumphant struggle that the forefathers of her first settlers maintained against the gigantic despotism of Spain!

APPENDIX.

NOTE A.

Translation of the first NEW NETHERLAND Charter, granted by the STATES GENERAL, on 11 October, 1614;—from Mr. Brodhead's Address before the N. Y. Historical Society, 20 November, 1844, p. 53, and from the New York Colonial Documents, volume I. pages 10–12.

SATURDAY, the Eleventh of October, 1614.
Present—The President, Mr. GHIESSEN.
Messrs. BIESMAN, WESTERHOLT, BRIENEN, OLDEN BARNEVELT, BERCKENRODE, DRIEL, TEYLINGEN, MAGNUS, MOESBERGEN, AYLOA, HEGEMANS.

THE STATES-GENERAL OF THE UNITED NETHERLANDS to all to whom these presents shall come, GREETING: Whereas Gerrit Jacobz Witssen, ancient Burgomaster of the City of Amsterdam, Jonas Witssen and Simon Monissen, owners of the ship named the *Little Fox*, whereof Jan de With was schipper; Hans Hongers, Paulus Pelgrom, and Lambrecht van Tweenhuysen, owners of the two ships named the *Tiger* and the *Fortune*, whereof Adriaen Block and Henrick Corstiaenssen were schippers; Arnolt van Leybergen, Wessel Schenck, Hans Claessen, and Berent Sweertsen, owners of the ship named the *Nightengale*, whereof Thys Volckertssen was schipper, merchants of the aforesaid City Amsterdam; and Pieter Clementssen Brouwer, Jan Clementssen Kies, and Cornelis Volckertssen, merchants of the City of Hoorn, owners of the ship named the *Fortuyn*, whereof Cornelis Jacobssen May was schipper, All now associated in one Company, Have respectfully represented unto Us, that they the Petitioners, after heavy expenses and great damages to themselves by loss of ships and other dangers, had, during the present current year, discovered and found, with the above-named five ships, certain New Lands, lying in America, between *New France* and *Virginia*, the sea-coasts whereof lie between Forty and Forty-five degrees of latitude, and now called NEW NETHERLAND: And Whereas We did, in the month of March last, for the promotion and increase of Commerce, cause to be published a certain General Consent and Charter, setting forth that whosoever should thereafter discover new havens, lands, places, or passages, might frequent, or cause to be frequented, for four voyages, such newly-discovered and found places, passages, havens, or lands, to the exclusion of all others from visiting or frequenting the same from the United Netherlands, until the said first discoverers and finders, shall themselves have completed the said four voyages, or caused the same to be done within the time prescribed for that purpose, under the penalties expressed in the said Charter,* &c., They pray that We would accord to them a proper Act to be passed in form, in pursuance of the aforesaid Charter; Which being considered, and WE having, in Our Assembly, heard the pertinent Report of the Petitioners relative to the discovery and finding of the said New Countries between the above-named limits and degrees, and also of their adventures, Have Consented and Granted, and by these presents Do consent and Grant, to the said petitioners, now united into One Company, that they shall be privileged exclusively to frequent or cause to be visited the above Newly-discovered Lands, situate in America, between *New France* and *Virginia*, whereof the sea-coasts lie between the Fortieth and the Forty-fifth degrees of latitude, now named NEW NETHERLAND (as can be seen by a Figurative Map hereunto annexed†), and that for four voyages within the term of Three Years, commencing the First of January Sixteen Hundred and Fifteen, next ensuing or sooner; without it being permitted to any other person from the United Netherlands to sail to, navigate, or frequent the said newly-discovered lands, havens, or places, either directly or indirectly, within the said three years, on pain of Confiscation of the vessel and cargo wherewith infraction hereof shall be attempted, and a fine of Fifty Thousand Netherland Ducats, for the benefit of the aforesaid discoverers or finders:—Provided, Nevertheless, that by these presents We do not intend to prejudice or diminish any of Our former Grants or Charters; And it is also Our intention that if any disputes or differences arise from these Our Concessions, they shall be decided by Ourselves:—We Therefore for this purpose expressly order and command all Governors, Justices, Officers, Magistrates, and inhabitants of the aforesaid United Lands, to allow the said Company peaceably and quietly to use and enjoy the whole benefit of this our Grant and Consent, refraining from all opposition and obstacles to the contrary: Inasmuch as we consider the same to be for the service and advantage of the country. Given under our Seal, and the Paraph and signature of our Secretary, at the Hague, the eleventh day of October, 1614.

---

* A translation of this Charter is in N. Y. Col. Doc., I. 5, 6.
† For a fac-simile of this map, see N. Y. Col. Doc., I. 13. See also the map compiled by Mr. Brodhead, for his History of New York, which illustrates this publication.

NOTE B.

New England writers, in their zeal to establish a paramount British title to the whole of North America between Virginia and Canada, appear to have overlooked the doctrine announced by Queen Elizabeth in 1580, and confirmed in the House of Commons in 1621, as stated *ante*, page 9. This doctrine was, that "*prescription without possession is of no avail;*" the logical consequence of which is, that the "prescription" arising from the voyages of the Cabots gave England no title except to such American territory, discovered by her subjects, as she might actually occupy. Under this rule, her title to Virginia was never questioned. But by King James's second Patent of May, 1609, the northern boundary of Virginia was fixed at about the fortieth parallel of latitude. The country between Virginia and Canada had been left a *vacuum domicilium*, after the abandonment of Maine by the Sagadahoc colonists in 1608. The discoveries of the Dutch in this intermediate and unknown region were followed by their permanent occupation of the most of it; and the only Englishman that seems to have visited NEW NETHERLAND, after those in the HALF MOON, was Dermer, in 1619. The New England Patent of November, 1620, by its express Proviso that no territory was intended to be granted which was "actually possessed or inhabited by any other Christian Prince or Estate," would appear to have clearly excepted New France and New Netherland, the actual possession of which by the French and the Dutch was undeniable. Yet, with the coolest audacity, one of the preliminary recitals of that Patent declared that there were "no other the subjects of any Christian King or State, by any authority from their Sovereign Lords or Princes, actually in possession" of any of the territory between the fortieth and the forty-eighth degrees of latitude! In the same spirit, the English Privy Council, in December, 1621, pretended that the King had "good and sufficient title" to the whole of that region, "*jure primæ occupationis*." If by this was meant the temporary and limited English "occupation" by the colony at Sagadahoc, it was a palpable absurdity; because that English "occupation" of a part of Maine was abandoned before the Dutch discovery of unknown New Netherland. To insist upon such a fallacy was simply to substitute "prescription" for "possession"—a doctrine which both Queen Elizabeth and Parliament had derided. Nevertheless, this transparent subterfuge of *constructive*, instead of *actual* possession, was the strongest ground upon which the English maintained their title as against the Dutch. See further on this subject, Brodhead's New York, I. 4, 15, 44, 92–96, 138–144, 189, 252, 633, 634; Hazard's Collections, I. 103–118; Trumbull's Connecticut, I. 547, 554; N. Y. Colonial Documents, I. 27, II. 287, 302, 325, 332, 379–382, 389, 412, III. 6–8, VII. 596; Smith's N. Y., I. 297; Dunlap's N. Y., II., Appendix, ccvi.—It could hardly, perhaps, have been expected that the Editor of the recent volume on "Henry Hudson the Navigator," published by the Hakluyt Society of London, in 1860, should have avoided the errors which deform his Introduction to that work.

NOTE C.

Translation of the Commission from the STATES-GENERAL of the UNITED NETHERLANDS to PETER STUYVESANT, as Director-General of NEW NETHERLAND, dated 28 July, 1646 :—from the New York Colonial Documents, vol. I. p. 178.

THE STATES-GENERAL OF THE UNITED NETHERLANDS.—To all those to whom these Presents shall come, or who shall hear them read, Health; BE IT KNOWN: Whereas we have deemed it advisable for the advancement of the affairs of the General Incorporated West India Company not only to maintain the trade and population on the coast of *New Netherland* and the places situate thereabout, also the islands *Curaçoa, Buenaire, Aruba*, and their dependencies, which have hitherto been encouraged thither from this country, but also to make new treaties and alliances with foreign Princes, and to inflict as much injury as possible on the enemy in his forts and strongholds, as well by sea as by land; For which purposes it becomes necessary to appoint a person Director: WE, Therefore, confiding in the probity and experience of Petrus Stuyvesant, formerly intrusted with our affairs in, and the government of, the aforesaid Island of Curaçoa and the places thereon depending, and We, being well pleased with his services there, Have commissioned and appointed and by these presents Do commission and appoint the said PETRUS STUYVESANT Director in the aforesaid countries of *New Netherland* and the places thereunto adjoining, together with the aforementioned Islands of *Curaçoa, Buenaire, Aruba*, and their dependencies; to administer, with the Council as well now as hereafter appointed with him, the said office of Director, both on water and on land, and in said quality to attend carefully to the advancement, promotion, and preservation of friendship, alliances, trade, and commerce; to direct all matters appertaining to traffic and war, and to maintain in all things there, good order for the service of the United Netherlands and the General West India Company; to establish regularity for the safeguard of the places and forts therein; to administer law and justice as well civil as criminal; And moreover to perform all that concerns his office and duties in accordance with the Charter and the general and particular Instructions herewith

APPENDIX. 63

given, and to be hereafter given him, as a good and faithful Director is bound and obliged by his oath in Our hands to do; Which done, WE, therefore, order and command all other officers, common soldiers, together with the inhabitants and natives residing in the aforesaid places as subjects, and all whom it may concern. to acknowledge, respect, and obey the said PETRUS STUYVESANT as our Director in the countries and places of *New Netherland*, and in the Islands of *Curaçoa, Buenaire, Aruba*, and their dependencies, and to afford all help, countenance and assistance in the performance of these things, as WE have found the same to be for the advantage of the Company. Done in our Assembly at the Hague, on the xxviii. July, 1646.

NOTE D.

Copy of the Commission from the DUKE OF YORK to Colonel RICHARD NICOLLS, dated 2 April, 1664, Recorded in Book of Patents, vol. I. pp. 116–118, in the Office of the Secretary of State at Albany.

JAMES, Duke of YORK and ALBANY, Earl of ULSTER, Lord High Admiral of ENGLAND and IRELAND, &c., Constable of Dover Castle, Lord Warden of the Cinque Ports, and Governor of Portsmouth, &c. WHEREAS it hath pleased the King's most Excellent Majesty, my Sovereign Lord and Brother, by His Majesty's Letters Patents, bearing date at Westminster the *Twelfth* day of *March* in the Sixteenth year of His Majesty's Reign, to give and grant unto me and to my Heirs and Assigns, All that part of the mainland of New England, Beginning at a certain place called or known by the name of *Saint Croix*, next adjoining to *New Scotland* in America, and from thence extending along the sea-coast, unto a certain place called *Petaquine* or *Pemaquid*, and so up the River thereof to the furthest head of the same, as it tendeth Northwards, and extending from thence to the River of *Kinebequi*, and so upwards by the shortest course to the River *Canada* northwards; And Also all that Island or Islands commonly called by the several name or names of *Matowacks* or *Long Island*, situate, lying, and being towards the west of Cape Cod and the Narrow-Higansets, abutting upon the mainland, between the two rivers there called or known by the several names of *Connecticut* and *Huason's* River; Together also with the said River called *Hudson's* River and all the land from the West side of *Connecticut* River to the East side of *Delaware* Bay; And Also all those several Islands called or known by the name of *Martin's Vineyards* and *Nantukes* otherwise *Nantucket*; Together with all the Lands, Islands, Soiles, Rivers, Harbours, Mines, Minerals, Quarries, Woods, Marshes, Waters, Lakes, Fishing, Hawking, Hunting, and Fowling, and all other Royalties, Profits, Commodities, Hereditaments, to the said several Islands, Lands, and Premises belonging and appertaining, with their and every of their Appurtenances; To Hold the same to my own proper use and behoof, With Power to correct, punish, pardon, govern, and rule the Inhabitants thereof, by Myself, or such Deputies, Commissioners, or Officers as I shall think fit to appoint; as by His Majesty's said Letters Patents may more fully appear: AND Whereas I have conceived a good opinion of the Integrity, Prudence, Ability and Fitness of RICHARD NICOLLS, Esquire, to be employed as my Deputy there, I have therefore thought fit to constitute and appoint, and I do hereby constitute and appoint him the said *Richard Nicolls*, Esquire, to be my Deputy-Governor within the Lands, Islands, and Places aforesaid, To perform and execute all and every the Powers which are by the said Letters Patents granted unto me, to be executed by my Deputy, Agent, or Assign. To HAVE AND TO HOLD the said place of Deputy-Governor unto the said *Richard Nicolls*, Esquire, during my will and pleasure only; Hereby willing and requiring all and every the Inhabitants of the said Lands, Islands, and Places to give obedience to him the said *Richard Nicolls* in all things, according to the tenor of His Majesty's said Letters Patents; And the said *Richard Nicolls*, Esquire, to observe, follow and execute such Orders and Instructions as he shall from time to time receive from myself. GIVEN, under my hand and seal, at *Whitehall*, this *Second* day of *April*, in the Sixteenth Year of the Reign of our Sovereign Lord *Charles* the Second, by the Grace of God King of England, Scotland, France, and Ireland, &c., *Annoque Domini*, 1664.

JAMES. (L. S.)

By Command of His Royal Highness,
W. COVENTRY.

NOTE E.

OFFICIAL DOCUMENTS RELATING TO THE SURRENDER OF NEW NETHERLAND, $\frac{\text{26-29 AUGUST,}}{\text{5-8 SEPTEMBER,}}$ 1664.

Copy of Stuyvesant's full power to his Commissioners, dated $\frac{\text{26 August,}}{\text{5 September,}}$ 1664;—from Albany Records, XVIII. 322, 323, and General Entries, I. 30, 31.

THE DIRECTOR-GENERAL and COUNCIL OF NEW NETHERLAND hereby make known;—To prevent the effusion of blood, plundering, murders, and for the good of the inhabitants, We are moved by the summons made by the honored Lord Richard Nicolls, General of his Majestie of England, being come with his men-of-war and soldiers before the port, promising freely (by his own proposition made) to re-deliver the Fort and City of Amsterdam in New Netherland, in case the difference of the limits of this Province be agreed upon betwixt His Majestie of England and the High and Mighty States-General likewise upon other equal and answerable conditions, to surrender and deliver; We have committed and do commit by this, John de Decker, Counsellor of State; Captain Nicholas Verlett, Commissary concerning matters of traffic; Samuel Megapolensis, Doctor of Physick; Cornelis Steenwyck, Burgomaster; Oloff Stevensen van Cortlandt, old Burgomaster; and James Cousseau, old Schepen of this City, to agree with the aforesaid Lord General Richard Nicolls or his deputies upon further articles; by these open letters promising that we will faithfully fulfill whatsoever shall by our fore-named Commissioners concerning these businesses be promised and agreed upon. In testimony of this it is confirmed by our Seale, in the Fort of Amsterdam in New Netherland, the 5th day of September, New Style, 1664.

Copy of Nicolls's full power to his Commissioners, dated $\frac{26 \text{ August,}}{5 \text{ September,}}$ 1664;—from General Entries, I. 32, 33.

I, Colonel RICHARD NICOLLS, Commander-in-Chief of all His Majesties forces now beleaguering the town on the Manhatans, Do accept of the proposal made by the Governor and his Council there residing, to treat of an accommodation by Articles of Surrender of the said Town and Forts thereunto belonging under His Majestie's obedience, to prevent the effusion of blood and to improve the good of the inhabitants; And whereas the Governor and Council are pleased to nominate and appoint John de Decker, Counsellor of State; Nicholas Varlett, Commissary concerning matters of traffic; Samuel Megapolensis, Doctor of Physick; Cornelis Steenwyck, Burgomaster; Oloff Stevensen van Kortlandt, old Burgomaster; and James Cousseau, old Sheriffe of this City, to agree and conclude with me or my Deputies, upon further Articles, promising they will faithfully fulfill whatsoever shall be by their fore-named Commissioners promised or agreed upon in the Treaty on their partes, I Do Therefore, on my part, nominate and appoint Sir Robert Carr, Knight; Colonel George Cartwright; Mr. John Winthrop, Governor of His Majestie's Colony of Connecticut; Mr. Samuel Willys, one of the Chief Councill of the said Colony; Captain Thomas Clarke, and Captain John Pincheon, Commissioners from the Court Generall of the Colony of the Massachusetts, To be my sufficient Deputys, to treat and conclude upon the Articles of Surrender of the aforenamed place, Promising that I will faithfully fulfill whatsoever they shall so treat and conclude upon. In Testimony Whereof, I have hereunto sett my hand and Seale, at the Camp before the Manhatans, this 26th day of August, Old Style, 1664.

RICHARD NICOLLS.

'Tis desired and agreed upon by the Commissioners on both parts above mentioned, that their meeting upon the premises shall be to-morrow morning, being the 27th of this month of August, Old Style, precisely at 8 o'clock in the morning, at a place called the Governor's Bowery, upon the Manhattans.

Copy of the Articles of Capitulation, agreed upon at the Governor's Bouwery, on Saturday, the $\frac{\text{27 August,}}{\text{6 September,}}$ 1664, and confirmed by Nicolls;—from N. Y. General Entries, I. 23–26, and from the Hollandtse Mercurius for September, 1664, 153, 154.

"These articles following were consented to by the persons hereunder subscribed, at the Governor's Bouwery, August 27th, Old Style [September 6th], 1664.

"I. We consent that the States-General, or the West India Company, shall freely enjoy all farms and houses (except such as are in the forts), and that within six months they shall have free liberty to transport all such arms and ammunition as now do belong to them, or else they shall be paid for them.

"II. All publique houses shall continue for the uses which they are now for.

"III. All people shall still continue free denizens, and shall enjoy their lands, houses, goods, shipps, wheresoever they are within this country, and dispose of them as they please.

"IV. If any inhabitant have a mind to remove himself, he shall have a year and six weeks from this day to remove himself, wife, children, servants, goods, and to dispose of his lands here.

"V. If any officer of state, or publique minister of state, have a mind to go for England, they shall be transported, freight free, in his majesty's frigates, when these frigates shall return thither.

"VI. It is consented to, that any people may freely come from the Netherlands, and plant in this country, and that Dutch vessels may freely come hither, and any of the Dutch may freely return home, or send any sort of merchandise home, in vessels of their own country.

"VII. All ships from the Netherlands, or any other place, and goods therein, shall be received here, and sent hence, after the manner which formerly they were before our coming hither, for six months next ensuing.

"VIII. The Dutch here shall enjoy the liberty of their consciences in divine worship and church discipline.

"IX. No Dutchman here, or Dutch ship here, shall, upon any occasion, be pressed to serve in war, against any nation whatsoever.

"X. That the townsmen of the Manhatoes shall not have any soldiers quartered upon them without being satisfied and paid for them by their officers, and that, at this present, if the fort be not capable of lodging all the soldiers, then the Burgomasters, by their officers, shall appoint some houses capable to receive them.

"XI. The Dutch here shall enjoy their own customs concerning their inheritances.

"XII. All publique writings and records, which concern the inheritances of any people, or the reglement of the church, or poor, or orphans, shall be carefully kept by those in whose hands now they are, and such writings as particularly concern the States-General may at any time be sent to them.

"XIII. No judgment that has passed any judicature here shall be called in question; but if any conceive that he hath not had justice done him, if he apply himself to the States-General, the other party shall be bound to answer for the supposed injury.

"XIV. If any Dutch living here shall at any time desire to travaile or traffique into England, or any place or plantation in obedience to his Majesty of England, or with the Indians, he shall have (upon his request to the Governor) a certificate that he is a free denizen of this place, and liberty to do so.

"XV. If it do appeare that there is a publique engagement of debt by the own of the Manhatoes, and a way agreed on for the satisfying of that engagement, it is agreed that the same way proposed shall go on, and that the engagement shall be satisfied.

"XVI. All inferior civil officers and magistrates shall continue as now they are (if they please) till the customary time of new election, and then new ones to be chosen by themselves, provided that such new chosen magistrates shall take the oath of allegiance to his Majesty of England, before they enter upon their office.

"XVII. All differences of contracts and bargains made before this day, by any in this country, shall be determined according to the manner of the Dutch.

"XVIII. If it do appeare that the West India Company of Amsterdam do really owe any sums of money to any persons here, it is agreed that recognition, and other duties payable by ships going for the Netherlands, be continued for six months longer.

"XIX. The officers military, and soldiers, shall march out with their arms, drums beating, and coulours flying, and lighted matches; and if any of them will plant, they shall have fifty acres of land set out for them; if any of them will serve as servants, they shall continue with all safety, and become free denizens afterwards.

"XX. If at any time hereafter the King of Great Britain and the States of the United Netherlands do agree that this place and country be redelivered into the hands of the said States, whensoever his Majestie will send his commands to redeliver it, it shall immediately be done.

"XXI. That the town of Manhatans shall choose deputyes, and those deputyes shall have free voyces in all publique affairs as much as any other deputyes.

"XXII. Those who have any property in any houses in the fort of Orange shall (if they please) slight the fortifications there, and then enjoy all their houses as all people do where there is no fort.

"XXIII. If there be any soldiers that will go into Holland, and if the Company of West India in Amsterdam, or any private persons here, will transport them into Holland, then they shall have a safe passport from Colonel Richard Nicolls, Deputy-Governor under his Royal Highness, and the other Commissioners, to defend the ships that shall transport such soldiers, and all the goods in them, from any surprizal or acts of hostility to be done by any of his Majestie's ships or subjects.

"XXIV. That the copy of the King's grant to his Royal Highness, and the copy of his Royal Highness's commission to Colonel Richard Nicolls (testified by two Commissioners more and Mr. Winthrop, to be true copies), shall be delivered to the Honourable Mr. Stuyvesant, the present Governor, on Monday next, by eight of the clock in the morning, at the Old Mill,* and also these articles consented to and signed by Colonel Richard Nicolls, Deputy-Governor to his Royal Highness; and that within two hours after, the fort and town called New Amsterdam, upon the island of Manhatoes, shall be delivered into the hands of the said Colonel Richard Nicolls, by the service of such as shall be by him thereunto deputed by his hand and seal.

"John de Decker,	Robert Carr,
Nicholas Varlett,	George Cartwright,
Samuel Megapolensis,	John Winthrop,
Cornelis Steenwyck,	Samuel Willys,
Jacques Cousseau,	Thomas Clarke,
Oloff S. van Cortlandt,	John Pinchon.

"I do consent to these articles,

"Richard Nicolls."

Copy of the Ratification of the Articles of Capitulation, by Stuyvesant and his Council, on Monday, the $\frac{29 \text{ August,}}{8 \text{ September,}}$ 1664;—from Albany Records, XVIII. 326, and General Entries, I. 31, 32.

The Director-General and Council of New Netherland, to all who shall hear or see this, Greeting: Be it known that we hereby ratify and confirm the Conditions agreed on and concluded, on the Sixth of this month, between our Commissioners, the Honorable John de Decker, member of our Council; Captain Nicholas Varlett, Commissary of wares and merchandises; the Reverend Samuel Megapolensis; the Honorable Cornelis Steenwyck, Burgomaster; Oloff Stevensen van Cortlandt, old Burgo-

---

* For the situation of this "Old Mill," see *ante*, p. 36. *note*.

APPENDIX.   69

master; and Jacques Cousseau, old Schepen of this city, with the Commissioners of the Honorable Governor Richard Nicolls, Commander of His Britannic Majesty's frigates and land forces who besieged this fortress and city; namely, Sir Robert Carr, George Cartwright, John Winthrop, Samuel Willys, John Pincheon, and Thomas Clarke; And We promise to execute the same. Done in Fort Amsterdam in New Netherland, on 8th September, 1664.

P. STUYVESANT.

N. DE SILLE.	JACOB BACKER.
MARTIN KRYGIER.	TIMOTHEUS GABRY.
PAULUS LEENDERTSEN VAN DER GEIST.	ISAAC GREVENRAET.
PIETER TONNEMAN.	NICOLAAS DE MEYER.

I certifie the same.

CORNELIS VAN RUYVEN,
Secretary.

NOTE F.

Translation of a letter from CORNELIS VAN RUYVEN, late Secretary of NEW NETHERLAND, to the Dutch Villages on Long Island, announcing the Surrender, dated, 8 September, 1664;—from the Bushwick Records, and from Thompson's Long Island, II. 165; —see also N. Y. Colonial Documents, II. 415, 445, 502, 509.

September 8, 1664, N. S.

BELOVED FRIENDS:

It has happened that New Netherland is given up to the English, and that Peter Stuyvesant, Governor for the West India Company, has marched out of the Fort with his men, by Beaver street (*Bevers Paed*) to the Holland shipping, which lay there at the time: And that Governor Richard Nicolls, in the name of the King of England, ordered a corporal's guard to take possession of the Fort. Afterwards, the Governor, with two companies of men, marched into the Fort, accompanied by the Burgomasters of the City, who inducted the Governor, and gave him a welcome reception. Governor Nicolls has altered the name of the City of New Amsterdam, and named the same NEW YORK, and named the fort, FORT JAMES.

From your friend.

CORNELIS VAN RUYVEN.

NOTE G.

Translation of a letter from the SCHOUT, BURGOMASTERS, and SCHEPENS of the City of NEW AMSTERDAM, to the WEST INDIA COMPANY, dated, 16 *September*, 1664, N. S.;—from New Amsterdam Records, V. 567–570, and Valentine's Manual for 1860, 592, 593.

RIGHT HONORABLE, PRUDENT LORDS, THE LORDS DIRECTORS OF THE HONORABLE WEST INDIA COMPANY, AT THE AMSTERDAM CHAMBER:

RIGHT HONORABLE LORDS :—

We, your Honors' loyal, sorrowful, and desolate subjects, cannot neglect nor keep from relating the event, which, through God's pleasure, thus unexpectedly happened to us in consequence of your Honors' neglect and forgetfulness of your promise; to Wit: The arrival here of late, of four King's frigates from England, sent hither by His Majesty and his brother the Duke of York, with commission to reduce not only this place, but also the whole of New Netherland under His Majesty's authority; whereunto they brought with them a large body of soldiers, provided with considerable ammunition. On board of one of the frigates were about four hundred and fifty, as well soldiers as seamen; and the others in proportion.

The frigates being come together in front of Najac in the Bay, Richard Nicolls the Admiral, who is ruling here at present as Governor, sent a letter to our Lord Director-General, communicating therein the cause of his coming, and his wish.

On this unexpected letter, the Heer General sent for us, to determine what was to be done in the matter. Whereupon it was resolved and decided to send some Commissioners thither, to argue the matter with the General and his three Commissioners; who were so sent for this purpose twice. But no answer was received, except that they were not come here to dispute about it, but to execute their order and commission without fail, either peaceably or by force; and if they had any thing to dispute about it, it must be done with His Majesty of England, as we could do nothing here in the premises. Three days' delay was demanded for consultation. That was duly allowed;—but meanwhile they were not idle. They approached with their four frigates, two of which passed in front of the Fort. The other anchored about Nooten Island, and with five companies of soldiers encamped themselves at the Ferry opposite this place; together with a newly raised company of horse and a party of new soldiers, both from the North and from Long Island, mostly all our deadly enemies—who expected nothing else than pillage, plunder, and bloodshed—as men could perceive by their cursing and talking when mention was made of a capitulation.

APPENDIX. 71

Finally, being then encircled round about, we saw little means of deliverance. We considered what ought to be done ; and after we had well inquired into our strength, and had found it to be full fifteen hundred souls in this place, but of them not two hundred and fifty men capable of bearing arms, exclusive of the soldiers, who were about one hundred and fifty strong ; wholly unprovided with powder, both in the city and in the Fort —yea, not more than six hundred pounds were found in the Fort besides seven hundred pounds that is unserviceable ; Also because the countrymen, the third man of whom was called out, refused, We, with the greater portion of the inhabitants, considered it necessary to remonstrate with our Lord Director-General and Council, that their Honors might consent to a capitulation. Whereunto we labored according to our duty, and had much trouble ; Laid down and considered all the difficulties which should arise therefrom, not being able to resist such an enemy, as they could also receive a much greater force than they then had under command.

The Director-General and Council at length consented thereunto. Whereupon Commissioners were sent to the Admiral, who notified him that it was resolved to come to terms, in order to save the shedding of blood, if a good Agreement could be concluded.

Six persons were commissioned on each side, for the purpose of treating on this matter ; which they have done and concluded in manner as appears by the Articles annexed. How that will result, time will tell.

Meanwhile, since we have no longer to depend upon your Honors' promises or protection, We, with all the poor, sorrowing, and abandoned commonalty here, must fly for refuge to the Almighty God, not doubting but He will stand by us in this sorely afflicting conjuncture, and no more depart from us.

And we remain your

Sorrowful and abandoned subjects,

Pieter Tonneman,	Jacob Backer,
Paulus Leendertsen van der Grist,	Timotheus Gabry,
Cornelis Steenwyck,	Isaac Grevenraet,
Nicolaas de Meyer.	

Done in Jorck, heretofore named Amsterdam, in New Netherland, Anno 1664, the 16th of September.

NOTE H.

Translation of a letter from the Reverend SAMUEL DRISIUS, one of the Collegiate Ministers of the Reformed Dutch Church at New Amsterdam, to the CLASSIS OF AMSTERDAM, dated 15 *September*, 1664, N. S.; from the *Original Manuscript* in the possession of the GENERAL SYNOD of the Reformed Protestant Dutch Church in North America.

TO THE REVEREND, LEARNED, AND PIOUS BROTHERS OF THE VENERABLE CLASSIS OF AMSTERDAM.

I cannot neglect to acquaint your Reverences with our present condition, namely that we are now brought under the government of the King of England. On the Twenty-sixth of August there arrived in the Bay of the North River, near Staten Island, four great ships-of-war or frigates, well equipped, manned with seamen and soldiers, having a Patent or Commission from the King of Great Britain to demand and receive this Province in the name of His Majesty, and, if the same should not be accomplished by amicable arrangement, then to attack the place by force; and that then all should be given over to the pillage, robbery, and spoil of the English soldiers. The people here were not a little amazed at the arrival of these frigates. Our Lords, the Director and Council, together with the Regents of the City, took this affair very much to heart; and with all diligence, by messages sent back and forth to the General Richard Nicolls, sought to delay these matters, and that they might be referred to his Majesty of England and the Lords States of Holland. But all was in vain! They landed their soldiers about six miles off, at Gravesend, and marched them on foot upon Long Island up to the Ferry, over against this place. And on the Fourth of September, the frigates came with full sail, as far as here, having their guns all ready on one side, charged and intending (in case any hostilities should be used against them) to discharge their full broadsides on this open place, and then to conquer this town by violence, and give over every thing to rapine and massacre. Our Noble Lords and Regents, as well of the Noble [West India] Company as of the City, were well disposed to defend the place. But they saw that it was impossible; because the town was not in a condition of defence, though it was now being fortified; that even then it could not be defended, seeing that each man would have to stand four rods from the other in the ramparts of the City; that there was little provision of powder, as well in the fort as in the town; and that there was no relief or assistance to be expected;—but, on the other hand, that a great concourse of Englishmen, as well foot as horse, came hitherwards daily out of New England, very ardent for the plundering of this place; also that six hundred Northern Savages, and one hundred and fifty French rovers, with English commissions, had offered their services against us. So it was that our authorities, under the strong urgency of the burghers and inhabitants, were compelled, in order to prevent plundering and bloodshed, to resolve (however unwillingly) to come to an Agreement; the which was accordingly concluded on the Sixth of September. And so the English marched into our City on the Eighth of September, according to the Convention.

After the surrender of this place, several Englishmen, whom we have long known, and who are well affectioned towards us, came to us, saying that God had particularly ordered this affair so that it was settled by a Convention; because otherwise nothing could have come out of it but plundering, murdering, and total ruin. The which, also, several soldiers confirmed; who said that they had come here out of England in hope of booty, and now that it had fallen out otherwise, they wished that they might go back again to England.

And whereas it was arranged in the Articles that the Church service and doctrine, together with the Clergymen, should remain and continue as they have been until now, we could not separate ourselves from our congregation and hearers, but have felt ourselves obliged by our duty to abide, yet for a time, with the same, so that they should not, all at once, be scattered, and dwindle away.

I have a moderate sum due to me from the Noble [West India] Company, which I hope and wish may be paid. And so I end, commending your reverend persons and labors to the blessing of God, and remain,

   Your Reverences' obedient Brother,

           SAMUEL DRISIUS.

Manhattans.
Anno 1664, Sept. 15.

PROCEEDINGS

OF THE

NEW YORK HISTORICAL SOCIETY

IN RELATION TO

THE COMMEMORATION

OF THE

CONQUEST OF NEW NETHERLAND,

ON ITS

TWO HUNDREDTH ANNIVERSARY.

NEW YORK:
PUBLISHED BY THE SOCIETY.
M DCCC LXIV.

OFFICERS OF THE SOCIETY.
1864.

President,
FREDERIC DE PEYSTER.

First Vice-President,
THOMAS DE WITT, D. D.

Second Vice-President,
BENJAMIN ROBERT WINTHROP.

Foreign Corresponding Secretary,
GEORGE BANCROFT, LL. D.

Domestic Corresponding Secretary,
SAMUEL OSGOOD, D. D.

Recording Secretary,
ANDREW WARNER.

Treasurer,
BENJAMIN H. FIELD.

Librarian,
GEORGE HENRY MOORE.

EXECUTIVE COMMITTEE.

AUGUSTUS SCHELL,
ERASTUS C. BENEDICT,
BENJAMIN W. BONNEY,
JOHN ROMEYN BRODHEAD,
WILLIAM CHAUNCEY,
CHARLES P. KIRKLAND,
GEORGE FOLSOM,
GEORGE GIBBS,
ROBERT L. STUART.

NEW YORK HISTORICAL SOCIETY.

COMMEMORATION

OF THE

CONQUEST OF NEW NETHERLAND.

OCTOBER 12, 1864.

THE New York Historical Society, at its meeting on the second of February, 1864, taking into consideration the importance of the event, resolved that it would commemorate, by suitable acts and proceedings, the Two Hundredth Anniversary of the Conquest of New Netherland, in the autumn of the year 1664.

A Committee of Arrangements, including some of its most distinguished members, was accordingly appointed, and JOHN ROMEYN BRODHEAD was selected to deliver the Commemorative Oration.

The Committee, in executing their duty, addressed the following letter of invitation to various Historical Societies and eminent citizens in New York and other States:—

NEW YORK HISTORICAL SOCIETY.

LIBRARY, *New York City, September 15th,* 1864.

SIR:—The NEW YORK HISTORICAL SOCIETY proposes to commemorate, by suitable Acts and Proceedings, the Two Hundredth Anniversary of the CONQUEST OF NEW NETHERLAND, in the autumn of the year 1664.

Next to the discovery in 1609, by the Dutch, of New Netherland—the original bounds of which included the present States of Maine, New Hampshire, Vermont, Massachusetts, Rhode Island, Connecticut, New York, New Jersey, Pennsylvania, and Delaware—its conquest by the English, in 1664, is the most interesting event in the Colonial History of New York. The consequences of this event were of momentous import, not only to the City and the State of New York, but to the American Union. It forms one of those great epochs in National existence which it is the special office of Historical Societies fitly to observe.

The time appointed for the proposed commemoration is WEDNESDAY, THE TWELFTH OF OCTOBER next, being just two centuries after the last Dutch Fort on the Delaware was taken by the English, and the conquest of New Netherland was completed.

An Oration will be delivered on that day, before the Society and its guests, at the Hall of the Union, Cooper Institute, in this City, by JOHN ROMEYN BRODHEAD, LL.D.; and other proceedings will take place.

In behalf of the New York Historical Society, the undersigned request the pleasure of your attendance on this occasion.

Awaiting your favorable reply,

    We have the honor to be, Sir,

      Your obedient servants,

GULIAN C. VERPLANCK,	FREDERIC DE PEYSTER,
GEORGE BANCROFT,	AUGUSTUS SCHELL,
HAMILTON FISH,	GEORGE FOLSOM,
JAMES W. BEEKMAN,	CHARLES P. KIRKLAND,
EVERT A. DUYCKINCK,	ANDREW WARNER,
GEORGE H. MOORE,	

Committee of Arrangements.

In pursuance of these arrangements, a special meeting of the Society was held at the Hall of the Union, Cooper Institute, at a quarter past seven o'clock, on Wednesday evening, the twelfth of October, 1864.

Notwithstanding the inclemency of the weather, the meeting was largely attended by a very respectable audience. Among those who occupied seats on the platform were many distinguished citizens, representing various departments in the State and municipal governments, the Army and Navy, and the learned professions. Delegates from several Historical Societies were also present. The New Hampshire Society was represented by the Rev. Dr. N. Bouton and Joseph B. Walker, Esq.; Maine, by the Rev. William Stevens Perry; Rhode Island, by Dr. Usher Parsons; Connecticut, by J. Hammond Trumbull, Esq.; New Jersey, by William A. Whitehead, Esq., and Solomon Alofsen, Esq.; Pennsylvania, by Thomas H. Montgomery, Esq.; Delaware, by Bishop Lee, Dr. Henry F. Askew, and William D. Dowe, Esq.; Long Island, by the Rev. Dr. R. S. Storrs, Charles E. West, LL. D., Joshua M. Van Cott, Esq., Dr. Henry R. Stiles, and Alden J. Spooner, Esq.; Buffalo, by William Dorsheimer, Esq., Dr. James P. White, George S. Hazard, Esq.

The meeting was called to order by FREDERIC DE PEYSTER, Esquire, the President of the Society, who addressed the audience as follows:—

MEMBERS AND GUESTS OF THE NEW YORK HISTORICAL SOCIETY:

We are assembled this evening to commemorate the Two Hundredth Anniversary of the Conquest of New Netherland, in the autumn of the year 1664. The circumstances and the consequences of this momentous event will be appropriately set forth to you by the Orator selected by the Society. A century after her conquest, New York was foremost among her sister colonies in taking measures which looked towards National Independence. Retributive justice, in 1783, followed slowly, but surely, the trespass of 1664. In our own day, when another century has passed away, our powerful and patriotic State is found putting forth gigantic efforts to maintain our National Union; assaulted as it is by domestic treason, which is fostered by foreign machinations. The Commemorative Oration, on this occasion, will be delivered by our fellow-member, JOHN ROMEYN BRODHEAD, Doctor of Laws, and well known as the historian of our State. The proceedings of this evening will begin by a Prayer, to be offered by the Reverend THOMAS DE WITT, Doctor of Divinity, Senior Minister of the Collegiate Reformed Protestant Dutch Church in this city, and First Vice-President of this Society.

The Reverend Doctor DE WITT then offered an appropriate Prayer.

After which, the President introduced Mr. BRODHEAD, who proceeded to deliver his Oration.

At the conclusion of Mr. Brodhead's Oration, the Honorable GULIAN CROMMELIN VERPLANCK rose to move a resolution of thanks.

Mr. VERPLANCK said, that in offering this Resolution, laboring as he was under a severe cold, and a hoarseness which must render his voice scarcely audible to most of this assembly, yet he could not refrain from expressing the high gratification he had felt in listening to the discourse just concluded. It contained much curious and instructive historical information, most of it not familiar even to the studious historical inquirer, and the fruit of large and accurate research. It was enriched throughout by a sagacious and clear-sighted historical philosophy, tracing out both the causes and the results of the most striking and the noblest peculiarities of the character and fortunes of our State and Nation. Above all, he could not but admire, as well as sympathize with, the glowing and grateful ancestral spirit which animated the Orator,—a worthy descendant of the compatriots of William the Silent,—and which had enkindled congenial emotions among his hearers. Mr. Verplanck added, that he was not able to expatiate on this rich and abundant theme, but must have recourse to the better voice of the Secretary, to make his resolution audible to the Society.

The Resolution offered by Mr. VERPLANCK having been read, as follows :—

Resolved, That the thanks of this Society are eminently due, and are hereby tendered, to JOHN ROMEYN BRODHEAD, LL. D., for his eloquent Oration, delivered this evening, in Commemoration of the Conquest of New Netherland, and that a copy be requested for the Archives of the Society, and for publication:—

The Honorable GEORGE BANCROFT said :—

I rise to second the vote of thanks which has been proposed for the admirable discourse to which we have just listened. It is marked by a thorough and comprehensive knowledge of the subject, and by a careful style; and it has been delivered with an earnestness which has enchained the attention of all.

We remind ourselves, with just pride, that Mr. Brodhead is one of the oldest members of our Society, and not surpassed by any in diligence and efficiency. It is to him that this State owes an invaluable collection of the Documents, gathered from many sources, to illustrate its History. To him, also, it owes the commencement of a work on its history, which is so full, so accurate, so marked by research, and an honest love of historic truth, that we have only to bid him go on and finish what he has so worthily begun.

We have all been pleased with the zeal with which he has, this evening, dwelt on the virtues of the Republic of the United Netherlands; and there can be no division of opinion as to the substantial fidelity of his picture. Such was always the opinion of New England. The founders of the first colony in Massachusetts, when they fled from the persecutions of their mother country, knew that Holland alone was the land where they could enjoy freedom of conscience; and in our day the hand that has portrayed, in the strongest and most lasting colors, the heroism and the sufferings of the Batavians, when, in pursuit of their liberties, they went unflinchingly through the baptism of fire and of blood, was that of a New Englander.

Our orator has set before our eyes a bright vision of the glory of New Netherland, when its territory, according to its claims, extended from some shadowy boundary in the distant north, beyond the southern Cape of the Delaware; and has set before us the successive aggressions by which that vast territory was dismembered, and formed into separate communities and States. Yet, as I listened to him, I seemed to think that the Providence which rules in human affairs, manifested in this a benevolent design. Had New Netherland remained undivided, it would have been so powerful, so opulent, and so self-relying, that it might have spurned at the thought of an equal union with other Colonies. It was broken into pieces, that New York, which by its position ought to be the eye of the country, might learn to feel its high vocation, to rally the many States of our Republic into superior union, to defend that union against all assailants, and to remain forever its spear and its shield!

The Resolution was unanimously adopted.

The Benediction was then pronounced by the Reverend Doctor DE WITT.

Immediately afterwards, a Reception was held at the Library of the Society, which was well attended. After some time spent in examining the Museum and Galleries, an entertainment was served in the Nineveh Room. At the call of the President, remarks were made by several of the invited guests, among whom were—

ALDEN J. SPOONER, Esq., of the Long Island Historical Society.

WILLIAM DORSHEIMER, Esq., of the Buffalo Historical Society.

THOMAS H. MONTGOMERY, Esq., of the Pennsylvania Historical Society.

ALFRED B. STREET, Esq., of Albany.

Attorney-General JOHN COCHRANE.

CORRESPONDENCE, ETC.

1. From Brantz Mayer, dated Baltimore, September 24, 1864, accepting the invitation of the Committee.
2. From John William Wallace, dated Philadelphia, September 25, 1864, accepting the invitation of the Committee.
3. From Henry R. Schoolcraft, dated Washington, September 25, 1864, accepting the invitation of the Committee.
4. From John M. Barbour, dated New York, September 26, 1864, accepting the invitation of the Committee.
5. From Millard Fillmore, President of the Buffalo Historical Society, dated Buffalo, September 26, 1864, accepting the invitation of the Committee.
6. From Charles J. Hoadley, dated Hartford, September 26, 1864, accepting the invitation of the Committee.
7. From William H. Bogart, dated Aurora, Cayuga Lake, September 27, 1864, accepting the invitation of the Committee.
8. From the Mayor of the City of New York, dated New York, September 27, 1864, accepting the invitation of the Committee.
9. From James Moncrief, dated New York, 29th September, 1864, accepting the invitation of the Committee.
10. From William H. Seward, dated Washington City, 29th September, 1864, acknowledging the invitation of the Committee:—

"I am profoundly gratified for the consideration which the New York Historical Society have manifested, by inviting me to attend their proposed Celebration of the Two Hundredth Anniversary of the Conquest of New Netherland. The changes in the condition of the American Continent which have followed, and in some respects are due to, that great Revolution, contribute a theme upon which I should like to hear the distinguished scholar you have chosen to be the Orator of the occasion. But, just now, I am encumbered with the cares incident to the effort of our country to save all that she has hitherto gained, and to secure for the continent a brighter and nobler future than we have before contemplated; and so, my respected and esteemed friend, I must ask you to have me excused."

11. From N. Bouton, Corresponding Secretary of the New Hampshire Historical Society, dated Concord, N. H., September 29, 1864, communicating the acceptance of the invitation of the Committee, and the appoint-

ment of the Rev. N. Bouton, D. D., and Joseph B. Walker, Esq., as delegates from that Society.

12. From Gideon J. Tucker, Surrogate, &c., dated New York, September 30, 1864, accepting the invitation of the Committee.

13. From D. T. Valentine, dated New York, October 1, 1864, accepting the invitation of the Committee.

14. From Charles W. Sandford, Major-General, &c., dated New York, October 1, 1864, accepting the invitation of the Committee.

15. From Henry E. Davies, Judge of the Court of Appeals, dated Albany, October 1, 1864, accepting the invitation of the Committee.

16. From Henry R. Selden, Judge of the Court of Appeals, dated Rochester, October 3, 1864, acknowledging the invitation of the Committee.

17. From William A. Whitehead, dated Newark, N. J., October 3, 1864, accepting the invitation of the Committee.

18. From William A. Whitehead, Corresponding Secretary of the New Jersey Historical Society, dated Newark, N. J., October 3, 1864, communicating the acceptance of the invitation of the Committee, and the appointment of the Hon. Richard S. Field, Solomon Alofsen, Esq., and William A. Whitehead, Esq., as delegates from that Society.

19. From Edward Ballard, Secretary of the Maine Historical Society, dated Brunswick, Me., October 4, 1864, communicating the acceptance of the invitation of the Committee and the appointment of the Hon. Edward E. Bourne, the Right Rev. George Burgess, D. D., the Hon. William Willis, the Hon. John A. Poor, and the Rev. Edward Ballard, as delegates from that Society.

20. From Robert C. Winthrop, President of the Massachusetts Historical Society, dated Boston, October 5, 1864, communicating the acceptance of the invitation of the Committee, and the appointment of delegates from that Society:—

"Your obliging communication, inviting the Massachusetts Historical Society to send a delegation to your most interesting Commemoration on the 12th instant, was gratefully received. As no meeting of our Society would take place until after the occasion was over, our Standing Committee have appointed several of our members to represent us on the occasion; and I trust that they will be present with you.

"I regret extremely that it will not be in my own power to attend this festival, agreeably to your kind request. I have not forgotten the prominent part which was played by Governor Winthrop, of Connecticut, in the events which you commemorate; and it would be particularly pleasant to me to be permitted to represent him on the occasion. But if your worthy Vice-President shall have returned from Europe in season for the celebration, you will have a representative of Winthrop and Stuyvesant in the same person. My worthy cousin would also be able to bring with him the original draft of the letter of Winthrop to Stuyvesant, which was the occasion of so much violent indignation. It was my good fortune to obtain possession of this letter, a few years since, and, after printing it in our Massachusetts Historical Collections, to transfer it to the ownership of one who had a double claim to its possession."

21. From Edward Everett, dated Boston, October 5. 1864, acknowledging the invitation of the Committee:—

"I have received your obliging invitation to attend the Celebration, by the New York Historical Society, of the Two Hundredth Anniversary of the Conquest of New Netherland by the English.

"The historical importance of that event—deciding, as it did, the nationality of North America—renders it a highly proper subject for commemoration; and your fortunate selection of an Orator for the occasion, my friend Mr. Brodhead, than whom no one is better acquainted with the history of that period, gives assurance that the treatment of the topic will be worthy of its intrinsic interest. I much regret that I must deny myself the pleasure of being present."

22. From Samuel Hazard, dated Germantown, October 5, 1864, acknowledging the invitation of the Committee.

23. From John R. Bartlett, dated Providence, R. I., October 5, 1864, acknowledging the invitation of the Committee.

24. From Henry C. Murphy, dated Brooklyn, October 5, 1864, accepting the invitation of the Committee.

25. From M. Romero, Mexican Minister, dated Washington City, D. C., October 5, 1864, accepting the invitation of the Committee.

26. From H. H. Van Dyck, Superintendent, &c., dated Albany, October 5, 1864, accepting the invitation of the Committee.

27. From W. K. Scott, Corresponding Secretary of the Buffalo Historical Society, dated October 5, 1864, communicating the acceptance of the invitation of the Committee, and the appointment of Millard Fillmore, Rev. Walter Clarke, G. R. Babcock, O. H. Marshall, Dr. J. P. White, H. W. Rogers, O. G. Steele, N. K. Hall, George B. Hibbard, and John Ganson, as delegates from that Society.

28. From Hiland Hall, President of the Vermont Historical Society, dated North Bennington, Vt., October 7, 1864, acknowledging the invitation of the Committee.

29. From E. A. Dalrymple, Corresponding Secretary of the Maryland Historical Society, dated Baltimore, October 7, 1864, communicating the acceptance of the invitation of the Committee, and the appointment of the Hon. John P. Kennedy, Philip T. Tyson, the Rev. Dr. John G. Morris, John H. Alexander, and John H. B. Latrobe, as delegates from that Society.

30. From J. Wingate Thornton, dated Boston, October 8, 1864, acknowledging the invitation of the Committee.

31. From Millard Fillmore, President of the Buffalo Historical Society, dated Buffalo, October 8, 1864, appointing Philip Dorsheimer a delegate from that Society.

32. From H. Denio, Judge of the Court of Appeals, dated Utica, October 8, 1864, acknowledging the invitation of the Committee.

33. From William Barnes, Superintendent, &c., dated Albany, October 8, 1864, accepting the invitation of the Committee.

34. From Horatio Gates Jones, dated Philadelphia, October 8, 1864, acknowledging the invitation of the Committee.

35. From William D. Dowe, Recording Secretary of the Historical Society of Delaware, dated Wilmington, Del., October 8, 1864, communicating the acceptance of the invitation of the Committee, and the appointment of Henry F. Askew, M. D., Rev. Charles Breck, and William D. Dowe, Esq., as delegates from that Society.

36. From the same, dated Wilmington, October 10, 1864, announcing the appointment of the Rt. Rev. Alfred Lee, Bishop of Delaware, &c., in place of the Rev. Charles Breck, as a delegate from that Society.

37. From Henry R. Stiles, M. D., Librarian of the Long Island Historical Society, dated Brooklyn, October 8, 1864, communicating the acceptance of the invitation of the Committee, and the appointment of the Rev. R. S. Storrs, Jr., D. D., the Hon. Henry C. Murphy, Charles E. West, LL. D., B. O. Silliman, Esq., Joshua M. Van Cott, Esq., Alden J. Spooner, Esq., and the President and Librarian, *ex-officio*. as delegates from that Society.

38. From William W. Campbell, dated Cherry Valley, October 10, 1864, acknowledging the invitation of the Committee.

39. From Andrew H. Green, Comptroller of the Central Park, dated New York, October 10, 1864, in behalf of the Commissioners of the Park, accepting the invitation of the Committee.

40. From J. Hammond Trumbull, dated Hartford, Conn., October 10, 1864, accepting the invitation of the Committee.

41. From George F. Houghton, Recording Secretary of the Vermont Historical Society, dated St. Albans, Vermont, October 10, 1864, communicating the acceptance of the invitation of the Committee, and the appointment of Messrs. Henry Hall and George F. Houghton, as delegates from that Society.

42. From Albert G. Greene, President of the Rhode Island Historical Society, dated Providence, October 10, 1864, acknowledging the invitation of the Committee.

43. From Charles J. Hoadley, Corresponding Secretary of the Connecticut Historical Society, dated Hartford, October 11, 1864, communicating the acceptance of the invitation of the Committee, and the appointment of the Hon. Henry C. Deming, and Messrs. Samuel H. Parsons and Erastus Smith, as delegates from that Society.

44. From John V. L. Pruyn, Chancellor of the University of the State of New York, dated Albany, October, 11, 1364, acknowledging the invitation of the Committee.

∗∗∗ The Committee desire to acknowledge their obligations to Messrs. Harper and Brothers, the Publishers of Mr. Brodhead's History of New York, for the use of the Map prefixed to that work, which illustrates this publication.

NEW YORK IN THE NINETEENTH CENTURY.

A DISCOURSE

DELIVERED BEFORE THE

NEW YORK HISTORICAL SOCIETY,

ON ITS SIXTY-SECOND ANNIVERSARY,

NOVEMBER 20, 1866.

BY

REV. SAMUEL OSGOOD, D.D.

PUBLISHED BY ORDER OF THE EXECUTIVE COMMITTEE.

NEW YORK:
PRINTED FOR THE SOCIETY.
MDCCCLXVII.

NEW YORK IN THE NINETEENTH CENTURY.

A DISCOURSE

DELIVERED BEFORE THE

NEW YORK HISTORICAL SOCIETY,

ON ITS SIXTY-SECOND ANNIVERSARY,

NOVEMBER 20, 1866.

BY

REV. SAMUEL OSGOOD, D.D.

PUBLISHED BY ORDER OF THE EXECUTIVE COMMITTEE.

NEW YORK:
PRINTED FOR THE SOCIETY.
MDCCCLXVI.

Officers of the Society, 1867.

PRESIDENT,
HAMILTON FISH, LL. D.

FIRST VICE-PRESIDENT,
THOMAS DE WITT, D. D.

SECOND VICE-PRESIDENT,
BENJAMIN ROBERT WINTHROP.

FOREIGN CORRESPONDING SECRETARY,
GEORGE BANCROFT, LL. D.

DOMESTIC CORRESPONDING SECRETARY,
JOHN ROMEYN BRODHEAD, LL. D.

RECORDING SECRETARY,
ANDREW WARNER.

TREASURER,
BENJAMIN H. FIELD.

LIBRARIAN
GEORGE HENRY MOORE.

EXECUTIVE COMMITTEE.

FIRST CLASS—FOR ONE YEAR.

AUGUSTUS SCHELL, ERASTUS C. BENEDICT,
BENJAMIN W. BONNEY.

SECOND CLASS—FOR TWO YEARS.

SAMUEL OSGOOD, WILLIAM CHAUNCEY,
CHARLES P. KIRKLAND.

THIRD CLASS—FOR THREE YEARS.

GEORGE FOLSOM, WILLIAM T. BLODGETT,
JOHN ADRIANCE.

AUGUSTUS SCHELL, *Chairman.*
GEORGE MOORE, *Secretary.*

[The officers of the Society are members, *ex officio*, of the Executive Committee.]

COMMITTEE ON THE FINE ARTS.

ABRAHAM M. COZZENS, WILLIAM J. HOPPIN,
JONATHAN STURGES, THOMAS J. BRYAN,
ANDREW WARNER, EDWARD SATTERLEE.

ABRAHAM M. COZZENS, *Chairman.*
ANDREW WARNER, *Secretary.*

[The President, Librarian, and Chairman of the Executive Committee are members, *ex officio*, of the Committee on the Fine Arts.]

DISCOURSE.

Mr. President and Brethren of the Historical Society, and Ladies and Gentlemen, our honored guests to-night:

In accepting the honor of your invitation to speak at this Anniversary, I find myself at once relieved and oppressed by the subject that forces itself upon me—relieved from all trouble in its choice, and oppressed by the utter impossibility of its adequate treatment. What topic can compare in importance and interest to this great city—our native or adopted home; and who shall presume to treat it adequately in all its vastness, variety, and constant evolution? As we gaze, the wonder grows! and not even our daily familiarity with its streets and manners and business and people can hide from us the truth that it is one of the striking facts of the nineteenth century—one of the marvels of the age, if not one of the wonders of the world.

The whole subject, of course, cannot be treated with any justness or fidelity in a single discourse; and to attempt to do it would be like trying to empty our great harbor with a single pump, or to condense a cyclopedia into an hour's reading. It will not be a presuming or thankless task to try to lay before you some thoughts and studies upon "New York in the Nineteenth Century," if only as the unambitious outline of a chapter of Universal History. I must be content with two points of view: the first, from the beginning of the century; the second, now.

Not a little motive for the effort is given, let me say, by the strange and broad gulf between our present population and the old New Yorkers, and the almost entire absence of historical landmarks from our city, now under the sweeping tide of business and enterprise. Only a few of the ancient buildings remain, and almost all that we see before us is new. This imperial city, with its palaces and churches, rises before most of its people like Melchisedec, king of Salem, without father, without mother; and they must confess his magnificence, who cannot tell his pedigree.

The nineteenth century may be defined as the age of liberty organizing itself, or as the period whose distinctive problem it is to construct or reconstruct society on the basis of freedom. The previous centuries have been the providential preparation for this task. It is probably safe to say, that the modern time, as a whole, since the invention of printing, the discovery of America, the inductive study of Nature, and the Protestant Reformation, has been most marked by the spirit of liberty; and its history is the record of the evolution of freedom, as the thousand years before, since Constantine gave the Cross the support of his sceptre, and made Christianity the law of the empire, was the age of authority, and its history is the record of obedience. Perhaps the four modern centuries may be designated thus, according to their part in the history of liberty: The sixteenth century was marked by the rise of religious liberty in protest against the Roman hierarchy, in connection with the revival of letters, and the awakening of industrial and commercial enterprise. The seventeenth century generally breathed a calmer spirit, and strove to settle the Protestant Church and State upon the new basis of Biblical doctrine or Reformed discipline. The eighteenth century, in great part, bolted from all Biblical doctrine and church discipline, and proclaimed radical or social and philosophical liberty in the face of priest and king, and was the jubilee of social and philosophical illuminism. The nineteenth century, the favored, and yet perplexed heir of such ancestors, has been trying to settle its great estate, and construct society and government upon the basis of the new liberty gained, and with all the lights of knowledge, experience, and faith. It has fallen to the lot of this city to have a conspicuous part in this great work of reconstruction, and the end is not yet. She has had the burden of the age upon her shoulders, and also her full share of the lessons and examples of the previous modern centuries to help her out. New York, in the beginning, was richly endowed in being the daughter and heir of one of the noblest nations of Europe; and when Henry Hudson first parted the waters of our noble bay and river, his signal, the Crescent or Half Moon, well and justly symbolized the predestined civilization of this New World. He opened here the pages of that history of liberty that is not yet finished;

and under that star of empire that shone above his ship, it did not need any marvellous divination to see the forms of the ruling spirits of the modern ages in his company. There were Columbus and Gutenberg and Luther and Bacon, with the compass and printing-press and open Bible and new organon of science signalling to him the new country and the new age coming, and his name marks still the river whose beauty and wealth and promise ask no borrowed honors from the fame of the Rhine or Danube, the Tiber or the Thames.

The Dutch who founded New Amsterdam on this island of Manhattan, not only brought their own individual characters and personal property hither, but also their national life with its historical traditions, institutions, and powers. They brought with them much of the old feudal age in their municipal laws and social traditions, that were in many respects so conservative, and all the fire of the New Reform in their thorough-going Calvinism, with its doctrines of justification by faith and direct election from God in the face of what they regarded as the Romish doctrine of salvation by merit and subjection to priests. Having passed through the terrible war for national life, they felt, at the time of the colonizing of New Amsterdam, the desire for stability so characteristic of the stormy century after the Reformation, the 17th, and they had all the conservatism of the old Catholicism on the new base of their reformed creed and discipline. They came here, indeed, for trade, yet their religion was none the less marked, because it did not send them hither, but simply came with them because they came, and lived with them as part of themselves. They were hospitable and tolerant; yet they never set forth any ideal standard of toleration, such as is the distinctive trait of Rhode Island. They did not affirm intellectual tolerance or intolerance here; but like practical merchants and kindly neighbors, they were disposed to welcome all settlers who would not interfere with their business, without troubling themselves much with their opinions. Their faith had nothing of the subjective turn of the New England Puritans, who were always looking into their own minds, and willing to do the same thing for their neighbors. The Dutch were not an introversial, but an objective, practical people, never or rarely moved to intolerance unless pushed by the fear of having their liberties or institutions interfered with; and it was probably from apprehended danger to the national life, rather than for mere opinion's sake, that the great acts of intolerance were perpetrated in Holland, such as the execution of Barneveldt and the exile of Grotius, and the persecution of the Baptists. The Dutch of New Amsterdam, though not wholly free from the charge of intolerance, were in advance of their mother country in charity, and in advance of their Puritan neighbors; and their temper and legislation here gave their colony a good place in the record of American liberty.

Their conservative temper had something in common with the spirit which the English rule brought with it in 1664; for then England, after Cromwell and the commonwealth, sought spiritual peace under the restored Stuarts, and afterwards, in 1688, she sought not to destroy, but to deepen that peace under the tolerant sceptre of William of Orange, who tried to bring Puritans as well as churchmen to truce, and who carried with him much of the moderate yet determined Dutch temper to the throne. The city, of course, was to be largely shaped by the English power; for in 1664 its future was not wholly with the existing population of fifteen hundred souls.

How far New York shared in the storm of radical opinion and passion that marked the eighteenth century, it is not easy to say. Theologically there was little latitudinarianism in the churches here, although there is ample proof that alike among leading men and the restless populace, there was a great deal of acquaintance and sympathy with the illuminism of France and Germany, though far more acceptance of its free spirit than of its destructive notions. Zenger, forty years before the Declaration of Independence, led on the Sons of Liberty in much of the temper of the destroyers of the Bastile, and Freneau had much of the French revolutionist in his pen, whilst such stormy radicals as Paine, Elihu Palmer, and John Foster, denounced the Bible and the Church in the spirit of Helvetius, Volney, Voltaire, and D'Holbach. Of these latter agitators, Paine and Palmer, and I think Foster also, were not natives, nor in any historical sense representatives of the old New York mind. The Revolution itself is proof of the power of radical, political ideas of the better class, and the very slowness of the leaders to join in the Declaration of Independence shows that the English Toryism that held the high places here during the British rule, was more than matched by the liberalism of the people and their favorite champions. The delay in adopting the federal Constitution—a delay that prevented New York from casting her first electoral vote for Washington, and from being represented in the first American Senate— was not from Tory leanings towards the old colonial times, but from jealousy of centralized power, and it called for all the sagacity and eloquence and personal influence of Hamilton, Jay, Madison, and the great Federalist leaders, to overcome the strong State feeling, and bring New York into that constitutional Union which she has never ceased to defend. It is interesting to read the names of the delegates from this city to the convention at Poughkeepsie in 1788, that met to act upon the National Constitution. New York, West Chester, Kings and Richmond Counties, chose federalists; the Counties of Albany, Montgomery, Washington, Columbia, Dutchess, Ulster, and Orange, chose anti-federalists, whilst the delegates from Suffolk and Queens Counties were divided. The New York delegates were John Jay, Alexander Hamilton, Chancellor Livingston, Richard Morris, then Chief Justice, and James Duane, Mayor of the city. Surely, we have not greatly improved on the year 1788, in the delegations of this year 1866. That delegation gave this city a great name in the history of liberty; for it undoubtedly overcame the majority of the delegates to the Convention who were opposed to the Constitution, and it brought New York into the Constitutional Union.

But we must not linger longer upon this preliminary view of the relation of this city to the three previous modern centuries. We take our stand now at the opening of the nineteenth century, the year 1801—a most memorable year alike in Europe and America, and memorable too in its bearing on the organization of liberty. In France, liberty, after having battled down the Bastile and Throne and nobles, had turned organizer, and taught conservatism in the person of the First Consul, who was now proud to join the name of pacificator to that of conqueror, and boasted of bringing tranquillity to Europe by the peace of Luneville in 1801. Here in America, Democracy, or, as it was then called, Republicanism, took something of the same position, and, after overthrowing Federalism, it lifted its idol, Thomas Jefferson, to the pedestal of national union under the Constitution which it had so vehemently assailed. Before, New York had been generally a federalist city, although all the power and influence of its great men were needed to keep it so. But in April, 1800, Aaron Burr and his republican allies put forth all their adroitness to carry the city for the democratic party, and nominated a ticket of memorable compass and attraction. Governor George Clinton, the most popular New Yorker of the day, the great States Rights man of that time, and the idol of the democrats, headed the ticket, and held out the banner of his party. Brockholst Livingston represented the wealth of his powerful family, and gave it the force of his personal talent. General Horatio Gates gave his name to kindle anew the old revolutionary passion. Samuel Osgood, a good type of a transplanted Massachusetts man, stood for the Cabinet of Washington, whose honored associate he had been, and was rewarded by being chosen Speaker of the Legislature, which, in November, 1800, virtually gave the electoral vote to Thomas Jefferson. So Federalism was defeated, yet not destroyed. Its characteristic idea lived and was vindicated by its nominal foes. Probably no men in America have done so much to carry out the cardinal principle of the American Union in the face of pressing dangers as the great democratic leaders, Thomas Jefferson and Andrew Jackson. Whatever they have meant to do, is less obvious than what God meant to do by them—the God of our liberty and our Union, who has determined that the wrath of man should praise Him, and that the popular passion for freedom shall secure the life and law of the nation. The old Federalists deserved honor, for they spoke out the calm wisdom of time, and were the historical statesmen of their day. So too they deserved rebuke, for they did not see, nor fully appreciate, the mind of the new age, and their distrust of the people with their own personal feuds had much to do with their downfall. We in our day have built their grandest monument in cementing their Union; yet we have a more cheerful philosophy than theirs, and see more of God in the people, "the plain people," than they saw. We can join the names of the old Democrats, Chancellor Livingston and George

Clinton, to those of their great federal antagonists, Hamilton and Jay, in our record of the architects of liberty in New York city.

It is amusing to look over the newspapers at the opening of the century, observe the items of news, and note the doleful tone of the leading conservatives as to the dark prospects of the age. The *Commercial Advertiser*, one of the seven daily papers issued here in 1801, and the only one, with the exception of the *Evening Post*, that has survived, begins the new year with the first of a series of articles by that noted and excellent man, Lindley Murray, on the nineteenth century, which are written in a spirit of croaking run mad, in a panic at the very name of liberty, especially the liberty of the press, and far more in the temper of the Pope's Encyclical Letter than of our modern thought; in fact, so gloomy and reactionary, that they would be laughed at now by moderate conservatives, in the old world and the new. There had been a green Christmas, and it was then a mild Winter; but to many like Murray, the political sky was dark and cold.

The leading editorial in the *Commercial Advertiser* of New Year's Day, 1801, begins thus:

> At the close of the eighteenth century, and near the close of the third Presidency in the American Administration, events have taken place that have excited no small surprise among men who are considered as possessing great political discernment. Men wonder and speculate! They are surprised at the issue of the elections, and look about them for the causes that have defeated their calculations.

The article thus continues towards the close:

We have no grounds to felicitate ourselves on advancing a single step in the theory or practice of government within two thousand years. The opinion that we *have advanced*, is derived from our pride, founded on our ignorance—an opinion that is a burlesk on our education, our pretended science, and our vanity.

In the *Commercial Advertiser* of January 18, 1801, we have this notice from President Adams, which is proof that he did not mean to see Thomas Jefferson inaugurated, and that our Presidents have mended the manners, if they have not outgrown the irritability, of the old times:

The President of the United States requests the several printers who have sent him their newspapers, to send in their accounts and receive their payments. He also requests that they would send him no more after the 3d of March next.

WASHINGTON, *January* 18, 1801.

A newspaper brings the past very near to us, and as we handle this old copy of the *Advertiser*, it recalls sixty-six years ago, and the New Year's Day when it was issued, and the New York of that day. It was then, as Irving said, a "handy city," where everybody knew everybody, and good neighborhood had not become a mere tradition. The city had about 60,000 inhabitants, 10,000 less than Philadelphia had, and was a little larger than the city of Providence now is, and considerably smaller than Newark is. Population had pushed up as far as Anthony Street, now Worth Street, a little above the present City Hospital, and a line of farm-houses seemed on their way to Stuyvesant's Bowery, our present place of meeting, and that St. Mark's Church, our near neighbor now, which had been lately erected without its present steeple. There was, of course, no gaslight, and but little coal, and not any of our Croton water. Great was the fame of the Tea Water Pump in Chatham Street, and bad was the name of the new reservoir on the east side of Broadway, between Pearl and White Streets, on the two-acre lot bought of the Van Cortlandts for 1,200 pounds; and great was the hope of the New Manhattan Water Works in Chambers Street near Centre—a hope quite vain. The city was healthy, as it always is to all who take care of themselves, and its death-rate was about half that of last year, which was thirty-five in one thousand.

Taxes were light, about one half of one per cent., and in 1796 the whole tax raised was 7,968 pounds, and the whole valuation of property was 1,261,585 pounds—estimates that were probably about half the real value, so that the tax was only about one fourth of one per cent. A man worth $50,000 was thought rich, and some fortunes reached $250,000. Mechanics had a dollar a day for wages, and a genteel house rented for $350 a year, and $750 additional would meet the ordinary expenses of living for a genteel family—such as now spends from $6,000 to $10,000, we have good reason to believe, from such authority as Mr. D. T. Valentine, Clerk of the Common Council. A good house could be bought for $3,000 or $4,000, and flour was four and five dollars a barrel, and beef ten cents a pound.

There were great entertainments, and men ate

and drank freely—more freely, apparently, than now —but nothing of present luxury prevailed in the high classes; and how rare the indulgence was, is proved by the common saying, "that the Livingstons give champagne," which marked their case as exceptional. Now, surely, a great many families in New York besides the Livingstons give champagne, and not always wisely for their own economy or their guests' sobriety.

These homely items give a familiar idea of old New York in 1801. We must remember that it was then a provincial city, and had nothing of its present back-country connection with the West, being the virtual capital of the Hudson River Valley rather than of the great Empire State. Buffalo, Syracuse, Utica, and the noted cities of Western New York, were but names then, and Albany was of so little business note, that the main communication with it was by dilatory sloops, such as Irving describes after his slow voyage in the craft that he long waited for, and which gave him ample time to study the picturesque on the Hudson, with such food for his humor as the Captain's talk in Dutch to his crew of negro slaves. What a contrast with a trip now in the St. John or the Dean Richmond— marine palaces that float you as in a dream by night through the charmed passes of the Hudson, to Albany! Irving's name does much to bring before us the living picture of New York in 1801, and we can fancy somewhat what the city then was, by looking in upon him—then a youth of seventeen, at 128 William Street—and going the rounds of society and sight-seeing on that New Year's Day. A few hours with him in his love of fun, and a few more with young Gulian C. Verplanck—who was then in the senior class at Columbia College and a little wild, according to the squibs of some of his political enemies, and whose social tastes were, of course, more mature, and in the line of all charming company— would tell more of those scenes and times than volumes of antiquarian research. We cannot paint the picture, nor try to describe the large diversity of nationalities, tastes, and characters, that even then made this city so universal in its affinities, and gave promise of its future comprehensiveness. Our task is rather in the sphere of general history, than of local and personal narrative; and perhaps enough has been said by Dr. Francis of the special features of old New York. Kindly thought of him here tonight; for, surely, if spirits ever walk the earth, the stout old Doctor's ghost is with us now, in this his loved and familiar haunt.

The historian seeks for universal laws, and is bound to search out the ideas and characteristics that connect a community with the nation and the race. It is not easy to say exactly wherein old New York represented the spirit of the nineteenth century. In some respects it seemed to ignore the nineteenth century, and surely, it was not conspicuous for science, art, philosophy, or poetry. Philadelphia and Boston, probably even Charleston, S. C., were in advance of it in literary spirit; and when Dr. Samuel Miller gave, on New Year's Day, 1801, in his Wall Street pulpit, his memorable retrospect of the eighteenth century—which he afterwards expanded into two volumes, published in 1803—he was far more complimentary to his remote than to his near neighbors in his portraiture of American science and literature. The title-page that styles him corresponding member of the Historical Society of Massachusetts, proves what he regarded as the representative of American history then, and is a sign that this Society of ours was needed and was to come the year after. His account of New York, in his chapter on "Nations Lately Become Literary," is very brief, and deals mainly with the founding of Columbia College, the Society Library, and the Medical School; and he has no higher name to record in science than that of Dr. Mitchill among the New Yorkers, who could claim such peerless statesmen and political writers. Dr. Miller, in speaking of the want of literary culture in America, mentions the causes, and naming among them defective collegiate instruction, want of books, want of leisure, and want of encouragement to learning, he perhaps tells the main reason when he says, "Besides, the spirit of our people is *commercial*. It has been said, and perhaps with some justice, that the love of gain peculiarly characterizes the inhabitants of the United States." This remark applied peculiarly to New York, which had been, from the first, especially a business city, and it has always been so. It is precisely in this direction that we are to look for its higher developments, and its rightful place in universal history, rather than to pure science or ideal philosophy or letters. It is business that has given this city its empire, and brought the imperial arts and sciences in its train.

There is reason to believe that soon after the Revolution, men of thought in New York saw the rising destiny of their City and State, and one reason of their reluctance to come into the constitutional union, was the fear of making over too much of their local power to the central Government; especially their great share of revenue from imports, and their commanding position between New England and the South and West. Very early the interest of the Colonies seemed to centralize here, and the Colonial Congress of 1765, and the Provincial Congress of 1776, and the inauguration of Washington in 1789, were all hints of the empire that was to be.

A gentleman who was here in 1787, when the whole State had a smaller population than North Carolina, wrote to his friends that the city was ruined by the war; but its future greatness was unquestionable. Truth must be told, even if it mortifies our ambition; and the development of the power of the State and City was not to be under the leadership of the great masters of its legislation. Hamilton fell sadly by an impious hand, and Jay retired from public life, and Gouverneur Morris too soon followed him. The masters of the future were men of business, and probably to Robert Fulton and De Witt Clinton, with their industrial friends and helpers, New York owes her imperial position in the nation and the world, more than to men of science or letters, scholars or statesmen. Even her great statesmen had much of business point and sagacity in their composition; and, surely, Hamilton was as much of a financier and soldier as a jurist, and perhaps was compelled to yield to the Virginia plan of the Constitution, because it came from Madison's more American mind, and embodied more of the instincts and traditions of the nation, than his more military and perhaps more European scheme of consolidation. Chancellor Livingston claims as much honor by his encouragement to Fulton as by his law and statesmanship, and deserves with him a high name among the organizers of liberty. Who shall say what steam navigation has done to emancipate mankind from drudgery, and construct society upon the basis of liberty? It is science turned liberator; and the saucy philosophy of the eighteenth century became the mighty and merciful helper of the nineteenth century. To us, individually and generally, how marvellous has been the gift! Wherever that piston-rod rises and falls, and those paddles turn, man has a giant for his porter and defender, and the liberty of the nation has been organized under its protection; and the great States of the Mississippi valley and the Pacific coast are brought within one loyal affinity, and build their new liberties upon the good old pattern of our fathers. Clinton and Fulton, the one identified with the rise of steam navigation, the other with the Erie Canal, are names that belong to universal history, as having given America its business unity, and brought its united wealth to bear upon the industry and commerce of the world.

We are somewhat surprised, in studying the old

New York mind, at seeing so little trace of speculative thinking, and it is not easy to say to what school of philosophy its intellectual leaders belonged. Here we must make an important distinction, and see the cause of the absence of the speculative, subjective habit of mind so common in New England. New York was more dynamic than ideal, or more busy with active forces than theoretic principles. New York itself was a historic force, and not a theological or philosophical school. It was a community that kept most of its historical continuity through three revolutions, and had no decided break in its evolution. Its people were never come-outers or radicals of the extreme type; but carried the old national life forward with them into new conditions. The Dutch colonists were Dutchmen still, and in the old church and nation; the English were English still, with all the old loyalty to church and state; and when the Dutch-English community crowned the old protest against Rome by the new protest against British despotism, they carried with them much of their old institutional habit. They did not go out and build anew under the open heavens from radical ideas; but kept as far as they could within the old walls. Their spirit was free, but their method was cautious and conservative, and they leaned much upon the leaders who walked in the old historical paths. Thus the Constitution of 1777 is a marvel of conservative caution, and shows the power of Jay and his associates over the mass, who were far more radical than he, and who consented to restricted suffrage and the aristocratic Councils of

Appointment and Revision as keeping them within the safe old paths, whilst they rejoiced in the untrammeled religious liberty given. Quite remarkable it is that the Convention of 1801 did little more than decide that the four Senators on the Council of Appointment should have concurrent voices with the Governor in making appointments to office. The people seemed to feel that they were a civic fact, a historic force, an actual institution, and it was a great thing to keep the life that came to them from their fathers.

In their own way, their historical life expanded into new enterprises and institutions, and the year 1804, that saw our Historical Society founded, the City Hall rising from its foundation, and the Public School Society virtually resolved upon, was a memorable date in the annals of the city. It was marked also by dark signs; for it brought the terrible fire of December, with its loss of $2,000,000 and forty stores and dwellings, and the death of Hamilton, and the loss of his brilliant gifts and guiding intellect.

In religion and theology there was much of the same spirit. The New York Churches were strong; but the clergy were little given to speculative thinking, and no commanding thinker appeared among them, such as abounded in New England. They kept the old creeds and usages with a strength that awed down dissent, and with a benign temper that conciliated favor. Latitudinarian tendencies were either suppressed, or driven into open hostility with the popular creeds under deistical or atheistical teachers. In all, the congregations numbered 30, and the Jews had one synagogue. Even the most radical congregation in the city, the Universalist, held mainly the old theological views, and had only one point of peculiar doctrine, and even with this single exception, and with all the orthodox habits, they had only a lay organization in 1801, and were without a regular minister till 1803.

The Dutch Reformed, Episcopalians, Presbyterians, and Methodists, numbered each five congregations; the Baptists three; the Friends two; the Lutherans two; the Roman Catholics, Huguenots, Moravians, and Universalists, one each. Some writers erroneously assign seven churches, instead of five, to the Episcopalians in 1801; by claiming for them the Huguenot Church Du Saint Esprit, which was established in 1704, and acceded to the Episcopal Church in 1804, and Zion Church, which was established by Lutherans in 1801, and joined the Episcopal communion in 1810.

As far as we can judge, the Presbyterian clergy had most of the new American culture of the severer kind, and Drs. Samuel Miller and John M. Mason were the intellectual leaders of the New York pulpit. The only man to be named with them in popular influence was John Henry Hobart, who was ordained in 1801, consecrated bishop in 1811, and who, in spite of his extreme views of Episcopal prerogative, is to be named among the fathers of the American Church, and a good specimen of what old Trinity Church has done to unite patriotism with religion.

The Episcopal Church had much accomplishment

in its clergy, and Bishop Prevoost, who received ordination in England, was a man of extensive knowledge, and Dr. Livingston of the Dutch Church was a good match for him in learning and dignity. It is said that when these clerical magnates met on Sundays and exchanged salutations, they took up the entire street, and reminded beholders of two frigates under full sail, exchanging salutes with each other.

Yet none of the New York clergy were patterns of the peculiar thinking of the nineteenth century, and the leaders steered clear of all traces of the rising rationalism. Dr. Miller touches upon the philosophy of the eighteenth century in his retrospect, and promises to deal with theology in a separate work, but did not fulfil the promise; and only indicates his own leanings and limited culture by praising Locke and Reid in the same chapter, and, in almost the same breath, accepting Jonathan Edwards and ridiculing Emanuel Kant. Very clearly New York religion was not speculative or philosophical, yet it was none the less a positive institution, a living force, and it made up by its kindly spirit and its historical life for the absence of the critical knowledge that sometimes is found apart from piety and charity—the knowledge that *puffeth up*. We are to look for the connections of the old New York religion with the new age in its powerful organizing spirit; and the great movements of piety and charity in America have come from the union of the institutional stability, order, and method of New York with the more subjective thought and culture of New England. Religious liberty has had its grandest organizations from this city, as a centre, and we have seen only the beginning of its mighty and benign work.

We may regard old New York as culminating in the year 1825, with the completion of the Erie Canal; and that great jubilee that married this city to the mighty west, began a new era of triumph and responsibility, that soon proved that the bride's festival is followed by the wife's cares and the mother's anxieties. New York had become the national city, and was so for a quarter of a century more, and then she became cosmopolitan, European as well as American, and obviously one of the few leading cities of the world—the third city of Christendom. We may fix this change upon the middle of the century as well as upon any date, and call the time from 1850 till now, her cosmopolitan era. The change, of course, was gradual, and the great increase of the city dates from the close of the Revolutionary war, and the evacuation of the city by the British troops. The population doubled nearly in the ten years after 1790, and went from 33,000 to 60,000. In 1825 it reached 166,086, and in 1850 rose to 515,515. All this increase could not but bring a new sense of power, and throughout all the bewildering maze of the old New York politics we can see traces of the desire of the people and their leaders to dispute the palm of empire with Virginia and its old dominion. The efforts seemed vain that were made to put New Yorkers into the presidential chair. Before 1825, the State had tried three times

to elect a President, and three times had raised one
of its sons to the Vice-Presidency. What could not
be done directly, was done indirectly, and it seems
to have been De Witt Clinton, before any leading
Northern man, who led the way to the nomination
of Andrew Jackson to the Presidency; and before
Van Buren had taken the same stand, he began the
movement that ended in breaking the old Virginia
line of power by reaching over into Tennessee and
bringing a successful soldier into the field of politics.
The line once broken, New York made way for its
own ambition, and twice has had the Presidency in
its hands; and had more reasons than state ambition for desiring to continue in power, when probably the ablest and purest of her new statesmen, Silas
Wright, lost his political prospects because he would
not strike hands with the propagandists of slavery;
carried forward democracy in the spirit of its anti-
slavery champion, Daniel D. Tompkins, who moved
the Liberty Bill of 1817; and the new age began
which has committed the Empire State to the dominion of freedom, and put her practically at the
head of the movement which identifies the democratic
idea in America with emancipation in the nineteenth
century.

The Constitutional Convention of 1821, with its
moderate liberalism, and the amendment of 1826, removing restrictions on white suffrage, and the Constitution of 1846, with its extreme radicalism, connect this city with general history, especially by
their bearing on universal suffrage, and the extension
of the elective powers of the people, and the decen-

tralizing of the State, to give more sway to local liberty, especially as to local magistrates and even judges. It is clear that the spirit of the nineteenth century was at work among the people; and, in some respects, has gone so far as to raise the question, whether liberty has not been disorganized under the hands of its dissectors, who have taken the body politic to pieces, with the promise of putting it together with complete equality among the members, without setting the intelligent voters, who should be the head, above the sots and dunces, who should be its foot; and without denying suffrage to a drunken ignoramus on account of his color, yet refusing it to an intelligent and sober patriot for having another skin.

It was in the period that we have called national, that the Constitutional Convention of 1846 was held, and entailed upon us, by its indiscriminate abolition of the old central safeguards, some of the mischiefs that stand in such contrast with the majestic triumphs of the city in wealth and culture during that period, and which called for some remedy, and found it, in part, in the new plan of centralized power, which, since 1849, has given the State at large a hand in our home affairs. How grand in other respects was the development of the city in that twenty-five years, 1825 to 1850, and what a new and marvellous world of wealth and splendor rose before the eyes of our people!

In 1830 the State, which in 1800 threw the same number of electoral votes as North Carolina, had risen from 586,756, to 1,918,608, and the city had gone from 60,489 to 202,589.

The introduction of gas and of the Croton water were grand illustrations of the power of organized industry, and mighty aids in throwing light, health, and purity into the lives of the people; and the rise of the great popular daily journals that almost created the national press of America, made an era in the free fellowship of public thought. The city pushed its triumphal march forward during that period, from Bleecker Street to Madison Square, and vainly tried to halt its forces at Washington and Union Squares, or to pause long anywhere on the way of empire. The whole period would make an important history of itself, and our task now is with the New York of to-day, as it has risen into cosmopelitan rank since 1850—the year which gave us a line of European steamers of our own, and opened the Golden Gate of California to our packets.

Look at our city now in its extent, population, wealth, institutions, and connections, and consider how far it is doing its great work, under God's providence, as the most conspicuous representative of the liberty of the nineteenth century in its hopes and fears. You are too familiar with the figures and facts that show the largeness of the city, to need any minute or extended summary or recapitulation. That we are not far from a million of people on this island, that began the century with 60,000; that the valuation of property, real and personal, has risen since 1805 from $25,000,000, to $736,988,058; that the real value of property here is about $1,000,000,-000, or a thirtieth part of the entire property of Great Britain; that our taxes within that time have risen from $127,000 to $16,950,767, over four and a half millions more than our whole national expenditure in 1801; that our banking capital is over $90,000,000, and the transactions of our Clearing Houses, for the year ending October 1, 1866, were over $29,000,000,000; that our Savings Banks have 300,000 depositors, and $77,000,000 of deposits; that our 108 Fire Insurance Companies and 38 Fire Agencies have a capital of $47,560,000, and our 18 Life Insurance Companies a capital of $2,938,000, whose premiums last year were nearly $9,000,000; that, by the census of 1865, the number of dwellings was 49,844, and the value of them was $423,096,918; that this city, by the census of 1860, returned a larger manufacturing product than any other city in the Union, and more than any State, except New York, Massachusetts, and Pennsylvania—the sum total of $159,107,369, from raw material worth $96,177,038 in 4,375 establishments, with 90,204 operatives, and $61,212,757 capital, and manufactured nearly one-eleventh of the sum total of the United States * manufactures in

---

* In justice to Philadelphia we quote the statistics of her manufactories from the census of 1860, which show a larger number of hands employed, and a larger capital invested, with less value, however, in raw material, and in the value of the product. Philadelphia had, in 1860, 6,298 manufacturing establishments, with a capital invested of $73,318,885; with the cost of raw material, $69,562,206; with 98,983 operatives, and with an annual product of value $135,979,677. It must be remembered, however, that Philadelphia, since 1854, is made to include the whole county of one hundred and twenty square miles— nearly six times the area of New York city—which is very much like annexing Brooklyn and Jersey City and the whole neighborhood that really contains New York people, business, and capital to the city itself, and setting their financial returns down under one head. It is to be desired that New York would make as good provision for mechanics and persons of moderate means, as Philadelphia makes by her many snug and cheap houses, and her light expenses and simpler habits.

1860, which was $1,885,861,676; that in twenty years we exported, from September 1, 1846, to September 1, 1866, to Europe, over 27,000,000 barrels of flour, over 164,000,000 bushels of wheat, 127,000,000 bushels of corn, nearly 5,000,000 bushels of rye; that the receipts for customs in this port for 1865 were $101,772,905; that this city is the great gold market of the world, and in 1865 received $61,201,108, and exported over $30,000,000 abroad, and received in twelve years, 1854 to 1866, from San Francisco $375,558,659 in gold; that our shipping, registered and enrolled in 1865, amounted in tonnage to 1,223,264 tons, and the number of arrivals of vessels in this port in 1865 was 12,634, of these 2,078 being steamers; that our exports for the year 1865 were $208,630,282, and our imports were $224,742,419; that, on an average, 35 tons of mail-matter are received here for our citizens, and 55 tons are sent out daily; that the average number of mail-bags received is 385, and the average number sent out is 713; that within three years and a half the mail correspondence of our citizens has doubled; that the number of letters and newspapers collected by the carriers for the quarter ending December 31, 1865, was over 3,000,000, and the number delivered by them was over 3,600,000, and the deliveries from Post-Office boxes for the same quarter were over 5,000,000; that the increase of letters is so marvellous that New York may soon rival London, which, in 1862, received by mail 151,619,000 letters; —these and the like plain statistics are sufficient to prove the imperial wealth and power of New York, and to startle us with the problem of its prospective growth, when we remember that $4\frac{6}{10}$ per cent. increase, which has been generally the actual rate of increase, will give us a population of some 4,000,000 at the close of the century.

Now, what are we to say of the city in its higher, intellectual, and moral relations to our nation and age? What features of cosmopolitan greatness is it manifesting? It is surely no small thing, that so many people live here in tolerable peace and comfort; yet, of course, mere numbers do not constitute greatness, else Pekin would excel us two to one, and Yeddo might throw Paris and London into the shade. Greatness is in quality, not quantity, and a rational man of five feet eight inches is greater than a rude giant of eight feet, or a whale of ninety feet, or a comet with a tail fifteen millions of miles long. Take the test of quality, and New York need not hide her head among the great cities of the world, nor shrink from comparing her best citizens with the best citizens of any other city, nor from asking for her daily work an honorable position in the history of human capital, labor, and skill. Every day the nation and the world are richer for what is done on this island, and the great army of workers here with the hand or head, presents a marvellous spectacle to the mind capable of putting their various sections together, and seeing at one view our New York at its daily work.

Let us pass in review the industrial army of the city, which General Barlow, Secretary of State, allows me to copy from the unpublished census of

1865, and let us imagine it divided into regiments, thus, of about a thousand persons each:

Blacksmiths, over two and one-half..........regiments or	....	2,621
Bookbinders, over one..................... "	....	1,134
Boiler Makers, nearly one................. "	....	910
Boot and Shoe Makers, over six............. "	....	6,307
Butchers, four .... "	....	3,998
Brokers, one and one-third........ .... "	....	1,348
Barbers, one .... "	....	1,054
Cabinet Makers and Dealers, two and one-half. "	....	2,575
Carpenters, over six.... .... "	....	6,352
Cartmen and Draymen, four and one-half.... "	....	4,675
Clerks, seventeen and one-half.............. "	....	17,620
Clergy, nearly one-half..................... "	....	429
Confectioners, nearly one................... "	....	756
Cooks, one................................ "	....	906
Coopers, one and one-half........ .... "	....	1,401
Dressmakers, etc., nine and one-half......... "	....	9,501
Drivers, nearly two........................ "	....	1,895
Engineers, over one........................ "	....	1,196
Grocers, one.............................. "	....	937
Hat and Cap Makers, one and one-half........ "	....	1,438
Jewelers, one.............................. "	....	925
Laborers, twenty-one and one-quarter........ "	....	21,231
Laundresses, three and one-half............. "	....	3,590
Lawyers, one and one-fourth .... "	....	1,232
Merchants, six............................ "	....	5,978
Machinists, three .... "	....	3,108
Masons, three............................. "	....	2,757
Milliners, one and one-third .... "	....	1,334
Musicians, nearly one...................... "	....	809
Painters and Glaziers, four .... "	....	3,801
Peddlers, two............................. "	....	1,988
Physicians, one and one-fourth.............. "	....	1,269
Piano Makers, nearly one .... "	....	855
Plumbers, one............................. "	....	1,108
Police, one and one-half.................... "	....	1,546
Porters, nearly three....................... "	....	2,729
Printers, two.............................. "	....	2,186
Saddlers and Harness Makers, one........... "	....	915
Sailors and Marines, over three............. "	....	3,288

Servants, thirty-three.....................regiments or	....	33,282
School-Children, one hundred............... "	....	100,000
Ship Carpenters, one....................... "	....	1,156
Stone Cutters, one and one-third............ "	....	1,342
Tailors, ten............................... "	....	9,734
Teachers, over one and one-half............. "	....	1,608
Tinsmiths, one............................ "	....	931

These occupations and others that I might present from the voluminous pages of the Census, reckon about 150,000 of the people, and with school-children a quarter of a million.

The measure of a man's dignity depends upon the degree in which he rises above his private wants and lives in universal principles, motives, and objects. Now, how far is the work of our city made to bear upon the business and welfare of the nation and the world, and how does a cosmopolitan spirit mark the temper of our people? Much, surely, and probably far more than we are apt to think. The truth is coming out, more and more, that we are working with the country and the race, and giving and receiving good of all kinds, by a perpetual and magnificent exchange of thought and incentive, as well as of merchandise. Our best merchants are obliged to hold the markets of the globe in their minds, and our commerce is the practical fellowship of the business of the world, and this city has much of the enterprise and wealth of the whole nation in its charge. I do not say that business is done wholly or mainly for disinterested aims, or that Wall Street and South Street are zealots for universal philanthropy or missionary sacrifice; but I do believe that they, in their best merchants, have a large sense of the grandeur of their work and a rising conviction of its relation to the nation and the world. Our best merchants and bankers do not neglect character as an essential attendant of capital, and commercial honor means as much here as anywhere in America or Europe. The city that is next to London in financial importance, and lately saved the credit of the Bank of England by her gold, is not behind London in the worth of a true business man's word. Business here in its best form is done with careful method as well as large enterprise, and the leading firms assure me that one per cent. in sales will cover the amount of their average losses in trade. Of course, wealth is no measure of greatness, and we all know how utterly contemptible a millionnaire may make himself by his utter treachery to the noblest principles; but it is the man that is mean, not the spirit of business, nor the nature of capital. The money is often nobler than the man, and capital, under the influence of the immense enterprise and world-wide relations of this city, has a certain grandeur in its tone, and cannot be sluggish, nor wholly mean, if it will follow bravely the lead of the age, and make its investments with the best promise of honest return. Surely, our New York capital is in marvellous relations with the industry of the nation and the globe, and the purse here is the sinew of peace, as it has been the sinew of war. Day by day it keeps its vast army and navy of industry on the land and sea, and no man can enter intelligently into the study of the relations of capital and labor here, without saying that the subject rises into imperial dignity, and a true merchant cannot be a churl or a dunce. Business itself here teaches large ideas, and breathes a brave spirit and a generous fellowship. The trades catch something of the same temper, and the mechanics of this city, so eminent for skill and thrift, have much sense of their part in the work of their time, as well as their craft.

The earnings of labor rise here into grandeur, and not only count up by millions in our Savings Banks, but defend the country and build up the city. New York was built up largely by money loaned to our merchants from our Savings Banks; and, when the nation's life was threatened, these husbanded wages, as will be seen by Colonel Warner's statement,* were transferred into loans to our Government, and thus our hard-handed industry sent its money as well as its men to the war; and, therefore, New York labor is imperial in its work, and has done a noble part in giving our America her place among the nations. How mightily New York labor, capital, and skill, met together in our iron-clad fleet! When the brave little Monitor steamed into Chesapeake Bay and struck the rebel bully, the Merrimac, the deadly blow that stopped its piratical work, the mechanics and merchants of New York were there in their might, and Fulton and Ericsson led them to their triumph under the good old flag of the Union. Our business surely rises into imperial proportions, and is training us to a certain sense of our belonging to the great empire of industry that is so vitally con-

* See Appendix.

nected with the republic of letters. It does some things that have a romantic grandeur, and read like chapters of a poem. What was it in the main but the business spirit, that carried through the last wonder of the world? It was not abstract philanthropy, nor priestly ambition, nor missionary zeal, nor scientific pride, nor intellectual curiosity, but simple business enterprise, far-seeing and plucky, that laid the Atlantic Cable, and gave the two hemispheres of the globe one pulse and brain. In the Great Eastern, Cyrus W. Field brought our Fulton and Morse to work together in a wonderful way, and Fulton's steam carried the cable, and Morse's lightning sent through the thought. So the spirit of business joined together the engine that carries bulk with the battery, that discharges brain; and New York has had a mighty hand in that organism of liberty of the nineteenth century, that emancipates man from the weight of his burdens and the bonds of distance and of time.

As to the bearing of New York upon government, which is part of the great work of life, there is much to say in various directions, lights, and shades. Yet this is surely true, that this city in its real historical life has been the guardian of liberty, order, and union, and the great scandals that have sometimes fallen upon its good name, have not been its own home production. The city has been wonderfully free from disorder, and when mobs have appeared, the fact that they have showed their heads reads less conspicuously in our history, than the fact that they were at once put down, and the heads disappeared more quickly than they came. The last of these mobs and the worst, because against the few and unoffending negroes, was most effectually put down, and the city at large applauded the magistrate whose decision was most conspicuous in giving the rioters their due, and he is now our honored Mayor. The logic of our history and conviction as to mobs, is simple and sufficient. It says to all assemblies that threaten person or property, "Disperse!" and if they do not go, then it says, "Fire!" In mercy, as well as in justice, that logic has worked well, and is not likely to die out.

The marvellous growth of population, within twenty years, has added half a million to our numbers, and called, of course, for new measures, and ought to be some excuse for some mistakes and disappointments. The charter bears the mark of many changes, and is destined to bear more. The original charter was given by James II. in 1686; was amended by Queen Anne in 1708; further enlarged by George II. in 1730, into what is now known as Montgomerie's Charter, and as such was confirmed by the General Assembly of the Province in 1732, and made New York essentially a free city. The Mayor was appointed by the Provincial Governor and Council, till the Revolution; by the State Governor and four members of the Council of Appointment, till 1821; by the Common Council, until 1834, and afterwards by the people. In 1830, the people divided the Common Council into two boards, and, in 1849, the government was divided into seven departments, the heads of each being chosen by the people, and the Mayor's term of office being extended to two years. In 1853, the Board of Assistant Aldermen was changed to a Board of sixty Councilmen, and the term of Aldermen extended to two years. In 1857, the number of Aldermen was reduced from twenty-two to seventeen, and the sixty Councilmen to twenty-four; and the present complex system of government was established, with its many disconnected branches and equivocal division of power between the city, county, and state. Strangely is the Mayor shorn of power, and the office which De Witt Clinton preferred to his place in the National Senate, is now little more than a name and position. Still, the essence of Montgomerie's old charter remains, and the true spirit can redress the new corruptions.

There are some ugly aspects of our city government that make it difficult to treat the subject in the dignified light of history, and difficult to keep silent upon the manifest wickedness of some of our officials and their accomplices. It is not necessary to take partisan ground to rebuke the wrong; for no party has the monopoly of the offence. Fair men of both parties now say that our citizens are robbed and our city is disgraced. It is clear that whilst we have many honest and effective men in office, we have also a set of knaves in power, whose conduct violates every principle of justice and patriotism. May I not say, that whilst this city is intensely American in feeling, we are afflicted with one institution peculiarly foreign? We have a royal family, whose maintenance is very dear, and whose title to their state and income it is hard to discover. They abound in brass and gold; but whilst the brass on their faces is their own, the gold in their pockets is stolen from yours. They have the costliest signet *ring* in Christendom, and it makes the dirtiest mark, and sullies the sacred motto of Liberty which it bears. It puts the stain of iniquity even upon the seat of judgment, and the millions ($2,243,340 60) expended on the unfinished Court-House, prove that the work has been managed in part by thieves. What to do is the universal question, and we all ask it with perplexity. The principle is clear, and the method will ere long show itself. The principle of our redemption is to be found in the sacred idea of freedom. It is not in party spirit, nor aristocratic pride, nor property prerogative; but in intelligent liberty and public spirit. We are oppressed, degraded, and robbed, and we ask to be liberated, and we shall be, if we trust more in the spirit of Zenger and his Liberty Boys than that of Lord Howe with his dragoons. The city belongs to the State, nation, and world, and not to any clique or ring or party; yet whatever is done, should aim to give our citizens self-respect, to train them as much as possible to manage their own affairs. Our people are intelligent, industrious, honest, and brave, and mean to have their rights, and shall. Careful legislation, with intelligent suffrage and a city government more on the plan of the national, and taking from the Common Council its temptations to base jobs, will set us right, and free us from being subject to the dynasty of dirt and sovereignty of sots. Of parties merely, as such, little is to be hoped. Of the people of the city and the State, all may be expected that is right, when existing wrongs are clearly seen, and all honest men are banded against them by the true principle of impartial suffrage, and universal liberty and law. Then, as elsewhere in America, liberty becomes conservative, and is settled into law, whilst law rises into liberty. Let all honest men take as much interest in our city affairs as thieves now take, and our city is saved.

With all the drawback of defective municipal government, the city is a great power in the Union, and gave its wealth and men to the nation. Nay, its very passion has been national, and the mass who deplored the war never gave up the Union, and might, perhaps, have consented to compromise rather than to disunion, and have gone beyond any other city in clinging to the Union as such, whether right or wrong. The thoughtful mind of the city saw the true issue, and, whilst little radical or *doctrinaire* in its habit of thinking, and more inclined to trust to historical tendencies and institutional discipline for the removal of wrong than to abstract ideas, it did not waver a moment after the die was cast, and the blow of rebellion and disunion was clear. The ruling business powers of the city gave money and men to the nation, when the Government was halting and almost paralyzed. The first loan was hazardous and the work of patriotism, and when our credit was once committed, the wealth of the city was wholly at the service of the nation, and the ideas of New England, and the enthusiasm of the West, marched to victory with the mighty concurrence of the money and the men of the Empire City and State. The State furnished 473,443 men, or, when reduced to years of service, 1,148,604 years' service; equal to three years' service of 382,868 three years' men; and the city alone furnished 116,382 men, equal to 267,551 years' service, at a net cost of $14,577,214 65. That our moneyed men meant devoted patriotism, it is not safe to say of them all. In some cases, their capital may have been wiser and truer than the capitalist, and followed the great current of national life. Capital, like water, whose currents it resembles, has its own laws, and he who owns it cannot change its nature, any more than he who owns a water-power can change the power of the water. The capital of this city is bound, under God, to the unity of the nation, and, therefore, has to do a mighty part in organizing the liberty of the nineteenth century. Led by the same large spirit, and true to the Union policy which has been the habit of the community from the old Dutch times, the dominant thought of our people will be sure to vindicate the favorite idea of States Rights *in* the Union against States Wrongs *out* of it; and the seceded States will be restored as soon as they secure the States that have never seceded the just fruits of the war for the national life—and guarantee them against all repetition of the treason. The end shall be liberty for all; for the white man and the black man, everywhere; for the South as well as the North.

It might be shown that the business mind of our city has had great aptitude for the organization and government of institutions of charity and reform, and that, with all their defects, these institutions are, in many respects, as remarkable for their efficiency as their extent. Here, moreover, where crime rises into gigantic proportions, our safeguards are by no means of pigmy shape, and our police system is justly a matter of pride with our good citizens, and makes their walks safe by day and their pillow tranquil at night. That 68,373 arrests were made for offences of all grades in the year 1865, and, of these arrests, 53,911 were for offences of violence or other harm towards the person, proves the vigilance of our police; and that so many who were arrested were discharged on insufficient grounds, has raised in some observers the suspicion that some of our judges are either not wise or not honest, and too near the interests of the culprits. Our police, although established by the State authority, represents the historical, legitimate mind of the city in itself and its rural connections; for the country and city are, in important respects, one, and a large part of our true democracy who have genuine and just interest in the city, live in the country. Aristotle* was wise, and seems to have had a foresight of our day, when over two thousand years ago he wrote: "When a country happens to be so situated, that a great part of the land lies at a distance from the

---

* Aristotle, Politics, Book vi., ch. iv.

city, there it is easy to establish a good democracy or a free State; for the people in general are obliged to form their settlements in the country." Our rural or territorial democracy may carry their jurisdiction too far; but their leading acts have tended to organize our liberty, not to bring us under the yoke of bondage. It is not the party, but the great heart of the people, that we must trust. Surely, viewing our city in all its public institutions, under the twofold aspect of urban and rural control, they present a great monument of organizing sagacity and force; and even the frauds that pervert their functions cannot blind us to the largeness of the organization and the frequent fidelity and effectiveness of the management. We must not exaggerate our miseries, nor allow a ring of thieves to shut us out from the knowledge of our faithful servants. Remember that if New York has rogues in office, other cities are not spotless, nor wholly frugal; that London prints ponderous volumes on municipal frauds, and Paris * has a yearly Budget, that, of late, approaches

* That Paris is like us in financial trouble, is evident from this passage from Kolb's admirable Handbook of Comparative Statistics, Leipsic, 1865. "The city of Paris alone has a Budget like an empire; but like one that finds itself in financial decline. In 1847, its levy was limited to 46,000,000 frs. In 1853, the impost was raised to 55,000,000 at the highest; but there was actually a demand, ordinary and extraordinary, for 90,000.000; on account of which a loan of 50,000,000 was negotiated. The Budget for 1859 closes with the figures 77,649,081 frs. The sum actually needed reached 97,720,545 frs. The Budget for 1864 is fixed at 81,586,376 frs. ordinary, and 52,714,936 extraordinary; to which were added 15¼ millions supplementary, and 1,337,630 special appropriations; amounting in all to the sum of 151,408,942 frs. The actual account in 1862 reaches the enormous sum of 175,712,566 frs." Kolb, page 68. I have seen a statement that sets the Budget of 1863 at 193 million frs. Yet for all this, Paris taxes property less than New York, and so does not drive her residents away by over taxation. She puts most of the burdens on

$40,000,000 in gold. Believe it, that we have the groundwork of a noble municipal order; and the poorest service that the citizen can render, is to despair of the republic or its metropolis. Its institutions of charity and reform have the outlines of imperial greatness, and need only to be filled up with an imperial mind and energy. Already munificent, voluntary associations have done a great work and given nobler promise. Their history would fill volumes.

Do not disdain to look upon our city upon another side, and consider how the great brain of business refreshes itself with what is generally called amusement. Rehearse all the records of excess and folly and utter wickedness that you can, and yet there is something else, and not by any means disheartening to say. Allow that in this city, in the year ending October 31, 1865, over 16,000 persons were arrested for intoxication, and over 7,000 more for intoxication and disorderly conduct; that there are some 10,000 places for intoxicating drinks, and dens of licentiousness in proportion. Let us not forget that there is something encouraging in the demand for the higher forms of recreation, the beautiful arts, sculpture, painting, music, the higher drama, and, above all, for that gift of God, fair and great Nature, as presented in our noble Park under the sagacious and powerful hand of art. We must rest our minds as well as our bodies, and beautiful

imports and sales, and in 1864 the Octroi tax was estimated at 84,281,000. New York would be a cheaply governed city, if we had our whole revenue from customs, &c., to draw from.

art gives the rest that soothes without stupefying, and cheers without maddening. God himself is opening a new world of loveliness. It is He that offers us the musical scale, after our brains are weary of the multiplication-table, and to man as to child he bids us to the drama that is called play, after we are worn down with the drama that is called work. Remarkable and interesting it is to see that beautiful tastes are rising with our utilitarian pursuits, and music and its sister arts follow in the track of mathematics and its severe paths. It is surely something to thank Heaven for, that we have so much beautiful art within our reach; that gifted men and women bring hither their choice works of sculpture and painting, and that we have heard Jenny Lind and other spirits of song, and seen the Keans and Kembles, Rachel, Ristori, and their peers in the higher walks of the drama. There is a Providence in it, and our city, with all its vices and follies, sets an example to the nation of the higher pleasures that cheer labor with recreation, and throw over care the charm of poetry and art. Happy will be the day when society learns the true lesson, and abandons its semi-barbarous extravagance and dissipation, for true companionship and exalting graces. Society is not well with us now, and the true union of men and women, social and domestic, is broken by an alarming secession. The men have, in great numbers, seceded to the clubs, and the women, in alarming array, have abandoned themselves to dress and jewels, in a devotion which makes the clothes primary, and the woman secondary; in a fashion that renders most visiting intolerable to sensible men, and ranks the lady according to the wardrobe, and the sociality according to the cook and dancing-master. We wait for the heroine, the feminine Grant or Sherman, who shall reduce the seceders to submission, plant the banner of Union on the Fort Sumters of their rebellion, and bring them to terms by force of such combined loveliness and goodness, as to make their loyal yoke more charming than their boasted and disloyal liberty. Then, perhaps, modern New York might recall, without blushing, what Mrs. Grant wrote long years ago of old New York: "These unembellished females had more comprehensiveness of mind, more variety of ideas, more, in short, of what may be called original thinking, than could be easily imagined."

And how shall we estimate the education of our people in its various forms; by schools, colleges, newspapers, books, churches, and, not least, by this great university of human life which is always before our eyes? Think of the 208,309 scholars reported in 1865 in our public schools, and the average attendance of 86,674 in those schools, and over 100,000 scholars in regular attendance in all our schools, both public and private. Think of our galleries of art, private and public, and our great libraries and reading-rooms like the Astor, the Mercantile, the Society, and the Cooper Union. Consider the remarkable increase of private libraries, such as Dr. Wynne has but begun to describe in his magnificent volume. Think of our press, and its constant and enormous issues, especially of daily papers, which are the peculiar literary institution of our time, and alike the common school and university of our people. Our 350 churches and chapels, 258 of them being regular churches of all kinds, can accommodate about 300,000 hearers, and inadequate as in some respects they are as to location and convenience, they can hold as many of the people as wish to attend church, and far more than generally attend.* Besides our churches and chapels, we have powerful religious instrumentalities in our religious press, and our city is the centre of publication of leading newspapers, magazines, and reviews, of the great denominations of the country. In these organs the best scholars and thinkers of the nation express their thought in a way wholly unknown at the beginning of the century, when the religious press of the country was not apparently dreamed of. The higher class of religious and theological reviews that are published here, are, perhaps, the best specimens of the most enlarged scholarship and severe thinking of America, and are doing much to educate an enlightened and

---

* The fullest statistics of New York religion that we can obtain, are given in the excellent Report of the City Mission for 1866, and give a list of 350 churches, chapels, and synagogues; 171 of them being below Fourteenth Street, and 179 above Fourteenth Street. The list of clergy resident numbers 537, and the number of pastors is 298: being of Baptists 30, Congregationalists 5, Dutch Reformed 21, Lutheran 9, Methodists 41, Presbyterians 56, Episcopalians 79, Roman Catholic 36, Unitarian 3, Miscellaneous 14. The number of Roman Catholic pastors is understated, by naming only one in connection with each church; whereas there are often several. The State Census of 1865 returns 258 churches in the city, valued at $12,859,500; with other real estate, to the amount of $8,477,800; with capacity for seating 266,980 persons, and with a usual attendance of 161,403. The salaries of the clergy, including use of real estate, are estimated at $504,400—being an average of $1,955 each.

truly catholic spirit and fellowship. If the question is asked, in view of all these means of education, what kind of mind is trained up here, or what are the indications of our New York intelligence, it may not be so easy to say in full, as to throw out a hint or two by way of suggestion. There is, certainly, what may be called a New York mind and character, and there must be from the very nature of the case. Some characteristics must mark each community, as the results of birth and breeding; and however great the variety of elements, some qualities must predominate over others in the people, as in the climate and fruits of a country. Where two tendencies seem to balance each other for a time, one is sure, at last, to preponderate, and to gain value and power with time, and win new elements to itself. It is not hard to indicate the essential New York character from the beginning. It is positive, institutional, large-hearted, genial, taking it for granted that all men are not of one pattern, and that we are to live by allowing others to have their liberty as we have ours.

Perhaps we make the portrait more distinct by comparing New York with New England; the Knickerbocker with the Yankee. There is this great difference in their antecedents. The old New Yorker began with his European national and church life, and was Dutch or English in church and state, without any radical non-conformity. The New Englander began with separation, and whilst bringing the noblest elements of European character, he started as a dissenter from church and state. Hence the obvious and remarkable difference. The New Yorker rested in the old institutions, and still rests in them, —in the Heidelberg Catechism and Dutch Church or in the Prayer Book and Anglican Church or Westminster Confession and Presbyterian Church; and, moreover, in civil matters, he trusts more in ancient and fixed law, than in radical principles. The New Englander was busy with reconstructing society and religion, according to his own convictions, and so became subjective, introversial, and *doctrinaire;* sometimes to such a degree as sadly to puzzle and annoy his old Dutch-English neighbors, and as still to draw from their representatives here the accusation of being over-subjective, opinionated, and dictatorial, if not over-fond of turning the world of institutions upside down, at the mercy of his remorseless ideas. One other difference marks the two in a way that is not often acknowledged, and may not be sufficiently appreciated. New England at first seceded not only from old England, but from old Europe, and undertook to give up the dominant Japhetic or Indo-European idea of God in history, and to return to Shem and the Law of Moses, with the idea of God over us rather than with us, and to reject or slight the European Christian year and round of worship that is based upon the Incarnation. The Puritan, of course, believed in the Gospel and its great truths of Incarnation and Atonement; but he made the expiatory Atonement and its subjective work more conspicuous, and was suspicious of the old church habits that are built upon the objective Incarnation, and keep the Christmas jubilee and its sequel. He was distrustful of the method of nurture, and trusted more to direct conversion. The New Yorker, whether Dutch or English, brought over the old Christian year with its educational discipline, and New York still keeps the habit, and is decidedly a Churchman's, and not a Puritan, city. The Dutch retained the Christian year with its Pinxter and Paas festivals, and great was the wrath of many when Dr. Laidlie denounced their old church ways, and drove scores of old Dutch families into the Episcopal church by his Puritanic radicalism.

The two churches are, indeed, wonderfully drawing near each other, the Puritan and the Churchman, as we shall see, and blending the calm method of church nurture with the Puritan method of individual conversion; yet these distinctions are nevertheless real, and are essential to a fair study of our subject. The Puritan has made up for the narrowness of his Semitic theism, by the new science and insight that discern God's immanence in nature and man; and the Churchman has quickened his objective conservatism by a large infusion of Puritan independence, intuition, and fire. In this and in other respects the elements of civilization are combining in our city, and are giving us promise of the imperial city and the imperial mind that shall be. Our literature shows the same process, and whilst all types of thought and styles of diction here centre, the most memorable combination is that of Puritan analysis and intuition with catholic largeness and repose. Irving well represents the calm, cheerful, old conservatism from his Sunnyside on the Hudson; and, perhaps, Hawthorne, at his old Puritan manse on Concord River, is his contrast in introversial insight and mystical fancy. How much their works are read here, and their tempers cross and modify each other! It seemed as if our people felt the worth and also the large affinities of their idol, by inviting good examples of Puritan intellects to honor his memory, when our leading Yankee poet and historian were called to pay their tributes at the obsequies of Irving. Then the two elements, the actual and the ideal, met together, and the two poles of the American mind were in unison. Our patriarch-poet was fitly chosen to give the eulogy over those fathers of our literature, Cooper and Irving; and the fact and the occasion brought the New York and the New England mind into striking contrast and also harmony. I may name him, William Cullen Bryant, without reserve here to-night, since age and absence from the country lift him into historical dignity, and I may characterize him as the noble and venerable exemplar of New England in New York—the prophet of Liberty as well as the poet of Nature, and combining in rare union the old Hebrew reverence with our modern largeness and freedom. Well may the nation honor him for singing so grandly the Dirge of Slavery, and at the same time protesting against all trespass upon the constitutional rights of our States and people, and all wrong to trade and commerce by unjust taxation and centralization. All honor to our poet and patriot for his service to our liberty and our law!

This affinity between the Puritan and Churchman mind, or between the New England subjective scholasticism and the New York Dutch-English objective institutionalism, has shown itself from the beginning. Jonathan Edwards, the Plato, as Franklin was the Aristotle, of New England thought, the first metaphysical mind of America, undoubtedly felt it, when, in 1722, a youth under nineteen, he came to preach to a little knot of Presbyterians in a hall in William Street; when he saw the face of God very near to him, as he mused on the banks of the Hudson; and when a ship arrived, "his soul eagerly catched at any news favorable to the interest and advancement of Christ's Kingdom." He much wished to stay here, and undoubtedly was as much calmed by the wholesome old-fashioned repose of Dutch and English institutions as cheered by the devotion and kindness of the people.

How far assimilation in its various forms of thought and life is to go, we can only conjecture; for the process has but begun. Our community, like every other community, must go through three stages of development to complete its Providential evolution: aggregation, accommodation, and assimilation. The first stage is aggregation, and that comes of course with the fact of residence. Here we are, about a million of us, aggregated on this healthy and charming island, and here we most of us expect and wish to stay. We are seeking our next stage, and wish accommodation not with entire success, and the city is distressed by prosperity, and is like an overgrown boy, whose clothes are too small for his limbs, and he waits in half nakedness for his fitting garments. In some respects, the city itself is a majestic organism, and we have light, water, streets, and squares, much to our mind, always excepting the dirt. The scarcity of houses, the costs of rent, living, and taxation are grievous, and driving a large portion of our middling class into the country. Yet the city is full and overflowing, and is likely to be. The work of assimilation is going on, and every debate, controversy, and party, brings the various elements together, and we are seeing each other whether we differ or agree. Great progress has been made in observing and appreciating our situation and population. Probably New York knows itself better to-day than at any time since its imperial proportions began to appear. In politics, police, philanthropy, education, and religion, we are reckoning our classes, numbers, and tendencies, and feeling our way towards some better harmony of ideas and interests. The whole population of the city was, by census of 1860, 813,669; and by the census of 1865, 726,386. The voters number 151,838; native, 51,500; foreign, 77,475. Over twenty-one years, they who cannot read and write are 19,199. Families number 148,683. Total of foreigners by census of 1860, was 383,717; and by census of 1865, 313,417. Number of women by census of 1865 was 36,000 more than of men, and of widows, over 32,000; being 25,000 more widows than widowers. The Germans, by the census of 1860, numbered 119,984; and by the census of 1865, 107,269. This makes this city not the third, but the eighth city in the world as to German population. These German cities have a larger population: Berlin, Vienna, Breslau, Cologne, Munich, Hamburg, and Dresden.* The Irish, by the census of 1860, number 203,700; and by the census of 1865, 161,334. New York now, we believe, has a million of residents, and either peculiar difficulties in the census commission of 1865, or peculiar influences after the war, led to the appearance of diminished population. Certainly we have, of late, gained numbers, and have not lost in variety of elements to be assimilated. The national diversities are not hostile, and we are seeking out their best, instead of their worst, qualities. Italian art and French accomplishment we can appreciate without forgetting that we are Americans. We are discerning in our New York Germany, something better than Lager Beer and Sunday Concerts, and learning to appeal to the sterling sense and indomitable love of liberty of the countrymen of Luther and Gutenberg. The Irish among us, who make this the second if not the first Irish city of the world, and who contribute so largely to our ignorant and criminal returns, we are studying anew, and discerning their great service to industry and their great capacity for organization. We find among them good specimens of the blood of the Clintons and the Emmets, and are bound to acknowledge that in purity, their wives and daughters may be an example to any class in America or Europe. Old

---

* Population of German cities by the last census (1864): Vienna, 578,525; Berlin, 609,733; Breslau, 156,644; Cologne, 117,000; Munich, 165,054; Hamburg, 135,339. The population of Hamburg is from the census of 1861 as that city does not belong to the Zollverein, and did not come into the Zollverein census of 1864. See Illustrirter Kalender, Leipzig, 1867, and Handbuch der Vergleichenden Statistik, von G. Fr. Kolb, Leipzig, 1865.

Israel is with us too in force, and some thirty synagogues of Jews manifest the power of the oldest organized religion, and the example of a people that cares wholly for its own sick and poor; willing to meet Christians as friends and citizens, and learn our religion more from its own gospel of love, than from its old conclaves of persecution. We often see other types of the Oriental mind in our streets and houses, and it will be well for us when Asia is here represented by able specimens of her mystical piety, and we learn of her something of the secret of her repose in God, and give her in return something of our art of bringing the will of God to bear upon this stubborn earth, instead of losing sight of the earth in dreams of pantheistic absorption. In many ways the various elements are combining to shape our ideas and society, and fill out the measure of our practical education.

Yet, probably, the most important assimilation, as already hinted, is that which is going on here between the various elements of our American life in this mother-city which is destined, apparently, to be to America what Rome was to the tribes that thronged to its gates. What has been taking place in England is taking place here, and the Independents and Churchmen are coming together here as in England since the Revolution of 1688, when extremes were greatly reduced, and the independency of Milton and Cromwell began to reappear in combination with the church ways of Clarendon and Jeremy Taylor. The most significant part of the process is the union here of Puritan individualism, and its intuitive thinking and bold ideas, with New York institutionalism, and its organizing method and objective mind. The Yankee is here, and means to stay, and is apparently greatly pleased with the position and reception, and enjoys the fixed order and established paths of his Knickerbocker hosts. It is remarkable that whilst New England numbered only some 20,000, or 19,517 of her people here, which is 7,000 less than the nations of Old England in the city, by the census of 1860, they are so well received and effective, and fill so many and important places in business and the professions. By the census of 1865, New York City has 17,856 natives of New England, and 19,699 natives of Old England; a balance of 1,843 in favor of Old England. Yet, in the State at large, the result is different, for the population numbers 166,038 natives of New England, and 95,666 natives of Old England; a balance of 70,372 in favor of New England. It is curious to note that the city had only 825 native Dutch in 1865, and the State 4,254. In a philosophical point of view, it is memorable that the Puritan mind is now largely in power, even in our church establishments that so depart from New England independency, and the leading Presbyterian and Episcopal preachers and scholars are largely from the Puritan ranks. Our best informed scholar in the philosophy of religion, who holds the chair of theological instruction in the Presbyterian Seminary, is a New England Congregationalist, transplanted to New York. Nay, even the leading, or at least the most conspicuous, Roman Catholic theologian of New

York, is the son of a Connecticut Congregationalist minister, and carries the lineal blood and mental habit of his ancestor, Jonathan Edwards, into the illustration and defence of the Roman creed. It is worthy of note that our most philosophical historian is the son of a Massachusetts Congregational minister, and a lover of the old scholastic thinking, and a champion of the ideal school of Edwards and Channing in its faith and independency; author, too, of perhaps the most bold and characteristic word of America to Europe, the oration of February 22, 1866, that was the answer of our new world to British Toryism, and Romish Obscurantism, whether to the Premier's mock neutral manifesto, or the Pope's Encyclical Letter. Some of the Puritans who keep their independency, catch the New York organizing passion; and Congregationalism, which, after making four unsuccessful attempts to win a footing, at last found it in 1819, has given to the city a body of clergy who understand the power of institutions as well as ideas. The pastor of the Tabernacle has written his name upon the roll of our patriotic leaders; and the pastor of All Souls, the First Congregational Church in New York, has led the grandest of our national charities, and written a chapter of humanity, that, in its way, has never been surpassed if equalled on earth, in the Sanitary Commission. On all sides New England independency works into the large organic methods of this metropolis and State. Large, indeed, is the hospitality that has been shown to us New Englanders in this city of our adoption, alike to our thought and our people. The press and the parlor have been alike generous, and we can ask no fairer treatment for our literature than has been given our authors in the admirable Cyclopedia of American Literature by our fellow-members of the Society—the brothers Duyckinck—one of whom we greet here cordially, and the other we tenderly remember, to-night.

It is not amiss to remember that of the 125 delegates to the Constitutional Convention of 1846, forty members were natives of New England, or nearly one third of the whole number—a fact quite remarkable, when we consider that in this State the New Englanders are but about a twentieth part of the population. A distinguished and truly honored historian of Massachusetts once, in the heat of party strife, called New York State a "soulless giant, whose honorable history is yet to be written." Without rehearsing the noble deeds of New York of old and of late, we trust that our excellent friend will remember that a great deal of New England soul has lived in New York, and that the community cannot be soulless that has harbored and honored such men as Rufus King, Postmaster-General Osgood, Judge Peck, Henry Wheaton, Silas Wright, Jonathan M. Wainwright, and William Ware, and hosts of other New England men. The honorable history of New York has not indeed been written; not because the topic is not honorable, but because it has not been fully, except in its early periods, written at all. Honor to old Massachusetts, who still keeps with New York the palm once shared with Virginia, that third of our three oldest States.

But how much harder the problem to solve here than there—New York here, with great nations pouring their immigrant hosts into her domain, whether to stay in her great city, where eighty dialects are said to be spoken, or make their way westward over her roads and canals—and Massachusetts there, with little comparative interruption of her old work of labor and education, and in comparative quiet and seclusion with her own sons and daughters about her. Massachusetts and New York! I name them gratefully and lovingly here to-night, and he is no true American who denies their foremost place among the architects of our Liberty and our Union. Virginia I would gladly name too with her ancient sisters, and God grant that some future orator here may be able in truth to note her new greatness, and restore her lost name. In 1800 she led New York in population by nearly 300,000, and in 1860 fell behind her about 2,300,000, and Pennsylvania succeeds to her honors, and approaches, but does not reach, the greatness of the Empire State. We shall be glad to greet the State of George Washington on the same platform of liberty as the State of William Penn, and so renew the old fellowship with fresh hope.

But why set any limit to our affinities, and not rather rejoice in the boundless fellowship of State with State, faith with faith, and nation with nation here opened? Here we may, if we will, find and meet on generous terms leading minds of every type and culture; and we ought to have a large humanity, an imperial conscience, purpose, and sympathy, worthy of our great liberty and opportunity. Here we may not only find the scattered truths that have been, to use Milton's figure, torn asunder like the mangled body of the fabled Osiris; but we ought to have what is better than abstract truth, the broken limbs of our great and glorious manhood here brought together, and in fellowship with the wise and good of every name and race, we should discern the true body of our completed humanity, in a catholic largeness that will not yield the palm to Paris or London, nor need to learn imperial breadth from Rome or Russia. Here already, in its best hours, our New York has glimpses of the true human fellowship, which is the organized liberty of the nineteenth century. We need some effective centre of public fellowship, where all elements of generous thought and life meet together, and bring the present and the past together in love and honor. Where should we find it but here, where sects and parties are ignored, and we meet as citizens and men?

It is the province of the New York Historical Society to keep up the connection of the New York of the past with the New York of to-day, and zealously to guard and interpret all the historical materials that preserve the continuity of our public life. It is to be lamented that so little remains around us to keep alive the memory of the ancient time; and everything almost that we see is the work of the new days. Sad it is that all the old neighborhoods are broken up, and the old houses and churches are mostly swept away by our new prosperity. But how impressive are our few landmarks! We all could join in the Centennial Jubilee of St. Paul's, and wish well to its opening future. So, too, we can greet our neighbors of the John Street Church in their Centennial, and thank God for the hundred years of New York Methodism. Who of us can pass without reflection by the old Middle Dutch Church, now our Post-Office, in Nassau Street, and without recalling the years and events that have passed since 1729, when it was opened for worship in the Dutch tongue? In March, 1764, the preaching there was, for the first time, in English, and in August, 1844, Dr. De Witt gave an outline of its history, and pronounced the benediction in Dutch; and that old shrine of the Knickerbockers is now the busy brain of the nation and the world, and receives and transmits some forty tons of thought a day. What would one of those old Rip Van Winkles of 1729 have thought, if he could have prolonged his Sunday afternoon nap in one of those ancient pews till now, and awoke to watch the day's mail, with news by the last steamers and the Atlantic cable for all parts of the great continent! Our Broadway, ever changing, and yet the same old road, is perhaps our great historical monument, and the historical street of America by eminence. All the men of our history have walked there, and all nations and tribes have trodden its stones and dust. In our day what have we seen there—what processions, armies, pageants! What work would be more an American as well as New York history, than Broadway described and illustrated with text and portraits, from the times when Stuyvesant astonished the Dutch with his dignity to the years that have brought the hearse of our murdered President and the carriage of his successor along its stately avenue? Thank heaven for old Broadway—noble type of American civilization—from the Battery to Harlem River! and may the ways of the city be as straight as the lines of its direction, and as true to the march of the Providence of God!

But is not our Society itself an historical monument, and does not the past combine with the present and future in our records and collections? This Sixty-second Anniversary revives the whole history of our Society since 1804. These busts recall the faces of Hamilton and Jay, George and De Witt Clinton,—and you, Mr. President, are not alone in your office, and we can almost hear the voice of Luther Bradish, and see the forms of your noted predecessors, Egbert Benson, Gouverneur Morris, Dr. Hosack, De Witt Clinton, James Kent, and Albert Gallatin, with you as you occupy your chair to-night. One aged member is here, whose life bridges over the chasm, and in him old New York and young are one before us now. He was born in 1786, when the city had but 23,000 inhabitants, and now he presides over the bureau of immigration, that sometimes receives that number in a month, and averages 16,000 or 17,000 monthly, or 200,000 a year. Stout specimen of a living man—we will not say venerable relic of the eighteenth century; contemporary of Hamilton and Jay, Morris, Livingston, and the Clintons; friend of Paulding, Irving, and Cooper; representative of the eighteenth century and the nineteenth; embodiment of the Dutch, English, and American times; master of our earliest literature and our last —Gulian Crommelin Verplanck! we, who are young New York, this goodly company of staunch men and fair women, a thousand strong, with a million behind us, we salute old New York in you to-night, and implore the blessing of God upon your venerable head. Heaven grant that the new generation may be able to transmit some such specimens of the sound mind in the sound body as yours!

What the orator who ushers in the twentieth century here, or who celebrates your One Hundredth Anniversary, may have to say as he reviews the nineteenth century, as Dr. Miller reviewed the eighteenth, I will not undertake to say. What we should wish and pray for is clear. Clear that we should wish the new times to keep the wisdom and virtue of the old with all the new light and progress; clear that after our trying change from the old quarters to the new, we may build a nobler civilization on the new base, and so see better days than ever before; that the great city that shall be here, should be not only made up of many men, but of true manhood, and be not only the capital of the world, but the city of God; its great Park, the central ground of noble fellowship; its great wharves and markets, the seat of honorable industry and commerce; its public halls, the headquarters of free and orderly Americans; its churches, the shrines of the blessed faith and love that join man with man, and give open communion with God and heaven.

APPENDIX.

The author has endeavored to gather all important information as to the present condition and prospects of the city, and is grateful to the many citizens and friends who have given him assistance in the effort. To meet the express wishes of judicious advisers, and to give more permanent historical value to the publication, he is induced to present in this Appendix the most important statistics in his possession as to the wealth and population, health, crime, charities and corrections, and education of the city.

I.
THE POPULATION AND WEALTH OF NEW YORK.

CENSUS OF THE CITY.

1860.

WARDS.	POPULATION.	DWELLINGS.	FAMILIES.
First	18,120	778	3,184
Second	2,507	202	353
Third	8,757	407	615
Fourth	21,994	1,015	3,631
Fifth	22,341	1,260	5,192
Sixth	26,698	1,386	5,300
Seventh	40,006	2,358	7,354
Eighth	39,722	2,755	8,110
Ninth	44,386	3,792	8,586
Tenth	29,051	2,045	6,282
Eleventh	59,963	2,743	13,054
Twelfth	30,647	3,296	4,881
Thirteenth	32,917	1,829	7,312
Fourteenth	28,087	1,490	5,969
Fifteenth	27,588	2,781	4,216
Sixteenth	45,182	3,412	3,364
Seventeenth	72,775	3,592	15,837
Eighteenth	57,464	3,685	9,928
Nineteenth	32,841	2,950	5,463
Twentieth	67,554	4,307	13,956
Twenty-first	49,025	4,226	8,621
Twenty-second	61,749	4,029	11,099
Total	814,254	54,338	155,707

POPULATION OF THE CITY AT VARIOUS PERIODS.

1656	1,000	1820	123,706
1673	2,500	1825	166,089
1696	4,302	1830	202,589
1731	8,628	1835	270,068
1756	10,381	1840	312,852
1773	21,876	1845	371,223
1786	23,614	1850	515,394
1790	33,131	1855	629,810
1800	60,489	1860	814,254
1810	96,373		

The falling off of the population, according to the State Census of 1865, is ascribed to various causes, such as the alarms and disasters of the war, and the reluctance of many persons to have their names known, in fear of military conscription. It is certain that the city has more inhabitants now than ever, and there is no vacant house on the island.

WEALTH OF NEW YORK.

STATEMENT *of Valuation of Property in the City and County of New York, from* 1805 *to* 1825, *both inclusive.*

DATE.	VALUATION.	CITY AND COUNTY TAX.	STATE TAX.	TOTAL OF CITY AND STATE TAX.	CTS. DOLS.
1805..	$25,645,867	$127,094 87	....	....	50 per 1.
1806..	26,529,630	127.814 97	....	....	48½ "
1807..	24,959,955	129,155 09	....	....	52 "
1808..	25,118,720	138,984 18	....	....	55 "
1809..	24,782,267	139,027 39	....	....	56 "
1810..	25,486,370	129,727 15	....	....	51 "
1811.	26,045,730	176,978 25	....	....	68 "
1812..	26,240,040	174,920 17	....	....	67 "
1813..	27,650,230	174,727 94	....	....	63 "
1814..	28,091,497	214,225 09	....	....	26 "
1815..	81,636,042	197,613 38	$163,372 08	$361,285 46	41½ "
1816..	82,074,200	180,653 94	164,148 50	344,802 54	42 "
1817..	78,895,735	216,720 44	157,591 27	374,311 71	47 "
1818..	80,254,091	255,740 70	80.254 09	335,994 88	42 "
1819..	79,113,061	250,140 21	79,113 61	329,453 82	41½ "
1820..	69,530,753	270,361 19	69,530 75	339,891 94	49 "
1821..	67,286,070	299,430 30	68,285 07	367,215 37	49½ "
1822..	71,285,141	303,105 61	71,289 14	374,397 75	52½ "
1823..	70,940,820	351,814 36	70,940 80	422,755 16	59½ "
1824..	83,075,676	353,329 89	41,537 84	394,857 73	47½ "
1825..	101,160,046	336,868 82	50,580 03	387,448 85	38¼ "

The debt of the city, December 31, 1865, was $33,326,524 50.

APPENDIX.

STATEMENT *of the Value of Real and Personal Estate in the City and County of New York, with the amount raised by Tax, from the year 1826 to 1866, both inclusive.*

DATE.	VALUE OF REAL ESTATE.	VALUE OF PERSONAL ESTATE.	TOTAL VALUE REAL AND PERSONAL.	AMOUNT RAISED BY TAX.
1826......	$64,804,050	$72,434,981	$107,238,931	$383,759 89
1827......	72,617,770	49,549,156	112,211,926	437,692 02
1828......	77,138,880	33,879,653	114,019,533	485,751 72
1829......	76,130,430	35,672,636	111,803,066	507,107 24
1830......	87,603,580	37,684,938	125,288,518	509.178 44
1831......	95,594,335	31,966,194	137,560,259	572,104 05
1832......	104,160,605	40,741,723	144,902,328	665,385 74
1833......	114,124,566	42,366,976	166,491,542	971,854 64
1834......	123,249,280	53,299,231	186,548,511	835,605 49
1835......	143,742,425	34.991,278	218,723,703	965,602 94
1836......	233,732,303	75,758,617	309,500,020	1,085,130 44
1837......	196,450,109	67,297,241	263,747,350	1,244,972 15
1838......	104,543,359	69,609,582	264,152,941	1,486,993 73
1839......	196,940,134	73,920,885	270,869,019	1,352,826 51
1840......	187,221,714	65,011,801	252,233,515	1,354,835 29
1841......	186,359,948	64,843,972	251,194,920	1,394,136 65
1842......	176,513,092	61,292,559	237,805,651	2,031,382 66
1843......	164,955,314	64,274,765	229,229,079	1,747,516 59
1844......	171,937,591	64,789,552	236,727,143	1,988,118 56
1845......	177,207,990	62,787,527	239,995,517	2,096,191 18
1846......	181,480,534	61,471,470	244,952,004	2,526,146 71
1847......	187,315,386	59,837,913	247,153,299	2,581,776 30
1848......	193,029,076	61,164,447	254,163,523	2,715,510 25
1849......	197,741,919	58,455,224	256,197,143	3,005,762 52
1850......	207,142,576	78,919,240	286,061,816	3,230,085 02
1851......	227,015,856	93,095,001	320,110,857	2,924,455 94
1852......	253,278,384	98,490,042	351,768,426	3,380,511 00
1853......	294,637,296	118,994,137	413,631,382	5,066,698 74
1854......	330,300,396	131,721,338	462,021,734	4,845,386 07
1855......	336,975,866	150,022,312	486,998,278	5,843,822 89
1856......	340,972,098	170,744,393	511,740,491	7,075,425 72
1857......	352,958,803	168,216,449	521,175,252	8,111,758 09
1858......	368,346,296	162,847,994	531,194,290	8,621,091 31
1859......	378,954,930	172,968,192	551,923,122	9,860,926 09
1860......	398,533,619	178,697,637	577,230,956	9,758,507 86
1861......	406,955,665	174,624,306	581,579,971	11,627,632 28
1862......	399,551,314	172,416,031	571,967,345	9,906,271 10
1863......	402,196,652	192,000,161	594,196,813	11,556,672 18
1864......	410,695,485	223,920,405	634,615,890	13,705,092 86
1865.	427,368,864	181,423,471	608,792,335	18,202,857 56
1866......	478,993,084	257,994,974	736,988.058	16,950,767 88

APPENDIX.

COMMERCE OF NEW YORK.

(From the Report of the Chamber of Commerce.)

TONNAGE OF THE PORT OF NEW YORK AND OF THE UNITED STATES.

STATEMENT *exhibiting the registered, enrolled, and licensed Tonnage belonging to the Port of New York, for each year, from 1857 to June 30, 1865, inclusive.* (*Official.*)

	REGISTERED.		ENROLLED AND LICENSED.		TOTAL.	
	Tons.	95ths.	Tons.	95ths.	Tons.	95ths.
1857	802,356	10	575,068	51	1,377,424	61
1858	840,449	08	592,256	33	1,432,705	41
1859	844,432	24	599,928	44	1,444,360	68
1860	838,449	51	625,551	47	1,464,001	03
1861	912,942	79	626,412	44	1,539,355	28
1862	921,983	03	645,232	57	1,567,215	60
1863	846,445	79	777,554	24	1,624,000	08
1864	723,812	49	931,157	85	1,654,970	39
1865	471,473	00	751,791	50	1,223,264	50
" new meas.	192,545	69	200,786	85	393,332	54

STATEMENT *exhibiting the tonnage of American and Foreign Vessels entered and cleared from the several districts of the State of New York, during the year ending June 30, 1865.* (*Official.*)

Districts.	ENTERED.			CLEARED.		
	American Vessels.	Foreign Vessels.	Total.	American Vessels.	Foreign Vessels.	Total.
	Tons.	Tons.	Tons.	Tons.	Tons.	Tons.
Genesee	27,540	92,016	119,556	76,682	92,197	168,879
Oswego	213,858	222,694	436,552	186,265	221,299	407,564
Niagara	56,378	49,698	106,076	932	49,683	50,615
Buffalo Creek	372,032	88,964	460,996	375,666	86,497	462,163
Oswegatchie	.....	33,665	33,665	....	33,625	33,625
Champlain	54,306	48,735	103,041	54,727	40,534	95,261
Cape Vincent	144,994	95,601	240,595	144,145	93,189	237,334
Dunkirk	571	1,305	1,876	232	1,305	1,537
Sag Harbor	.....	....	....	614	....	614
New York	774,136	1,301,341	2,075,477	629,186	1,473,729	2,102,915
Total State of New York.	1,643,815	1,934,019	3,577,834	1,468,449	2,092,058	3,560,507
Other States	1,299,846	1,282,948	2,582,794	1,556,685	1,503,065	3,059,750
Total United States	2,943,661	3,216,967	6,160,628	3,025,134	3,595,123	6,620,257

APPENDIX. 69

ARRIVALS OF SHIPPING AT NEW YORK IN 1865.

FROM FOREIGN PORTS.

Steamers.	*Ships.*	*Barks.*	*Brigs.*	*Schooners.*
454	479	1,024	1,635	1,070

COASTWISE.

Steamers.	*Ships.*	*Barks.*	*Brigs.*	*Schooners.*
1,604	85	144	299	5,840

Total, foreign ports 4,662
" coastwise....................................... 7,972

Grand total for 1865 12,634
Whole number, 1864.................................. 12,825

Decrease... 191

ARRIVALS DURING PREVIOUS YEARS.

	Foreign, all Classes.		Coastwise, all Classes.
1865	4,662	....	7,972
1864	4,841	....	7,984
1863	5,173	....	7,937
1862	5,487	....	7,148
1861	5,122	....	6,977
1860	4,451	....	8,445
1859	4,027	....	7,809
1858	3,483	....	7,243
1857	3,902	....	6,097
1856	3,869	....	6,109

COMMERCE OF NEW YORK FOR THE YEAR 1865.

IMPORTS AND EXPORTS OF THE PORT OF NEW YORK FOR THE YEAR 1865.

THE following statistics of the commerce of the port of New York for the year 1865, showing the imports and exports classified, with a comparison with previous years, have been compiled from the official returns at the Custom House:

FOREIGN IMPORTS AT NEW YORK.

	1862.	**1863.**	**1864.**	**1865.**
Dry-Goods	$56,121,227	$67,274,547	$71,589,752	$91,965,138
General Merchandise	117,140,813	118,814,219	144,270,386	130,654,000
Specie	1,390,277	1,525,811	2,265,622	2,123,281
Total imports	$174,652,317	$187,614,577	$218,125,760	$224,742,419

It appears from this statement that the total for the year exceeds the total of any year since the war, because of the very heavy dry-goods imports last year. Our imports of cotton alone have decreased about six millions. We now give, for comparison, the previous years since 1851, classifying them into dutiable, free, and specie. Under the head of dutiable is included both the value entered for consumption and that entered for warehousing. The free goods run very light, as nearly all the imports now are dutiable.

FOREIGN IMPORTS AT NEW YORK.

	Dutiable.	Free Goods.	Specie.	Total.
1851	$119,592,264	$9,719,771	$2,049,543	$131,361,578
1852	115,336,052	12,105,342	2,408,225	129,849,619
1853	179,512,412	12,156,387	2,429,083	194,097,882
1854	163,494,984	15,768,916	2,107,572	181,371,472
1855	142,900,661	14,103,946	855,631	157,860,238
1856	193,839,646	17,902,578	1,814,425	213,556,649
1857	196,279,362	21,440,734	12,898,033	230,618,129
1858	128,578,256	22,024,691	2,264,120	152,867,067
1859	213,640,363	28,708,732	2,816,421	245,165,516
1860	201,401,683	28,006,447	8,852,330	238,260,460
1861	95,326,459	30,353,918	37,088,413	162,768,790
1862	149,970,415	23,291,625	1,390,277	174,652,317
1863	174,521,766	11,567,000	1,525,811	187,614,577
1864	204,128,236	11,731,902	2,265,622	218,125,760
1865	212,208,301	10,410,837	2,123,281	224,742,419

IMPORTS OF DRY-GOODS AT THE PORT OF NEW YORK FOR THE YEAR 1865.

	Wool.	Cotton.	Silk.	Flax.	Miscellaneous.	Total Value.
1865	36,074,585	15,350,064	20,556,261	15,402,602	4,581,626	91,965,138

The following statement shows the receipts for duties for the last four years:

RECEIPTS FOR CUSTOMS AT NEW YORK.

1862.	1863.	1864.	1865.
$52,254,116 72	$58,886,054 42	66,937,127 71	$101,772,905 94

The annexed detailed statement shows the exports of domestic produce, and specie and bullion, during each month of the last four years:

APPENDIX. 71

EXPORTS OF DOMESTIC PRODUCE.

1862.	1863.	1864.	1865.
$149,179,591	$164,249,177	$201,855,989	$174,247,454

EXPORTS OF SPECIE AND BULLION.

1862.	1863.	1864.	1865.
$59,437,021	$49,754,066	$50,825,621	$30,003,683

TOTAL EXPORTS.

1862.	1863.	1864.	1865.
$216,371,843	$220,465,034	$272,648,163	$208,630,282

BANKING IN NEW YORK.

THE NEW YORK CLEARING HOUSE.

OPERATIONS OF THE YEAR 1865–1866.—AGGREGATE OPERATIONS OF THE THIRTEEN YEARS, 1853–1866.

This institution has been organized thirteen years, during which time its aggregate transactions have amounted to $158,070,344,871.33.

Its transactions for the year ending Oct. 1, 1866, were $29,783,282,020.44, being in excess of the year ending Oct. 1, 1865, $2,715,132,570.86; $4,800,366,159.59 greater than the year ending Oct. 1, 1864, and $17,624,024,722.65 more than the average for thirteen years.

The association numbers fifty-seven banks, with a capital of $81,777,000. Of this number, nine are organized under the banking laws of the State of New York, and the remainder (forty-nine) under the National Banking Law.

At the time of its organization, fifty-two banks composed the association, with an aggregate capital of $49,103,362; $32,666,638 less than its present capital.

The first weekly statement published by the associated banks was on October 15, 1853, and was as follows:

Capital, $49,103,362; *Loans and Discounts*, $87,837,273; *Specie*, $11,330,172; *Circulation and Net Deposits*, $46,900,212.

APPENDIX.

The statement on October 13, 1866, was:

Capital, $81,770,000; *Loans and Discounts,* $276,443,219; *Specie and Legal Tenders,* $88,756,424; *Circulation and Net Deposits,* $257,035,895.

The percentage of specie to net liabilities on October 15, 1853, was 24.16 per cent. The percentage of specie and legal tenders, October 13, 1866, was 34.53 per cent.

The circulation of the banks of the association, previous to the passage of the "National Currency Act," averaged about $8,000,000. The smallest amount of circulation reported in the weekly statement was $2,720,666, on March 4, 1865.

The largest amount was in the last statement, October 15, 1866, viz., $28,940,538, an increase of $26,219,872 in nineteen months.

The following banks are the only ones in the city that are not members of the association:

1. Dry Dock Bank.
2. Bull's Head Bank.
3. New York County Nat. Bank.
4. Fifth National Bank.
5. Sixth National Bank.
6. Eighth National Bank.
7. Manufacturers' National Bank.
8. American National Bank.
9. Croton National Bank.
10. Bowery National Bank.
11. National Currency Bank.
12. Wooster Sherman Bank.

Aggregate operations for thirteen years—October,1853, to October, 1866. I.—The aggregate exchanges. II.—The aggregate cash balances. III.—The average daily exchanges.

	Exchanges.	*Cash Balances Paid.*
Oct., 1853 to Oct., 1866..	$151,290,133,640 51	$6,780,211,230 82

	Average Daily Exchanges.	*Average Daily Bal.*
Oct., 1865 to Oct., 1866......	93,541,195 16	3,472,752 79

The Clearing House is one of the important financial institutions of the City of New York. The amount of labor, time, and expense saved to the banks by this medium is almost incalculable. In the first place, over twenty-five hundred accounts on the ledgers of the banks were instantly closed. The daily exchanges formerly occupied the time of one or two bank clerks five or six hours per day, accompanied with frequent disputes. Now the daily transactions of over one hundred millions are accomplished in one hour, and with perfect accuracy and satisfaction.—*J. S. Homans, Bankers' Magazine.*

RELATIVE VALUE OF THE REAL AND PERSONAL ESTATE
IN THE CITY AND COUNTY OF NEW YORK, AS ASSESSED IN 1865-66.

WARDS.	ASSESSMENTS OF 1865.	ASSESSMENTS OF 1866.	INCREASE.
First	35,249,250	40,077,550	4,828,300
Second	19,986,200	21,295,500	1,309,300
Third	25,722,800	28,559,900	2,837,100
Fourth	9,411,200	9,488,350	77,150
Fifth	21,217,300	22,182,900	965,600
Sixth	13,416,600	13,734,600	318,000
Seventh	12,417,599	12,562,799	145,200
Eighth	18,391,600	18,866,700	475,100
Ninth	15,940,200	16,295,600	355,400
Tenth	9,124,600	9,691,800	567,200
Eleventh	9,460,325	11,042,000	1,581,675
Twelfth	18,177,305	18,381,650	204,375
Thirteenth	5,553,400	5,645,700	92,300
Fourteenth	12,686,300	13,379,300	693,000
Fifteenth	28,277,000	31,570,300	3,293,300
Sixteenth	18,867,450	19,807,310	939,860
Seventeenth	18,768,200	22,022,300	3,254,100
Eighteenth	38,387,050	41,004,200	2,617,150
Nineteenth	23,070,940	37,636,050	14,565,110
Twentieth	18,177,900	18,990,910	813,010
Twenty-first	35,322,250	42,704,950	7,382,700
Twenty-second	19,825,515	24,052,715	4,227,200
Total	427,450,984	478,993,084	51,542,100
	PERSONAL ESTATE.	PERSONAL ESTATE.	PERSONAL ESTATE.
Resident	162,982,154	206,609,278	43,627,124
Non-Resident	18,441,317	51,385,696	32,944,379
Total	181,423,471	257,994,974	76,571,503

Total Real and Personal for 1865......................608,874,455
Total Real and Personal for 1866......................736,988,058

Total Increase...................................128,113,603

Total Valuation for 1865. 608,874,455
Total Valuation for 1866.............................736,988,058

Increase in 1866 128,113,603
Total Valuation in County.......................... 736,988,058

   A. J. WILLIAMSON,   *Commissioners*
   J. W. ALLEN,   *of*
   J. W. BROWN,   *Taxes and Assessments.*

APPENDIX.

This paper, from Colonel Andrew Warner, is important as illustrating the relation of Savings Banks to the property of the city and the credit of the nation.

ABSTRACT OF OFFICIAL REPORTS OF SAVINGS BANKS IN THE CITY OF NEW YORK, VIZ.:

Jan. 1.	No. of Banks.	Open Accounts.	Amount due Depositors.	INVESTMENTS.		Surplus.	Invested in Real Estate.
				Bonds and Mortgages.	Public Stocks.		
1855.	16	122,921	26,111,719 20	13,265,515 27	11,424,885		686,867 15
1856.	16	132,737	28,138,578 25	12,987,581 60	12,895,896 22		715,468 44
1858.	16	154,443	32,615,184 53	15,400,206 80	14,983,874 94	1,957,283 02	720,421 29
1859.	16	169,997	36,806,426 29	15,750,382 89	18,883,860 04	1,931,369 74	828,030 56
1860.	17	196,619	43,410,090 88	16,466,964 76	24,508,582 61	1,942,394 71	854,528 97
1861.	21	217,964	48,988,836 79	18,528,817 42	27,618,651 48	2,267,000 47	789,589 24
1862.	21	205,169	45,085,026 83	17,618,330 02	23,923,133 03	2,278,581 54	746,808 25
1863.	21	229,468	51,035,233 27	17,134,349 90	29,266,917 94	2,912,906 86	812,186 23
1864.	22	269,570	62,174,628 97	16,181,279 38	41,760,255 10	3,716,981 45	905,664 33
1865.	23	294,290	72,928,854 59	15,687,091 10	52,444,159 57	5,249,107 49	1,055,878 28
1866.	23	299,538	76,989,505 56	16,559,602 54	57,300,441 96	6,017,828 38	1,105,773 29

The first bank established in this city was the Bank for Savings, which commenced operations in Chambers Street, 3d July, 1819.

The Seamen's, the next chartered, in..........................1829
The Greenwich................   " 1833
The Bowery....................   " 1834
East River....................   " 1848
Inst. for Sav. Merch. Clerks.....   " 1848
Dry Dock.....................   " 1848
Manhattan....................   " 1850
Emigrant Industrial............   " 1850
Broadway....................   " 1851
Irving........................   " 1851
Mariners'....................   " 1852
Mechanics' and Traders'........   " 1852
Sixpenny.....................   " 1853
Bloomingdale.................   " 1854
Rose Hill.....................   " 1854
German.......................   " 1859
Union Dime..................   " 1859
Citizens'.....................   " 1860
Atlantic......................   " 1860
Franklin......................   " 1860
Harlem.......................   " 1863
Market.......................   " 1863
Peoples'.....................   " 1863

II. HEALTH OF THE CITY.

DEATHS IN 1865: GENERAL SUMMARY.

Total number of deaths reported in 1865, was..................24,843	Total number of adults............10,039
Divided thus:	Total number of children............14,804
White persons......................24,421	Total number of deceased persons..................24,843
Colored persons.................... 422	From which deduct:
Total..................24,843	Premature births...................233
	Malformations...................... 31
Male adults.........................5,433	Old age............................390
Male children......................7,902	Suicides, various.................. 42
	Casualties.........................352
Total males.................13,335	Drowned............................175
	Sunstroke.......................... 11
Female adults......................4,606	Burned or Scalded..................105
Female children...................6,902	Killed or Murdered................. 7
	Heat, effects of................... 3
Total females................11,508	Poison............................. 12
Total..................24,843	Total............................1,361
	Total number of deaths from disease..23,482
	Total............................24,843

N. B.—*Age for division of adults and children, 20 years.*

F. A. BOOLE, *City Inspector.*

LETTER FROM DR. ELISHA HARRIS.

To REV. S. OSGOOD, D. D.

DEAR SIR: The population of the City of New York, according to the Census of 1790, was, at the beginning of the last decennium of the 18th century, 33,131. In the year 1800, the Census returned 60,489, which showed an increase of 83 per cent. upon the city's population in 10 years. The next decennial period—the first of the present century—there was an increase of 59 per centum; but during the succeeding four years, a brief period of war, there was a *decrease* amounting to 1 per centum, or a retrogression of nearly 10,000 in the total population. Since that period there has been a steady and rapid increase in the population, until the commencement of the war of the Rebellion.

In a retrospective estimate of the state of the public health, the Mortuary Record is a trustworthy index, if we note the nature and fatality of each great epidemic visitation. The following statement, in columns of population, deaths, and death-rates on population, are authentic:

	Total percentage of the increase in population in the previous years.	Total population of the city.	Total mortality that year.	Death-rate estimated by number deaths in 1,000 of population.
1814	Decrease of about 0.1 in three years.	95,519	1,961	$20\frac{5}{9}$
1820	Increase in six years 30 per cent.	123,706	3,522	$28\frac{1}{2}$, Two epidemics.
1825	Increase in five years 34 per cent.	166,086	4,920	$23\frac{4}{5}$
1830	Increase in five years 19 per. cent.	197,112	5,522	28, One epidemic.
1835	Increase in five years 36 per cent.	268,089	7,096	$26\frac{1}{2}$
1840	Increase in five years 17 per cent.	312,710	8,469	$27\frac{1}{14}$
1845	Increase in five years 16 per cent.	371,223	9,652	26
1855	Increase in ten years 59 per cent.	629,810	24,448	$38\frac{5}{8}$, Including two epidemics of cholera, 9,000 killed.
1865	Increase in ten years 10.53 per ct.	726,354	25,767	$35\frac{4}{10}$

The accuracy or inaccuracy of the census returns need not be mentioned here. But we cannot fail to note the marked increase in the death-rate, year by year, for nearly twenty years past. This general increase of mortality must not be assumed to indicate a decrease in the expectation and length of life in the more favored classes of the population. There is reason to believe that all this increase of the death-rate is caused in particular classes of inhabitants. It is found to be mainly in those classes from which the paupers are derived, viz.: the ignorant and poor *classes*. Methods of classification, and analysis of causes of death at the various periods of life, are now so employed in the Bureau as to set forth, after a year or two, the actual conditions under which occur all the great excesses of mortality in the different classes and occupations, and at the several periods of life. Already we know that, as regards periods of life, the excess of mortality is in children under five years of age. The chances of life after that early period, are as good in New York as in most maritime cities.

London, Paris, and Liverpool are the chief great capitals with which the increase and movement of population, the physical influences of commerce and the trades, and the rates of mortality in New York can be justly compared; yet none of those cities feels so greatly the influence of a *foreign* and *unacclimated* element in the population.

In London, with a population, now, of 3,067,000 and upwards upon 121 square miles, the death-rate, for twelve or fourteen years, has not varied much from $23\frac{2}{3}$ per 1,000 annually. In Paris the death-rate is, year by year, about 1 in the 1,000 higher than that of London.

Liverpool last year had a death-rate of $36\frac{2}{3}$ per 1,000 inhabitants.

The city of Dublin, last year, had a death-rate of 28 per 1,000.

In the thirteen chief cities of Great Britain, the average rate is a little more than 24 per 1,000 annually. England and Wales suffer yearly a loss of $22\frac{1}{5}$ lives to every 1,000 inhabitants.

Austria, in 1853, buried $34\frac{1}{4}$ out of every 1,000; in 1858, $31\frac{2}{3}$; and in 1863 $31\frac{1}{10}$ to the 1,000 of her population.

France, in the same years, lost only 22, $24\frac{1}{8}$, and $22\frac{1}{2}$ to the 1,000 respectively.

Most of the countries of Europe have, for years, been increasing their population at the rate of about 1 *per cent.* per annum. The most rapidly growing capitals have increased at a much more rapid rate, but even London has less than half the average rate of population growth which New York has.

The standards of life-endurance in Europe are not high standards, though in cities they have risen to nearly double the length of European city lives two hundred years ago. Even in the notorious Parish of St. Giles, in London, a district has been so renovated the past ten years that the chances of life have more than doubled.

New York should have its own standard, and, with its healthful climate, and great advantages, the motto of its sanitary government should be EXCELSIOR.

In the Fifteenth Ward of this city, with a dense and well-mixed population, the present standard of life, in that ward, has, for six years, averaged nearly twice as high as the average of the city. The mean death-rate in the ward has been but 17 per 1,000. And in this epidemic year, life has been more secure in that ward than ever before, the death-rate having thus far been as 16 per 1,000 annually.

Let me express the belief that, unless sanitary science and social improvements are delusions, New York will, at some future day, contain a population of 2,000,000, and the metropolitan district 4,000,000, *with a death-rate not exceeding* 16 per 1,000 annually,—but half the present rate!

Our war has demonstrated the wonderful endurance and vitality of the *American man*. The metropolis of our country can yet present the healthiest of all the crowded populations; for all the resources of sanitary science and medicine have become tributary to social progress in the civilization and Christianity of our day.

With highest regard, I remain, very truly yours,

E. HARRIS.

BUREAU OF RECORDS AND VITAL STATISTICS,
METROPOLITAN BOARD OF HEALTH, *November 19th*, 1866.

MORTALITY OF THE CITY OF NEW YORK IN 1864 AND 1865.

YEAR.	1864.	1865.	
Total	25,645	24,843	Decrease....802
Males	13,662	13,335	" 327
Females	11,983	11,508	" ...445
Men	5,959	5,433	" ...526
Women	5,114	4,606	" ...508
Adults	11,073	10,039	" ...1,034
Children	14,572	14,804	Increase....232
" under 1 year	6,058	6,217	" ...159

Ratio to 1,000 living in 1864, 23.7; in 1863, 25.1; decrease, 1.4.

These returns indicate the city to have been entirely free from any epidemic or even endemic, and the general health to have been unusually good.

A TABLE, *showing the total* DEATHS *from* 1850 *to* 1866, *also the number of* ADULTS, CHILDREN, *and* CHILDREN *under one year of age who died in the same period.*

Year.	Deaths.	Adults.	Children.	Children under 1 year.
1851	21,748	7,775	13,973	6,891
1852	20,296	8,002	12,294	6,351
1853	21,137	8,124	13,003	6,661
1854	26,953	10,681	16,271	7,551
1855	21,478	7,289	14,189	6,771
1856	20,102	6,769	14,889	6,437
1857	21,775	7,558	14,217	6,905
1858	22,196	8,081	14,105	7,109
1859	21,645	8,182	13,463	6,599
1860	22,710	8,752	13.958	6,087
1861	22,117	8,503	13,614	6,189
1862	21,244	8,618	12,626	5,720
1863	25,196	10,596	14,600	6,118
1864	25,645	11,073	14,572	6,058
1865	24,843	10,039	14,804	6,217

CHOLERA MORTALITY DURING SIX YEARS.

Year.	January.	February.	March.	April.	May.	June.	Total for six months.
1861......	22	21	15	23	29	66	176
1862......	18	22	34	26	32	68	199
1863......	49	27	23	36	60	69	267
1864......	51	36	38	58	54	111	348
1865......	41	46	37	40	45	141	350
1866	55	33	45	90	84	196	598
Total..	236	190	195	272	304	651	1,848

The number of deaths in the Cholera Hospitals is stated to have been:

In the Battery Hospital..............................109
In the Red House Hospital........................ 32

Total........... 141

DEATHS IN THE CITY BY WARDS.

The following table shows the number of deaths from cholera in this city, by wards, from May 1 to December 1, 1866, inclusive, showing the rate of those deaths to the 10,000 inhabitants living:

Wards.	Total..............	Total population (in wards,) census of 1865...	Total cases of cholera to 10,000 people...........	Rate of population to square mile	Total cholera deaths, in each ward, including fatal cases sent to cholera hospitals...............	Total deaths, (inclusive of cholera hospital cases) to 10,000 inhabitants.....
First...............	14	9,852	14	41,010	37	$37\frac{1}{2}$
Second.............	2	1,154	$16\frac{3}{4}$	9,950	2	$16\frac{3}{4}$
Third...............	1	3,367	$2\frac{3}{4}$	22,447	2	$5\frac{9}{10}$
Fourth..............	25	17,352	$14\frac{1}{4}$	133,477	38	$29\frac{9}{10}$
Fifth................	12	18,205	$6\frac{1}{2}$	69,904	18	$9\frac{1}{5}$
Sixth................	90	19,754	$45\frac{1}{2}$	151,954	125	$63\frac{1}{4}$
Seventh.............	18	36,962	$4\frac{3}{4}$	119,232	22	$5\frac{9}{10}$
Eighth..............	19	30,098	$6\frac{1}{4}$	103,786	22	$7\frac{3}{10}$
Ninth...............	12	38,504	3	77,004	14	$3\frac{6}{10}$
Tenth...............	13	31,537	4	185,512	14	$4\frac{2}{5}$
Eleventh...........	13	58,953	2	196,510	13	2
Twelfth............	25	28,259	$8\frac{3}{4}$	5,195	39	$13\frac{4}{5}$
Thirteenth..........	10	26,388	$3\frac{3}{4}$	155,224	10	$3\frac{3}{4}$
Fourteenth.........	28	23,382	$11\frac{3}{4}$	155,880	37	$15\frac{4}{5}$
Fifteenth	3	25,572	1	82,490	4	$1\frac{1}{2}$
Sixteenth...........	14	41,972	$3\frac{1}{4}$	69,953	15	$3\frac{6}{10}$
Seventeenth........	22	79,563	$2\frac{3}{4}$	153,656	24	3
Eighteenth..........	10	47,613	2	51,197	11	$2\frac{3}{10}$
Nineteenth	20	39,945	5	16,713	25	$6\frac{1}{4}$
Twentieth..........	33	61,884	$5\frac{1}{4}$	91,006	35	$5\frac{2}{3}$
Twenty-first........	8	38,669	2	52,255	8	2
Twenty-second	66	47,361	$23\frac{3}{4}$	21,334	76	16
Total.........	458	726,385	$6\frac{1}{4}$	43,364	591	$8\frac{1}{10}$

JUNE, JULY, AUGUST, AND SEPTEMBER.

Of the 342 persons who died from cholera, in the months of June, July, August, and September, there were born in Ireland, 190; United States, 73; Germany, 36; England, 21; Scotland, 5; France, 4; Sweden, 3; Canada, 2; China, 1; Italy, 1; Australia, 1; at sea, 1; not stated, 2.

The ages at which these 342 persons died were as follows:

Years.	Number of persons.	Years.	Number of persons.
10 to 15	3	45 to 50	32
15 to 20	13	50 to 55	25
20 to 25	39	55 to 60	24
25 to 30	47	60 to 65	16
30 to 35	50	65 to 70	12
35 to 40	37	75 to 80	2
40 to 45	41	80 to 85	1

OCCUPATION OF THE DEAD.

Among the persons who died in the four months last alluded to, 88 are returned as "laborers," 65 as "domestics," 16 as "housekeepers," &c.

CHOLERA DEATHS IN THE PUBLIC INSTITUTIONS.

The following statement gives the number of deaths from cholera in the public institutions of New York from July 7 to December 1, 1866:

Ward's Island, 172; Workhouse, Blackwell's Island, 151; Almshouse, Blackwell's Island, 95; Charity Hospital, Blackwell's Island, 41; New York City Lunatic Asylum, Blackwell's Island, 74; Penitentiary, Blackwell's Island, 6; Randall's Island, 20; Bellevue Hospital, 33; New York Hospital, 3; City Prison, 2; Castle Garden, 3; Fort Columbus, New York Hospital, 2; Small-pox Hospital, Blackwell's Island, 2; Colored Home, 1; Nursery and Child's Hospital, 8; Battery Hospital, 107; Red House Hospital, 32. Total, 752.

CHOLERA GROUPS.

From the list of streets in which fatal cholera cases occurred, we extract all numbering over five, as follows:

Baxter Street, 35; Broadway, 9; Cherry Street, 8; Franklin Street, 6; Greenwich Street, 10; Mott Street, 15; Mulberry Street, 67; Ninth Avenue, 7; Third Avenue, 10; Thomas Street, 6; Washington Street, 17; Water Street, 6; West Twenty-sixth Street, 9; West Forty-first Street, 7; West Fifty-fourth Street, 7; West Sixty-seventh Street, 6.

APPENDIX. 81

The total number of houses in which the deaths occurred at home and in the cholera hospital, was 440.

The number of houses in which only one death occurred, was 362.
The number of houses in which two deaths occurred, was 61.
The number of houses in which three deaths occurred, was 16.
The number of houses in which four or more deaths occurred, was 10.

SANITARY DEDUCTION.

The progressing demands and appliances of sanitary science went beyond such general and vague, though practical and just, conclusions. But it was not until the results of the more exactly defined experiences and researches in the epidemics of 1854, 1859 and 1865 in Europe had been logically analyzed and compared, that this most valuable of all conclusions was reached, namely: That the diarrhœal excreta of the sick when impregnating the soil, the drinking water, or any kind of decomposing matter, especially that of privies, cesspools, sewers, drains, and the ground about dwelling houses, constitute the positive, the chief, and, for aught that is yet known, the only means for propagating and spreading Asiatic cholera.

BOARD OF HEALTH.

December 4th, 1864.

DEAR SIR: Enclosed I send you an extract from the forthcoming report of the Board of Health, which will give some idea of the kind and amount of detailed labor which it has performed in the eight months since its organization. Yet, without far greater space than you can afford, you can give but a meagre idea of its great and varied labors and influences.

The extent to which it has coerced and stimulated the public schools and other institutional authorities of the district, to regard sanitary laws; the efficient manner in which it has compelled offal and garbage contractors to discharge their duties; the powerful stimulant it has been to landlords to put their buildings in better order for poor tenants; the suppression of cattle-driving in the day-time in this city; the great controlment of the slaughtering of animals in New York; the important fact that it has caused some of the largest abattoirs to be built in the open country, some miles distant; the better care it has caused to be taken to prevent the spread of typhoid and ship fever; above all, its effectual and energetic treatment of cholera; the noble exhausting and self-sacrificing labors of the commissions, during the hot summer months, worth so much as a public example, are not alluded to in the extract, nor, I think, have you any space for them.

82   APPENDIX.

Considering the embarrassments the Board has had to encounter, the suddenness with which the cholera came, the work done, I think its full record in its report will be one of which New York may be proud.   Yours, very truly,   D. B. EATON.

The first orders of the Board were issued on the 14th of March, between which date and the 1st of November, 31,077 orders were issued, and were duly served by the Sanitary Police. Of these orders, 5,325 were under the *first subdivision* of Section 14, of Chapter 74, of the Session Laws of 1866, by the terms of which the party served is allowed three days in which to demand a " *hearing* " by the Board of the testimony which may be presented to show that the order should be revoked and not enforced. In cases where no hearing has been asked for, and the order has not been obeyed by the proper party, "*final*" orders in the original or an amended form, to the number of 3,160, have been issued and forwarded to the Board of Metropolitan Police for execution. All other written orders, in number 22,592, have been issued under the *second subdivision* of Section 14, of Chapter 74, of the Session Laws of 1866, and are of a peremptory character, requiring that the nuisance be abated within five days, and, if not obeyed, directing the Board of Metropolitan Police to enforce the same without further notice. The following is a statement of the subjects of the orders above referred to, other than the "*final*" orders, and of the work performed in the execution of the same, either by the party upon whom the order was served, or by the Metropolitan Board of Police, or by the officers or agents of this Board.

We select the principal items of the work done by the Board from the full list of 180 classes of work:

Alleys cleaned..............	381
Ashes, garbage, and rubbish removed..................	1,335
Areas cleaned..............	701
Basements cleaned.........	230
" whitewashed...	66
Bone and offal boiling (business of) discontinued....	12
Cellars cleaned............	3,067
" connected with sewer...............	62
" filled................	182
" whitewashed........	653
Cesspools cleaned..........	686
" connected with sewer..........	45
" disinfected.......	56
" emptied..........	25
" filled............	111
Cesspools made............	131
" repaired.........	28
Cisterns cleaned and emptied............	771
" disinfected.......	76
" filled.............	328
" repaired..........	38
Cows removed (No. of orders)..................	110
Ditches cut................	49
Drains cleaned.............	38
" made.............	136
" (obstructions in) removed............	99
" repaired............	138
Fat boiling (business of) discontinued...............	54
Halls cleaned...............	260
" whitewashed.........	161

APPENDIX.   83

Hide curing and storing (business of) discontinued	15
Hydrants repaired	159
Hydrant-waste drained, &c.	209
Leaders repaired	254
Lime burning (business of) discontinued	6
Lots cleaned	479
" filled	143
" graded	57
Manure removed	991
" vaults cleaned	22
" " constructed	492
" " (covers for) made	38
" " repaired	53
Market stalls removed	128
Offal boiling (business of) discontinued	1
Oil manufacturing (business of) discontinued	1
Packing rancid butter (business of) discontinued	1
Pickles manufacturing (business of) discontinued	2
Piers cleaned	30
" repaired	18
Pigs' feet and tripe boiling (business of) discontinued	2
Pig-pens cleaned	299
Pigs removed (No. of orders)	381
Pipe (water, waste, and hydrant) obstructions removed	46
Pipes (waste) cleaned	149
" " repaired	427
" (water) "	248
Plastering removed and walls re-plastered	47
Ponds filled	42
Premises cleaned	2,581
" disinfected and fumigated	194
" connected with the sewer	521
" whitewashed	871
Privies disinfected	6,418
" emptied and cleaned	15,214
Privy houses removed	31
" " repaired	195
" seats repaired	44
" sinks connected with sewer	2,056
Privy sinks filled	577
" " made	2,085
" vaults repaired	442
Privies built	4
Rags removed	78
Rag sorting and cleaning (business of) discontinued	6
Sausage case and gut cleaning (business of) discontinued	13
Sausage and tripe manufacturing (business of) discontinued	11
Sewers built	28
" cleaned	157
Sewer connections cleaned	136
Sewers repaired	338
Sewer pipes (obstructions in) removed	1,493
Sewer pipes repaired	505
Sidewalks repaired	130
Sinks emptied and cleaned	2,625
Slaughtering (business of) discontinued	36
Slaughter houses cleaned	20
Soap boiling (business of) discontinued	5
Spaces (vacant) cleaned	162
" disinfected	11
Stables cleaned	657
" disinfected	6
Stagnant water removed	354
Stairways cleaned	68
" repaired	30
Streets cleaned	17
" (obstructions in) removed	78
Superphosphate lime manufacturing (business of) discontinued	4
Swill boiling (business of) discontinued	7
Tanks constructed	24
Varnish manufacturing (business of) discontinued	3
Vaults cleaned	95
Walls and ceilings repaired	18
Water closets cleaned	413
" " repaired	66
" " and urinals constructed	45
Yards cleaned	3,949
" graded and repaired	245

III. CRIME IN NEW YORK.

Nativity of those arrested, classified for the year ending Oct. 31st, 1865.

Nativity.	Num.	Nativity.	Num.
United States (white)	21,852	Sweden	86
" (black)	1,184	Norway	31
Ireland	32,867	Hungary	13
Germany	7,162	Wales	46
England	2,819	Mexico	4
France	639	Bermuda	3
Scotland	901	Greece	2
Spain	57	Nova Scotia	44
Russia	24	Portugal	13
Prussia	87	Bohemia	5
Austria	18	Cuba	35
Canada	409	South America	12
Holland	25	Sandwich Islands	1
Italy	189	China	7
Denmark	43	Bavaria	1
Poland	139	Turkey	1
British Provinces	61	Africa	1
East Indies	11	Sicily	1
West Indies	29		
Belgium	11	Total number of arrests	68,873
Switzerland	40		

Recapitulation of Offences against the Person for the year ending October 31st, 1865.

Offences against person.	Males.	Fem's.	Total.	Offences against person	Males.	Fem's.	Total.
Assault	106	14	120	Insanity	304	184	488
Assault and Battery	6,077	1,667	7,744	Interfering with policemen	178	14	192
Assault with intent to kill	197	1	198	Insulting females in the streets	18	....	18
Assault, felonious	546	54	600	Indecent exposure of the person	116	3	119
Assault on policemen	36	....	36	Intoxication	11,482	4,936	16,418
Abandonment	253	5	258	Intoxication and disorderly conduct	4,866	2,445	7,311
Accessory to murder	9	....	9	Juvenile delinquents	154	25	179
Aiding prisoner to escape	5	1	6	Kidnapping	20	5	25
Attempt at rape	40	....	40	Libel	5	....	5
Abduction	3	....	3	Miscellaneous misdemeanors	80	34	114
Abortion	2	2	4	Maiming	14	....	14
Attachment or bench warrant	100	40	140	Personating policemen	16	....	16
Bastardy	141	....	141	Runaway apprentices	10	12	22
Bigamy	14	5	19	Rescuing prisoners	18	2	20
Contempt of Court	23	6	29	Rape	38	....	38
Carrying concealed weapons	58	1	59	Suspicious persons	1,617	440	2,057
Disorderly conduct	8,542	5,412	13,050	Seduction	21	....	21
Deserters	254	....	254	Sodomy	5	....	5
Escaped convicts	95	4	99	Threatening life	88	8	96
Fighting in streets	613	94	767	Trespassing	9	....	9
Fugitives from justice	5	1	6	Truancy	188	18	206
Habitual drunkards	52	139	191	Vagrancy	978	838	1,816
Homicides in all degrees	65	4	69	Witnesses	28	8	36

Offences against the person.................37,489 16,422 53,911

APPENDIX.

Recapitulation of Offences against Property for the year ending October 31st, 1865.

Offences against property	Males.	Fem's.	Total.	Offences against property	Males.	Fem's.	Total.
Arson	35	....	35	Obtaining goods by false pretences	108	23	131
Attempt to steal	236	9	245	Offences against the Government	122	2	124
Attempt at burglary	53	....	53	Picking pockets	255	20	275
Burglary	291	3	294	Petit larceny	3,380	1,860	5,240
Constructive larceny	43	12	55	Perjury	14	....	14
Conspiracy	6	....	6	Passing counterfeit money	414	46	460
Compounding felony	2	....	2	Rece v'g stolen g'ds	166	51	217
Embezzlement	42	....	42	Robbery, first degree	109	6	115
Forgery	151	3	154	Rioting	10	....	10
Fraud	104	17	121	Smuggling	5	....	5
Forfeited bail	7	....	7	Shoplifting	5	3	8
Felony	2	....	2	Swindling	104	3	107
Grand larceny	1,675	946	2,621	Violations of corporation ordinances	2,417	415	2,832
Gambling	249	3	252	Violations of the Sunday law	183	20	203
Highway Robbery	199	6	205	Violations of the election law	30	....	30
Horse stealing	6	....	6	Violations of the State law	75	1	76
Keeping disorderly house	177	165	342				
Larceny upon the person	102	35	127				
Mutiny	52	....	52				
Malicious mischief	436	48	484				
Offences against property					11,265	3,697	14,962
Offences against the person					37,489	16,422	53,911
Total number of arrests					48,754	20,119	68,873

HOUSE OF REFUGE.

The last report states that the whole number of children received into the House of Refuge since its opening in 1825, is 10,853.

That the number of children in the House on the 1st day of January, 1865, was... 718
That there have been received during the year 1865............... 824

Making a total of..1,542
That there have been indentured and discharged during the year.. 603

And there remain in the House on the 1st of January, 1866...... 939

The Superintendent's statement thereto annexed contains all the particulars required by the act referred to, as to the sources from which the inmates of the House have been received, and the disposition that has been made of them, as well as many other facts and statistics of interest in the history of the institution during the past year.

The very large increase in the number of the children committed to the House, being nearly fifty per cent. on the number committed during 1864, and about seventy-five per cent. on the average of three years preceding, is a fact calculated to excite inquiry.

IV. PUBLIC CHARITIES AND CORRECTION.

SIXTH ANNUAL REPORT OF THE COMMISSIONERS OF PUBLIC CHARITIES AND CORRECTION FOR THE YEAR 1865.

BOARD OF COMMISSIONERS OF PUBLIC CHARITIES AND CORRECTION.

Isaac Bell, *President*,   James B. Nicholson,
James Bowen,   Owen W. Brennan.

The Institutions in charge of the Commissioners are the

City Prison in the City of New York,
Bellevue Hospital   "   "
Small Pox and Fever Hospitals, Blackwell's Island,
Island Hospital,   "   "
Penitentiary,   "   "
Alms Houses,   "   "
Work House,   "   "
Lunatic Asylum,   "   "
Children's Nurseries, Randall's Island,
City Cemetery and Farm, Ward's Island.

The Colored Home and Colored Orphan Asylum in the city of New York are under the supervision of the Commissioners, though in direct charge of their respective Boards of Managers.

Detailed statements of the expenses for maintaining the several institutions will be found in the tables accompanying this report, but they may be generally classified as follows:

Provisions	$314,186 29
Clothing, Beds, and Bedding	63,148 20
Medicines	38,055 07
Coal and Wood	105,031 77
Erection of New Buildings	39,868 72
Repairs—Buildings	6,082 16
Salaries	139,073 81
Steamboat	29,809 38
Donations to Out-Door Poor	32,438 75
Colored Orphan Asylum and Nursing Children	20,712 62
Furniture	6,307 08

Hardware, Steam and Gas Fixtures	$15,198	69
Rents	7,549	79
Lumber and Mason Work	14,102	99
Plumbing, Paints, etc	5,292	86
Leather and Shoes	10,670	81
Soap	8,882	28
Stationery, Printing, and Advertising	10,646	77
Transportation of Prisoners and Paupers	7,140	58
Miscellaneous	68,134	80
	$942,243	42

CITY PRISONS.

The total number of prisoners who were committed to the city prisons during the past year was thirty-nine thousand six hundred and sixteen (39,616), being an increase over the previous year of eight thousand three hundred and eighty-three (8,383). The increase has been principally among the prisoners who were charged with high crimes.

NATIVITY OF THE PRISONERS COMMITTED DURING THE YEAR 1865.	MALES.	FEMALES.	TOTAL.
Ireland	10,638	8,998	19,636
United States	8,111	4,199	12,310
Germany	3,195	1,210	4,405
England	1,076	560	1,636
Scotland	369	171	540
Canada	220	99	319
France	268	35	303
Italy	113	6	119
Prussia	49	..	49
Poland	49	..	49
Sweden	42	..	42
Switzerland	29	1	30
Denmark	29	..	29
Wales	24	4	28
Cuba	24	1	25
Spain	22	2	24
Austria	20	..	20
Russia	14	1	15
Norway	14	..	14
Portugal	8	..	8
China	6	..	6
Greece	6	..	6
Mexico	3	..	3
Total	24,329	15,287	39,616

BELLEVUE HOSPITAL.

The number of Patients remaining in Hospital, January 1st, 1865, 648
The number of admissions for the year (including 590 births) were...6,425

The total number of patients treated during the year......7,073

The number discharged, cured, and relieved for the year were....5,801
The number of deaths for the year were........................ 658

6,459

The number of Patients remaining in Hospital under treatment, December 31st, 1865..................... 614

NATIVITY OF THOSE ADMITTED,

INCLUDING BIRTHS.

COUNTRY.	MEN.	WOMEN.	BOYS.	GIRLS.	BIRTHS.		TOTAL.
					BOYS.	GIRLS.	
United States.......	676	601	21	15	297	293	1,903
Ireland............	1,603	1,844	..	..	..	..	3,447
England...........	147	126	..	..	..	..	273
Scotland	61	43	..	..	..	..	104
Germany	323	148	..	..	..	..	471
France............	41	11	..	..	..	..	52
Canada............	40	24	..	..	..	..	64
Wales	2	2	..	..	..	..	4
Belgium...........	3	1	..	..	..	..	4
Italy..............	5	..	..	..	..	..	5
Prussia........ ..	6	1	..	..	..	..	7
Spain..............	3	..	..	..	..	..	3
At Sea	1	..	..	..	..	..	1
Unknown Countries.	15	3	..	..	..	..	18
Other Countries....	51	18	..	..	..	..	69
Total...........	2,977	2,822	21	15	297	293	6,425

ISLAND, FEVER, AND SMALL POX HOSPITALS.

During the year both Hospitals have been over-crowded with patients, and the experience of the past will justify your Board in making further provision for the care of Small Pox and Typhus Fever patients.

The Island Hospital, with its pavilion and tents, has received during the year 8,893 patients, the whole number treated in the same period being 9,877.

In February the number of fever cases under treatment at one time was 155; the whole number treated during the year was 1,330. A large item in the expenses of Island Hospital was caused by the erection of the building and maintenance of these fever patients.

There has been received and treated in Small Pox Hospital 1,116 patients, an increase of 397 over the number treated during 1864.

Of this number, 358 were emigrants, 48 United States soldiers, and 620 residents of New York city.

PENITENTIARY.

The health of the prisoners generally, for the past year, has been very good. The number of convicts is large compared with last year. On December, 1864, there were 280, and at the close of 1865, 596.

The following Table shows the Crimes committed by the Male and Female Convicts received from 1st of January to 31st December, 1865, inclusive:

CRIMES.	MALES.	FEMALES.	TOTAL.
Assault.	40	..	40
Assault and Battery	215	166	381
Assault with intent to steal	196	23	219
Disorderly House	18	5	23
Grand Larceny	82	52	134
Grand Larceny, attempt at	105	68	173
Indecent Assault and Battery	15	..	15
Indecent Exposure of Person	13	..	13
Manslaughter, fourth degree	2	..	2
Petit Larceny	398	260	658
Forgery, fourth degree	3	..	3
Forgery, third degree	1	..	1
Illegal Voting	8	..	8
Total	1,096	574	1,670

The following Table shows the Nativities of the Male and Female Convicts received from 1st January to 31st December, 1865, inclusive:

NATIVITIES.	MALES.	FEMALES.	TOTAL.
United States	235	135	370
England	193	71	264
Ireland	355	240	595
Scotland	31	16	47
Canada	35	14	49
France	38	5	43
Prussia	35	2	37
Germany	159	91	250
Spain	15	..	15
Total	1,096	574	1,670

WORK HOUSE.

Census for the Year.

	MALES.	FEMALES.	TOTAL.
Number on hand December 31st, 1864	217	1,016	1,233
Number received during the year	4,100	7,013	11,113
Total	4,317	8,029	12,346

	MALES.	FEMALES.			
Number discharged	3,691	6,835			
Number eloped from this and other Institutions	187	295	3,917	7,170	11,087
Number died at this and other Institutions	39	40			
Number remaining on Register			400	859	1,259
And of this number there are transferred to other departments, at work, sick, etc			97	390	487
Leaving in building			303	469	772

The daily average number of inmates for the year was $772\frac{227}{365}$, showing a decrease of $111\frac{332}{365}$ since the previous year.

ALMS HOUSE.

The following is a comparative Statement of Admissions during the last ten years.

	NATIVES.	FOREIGNERS.	TOTAL.
There were admitted in 1856	723	2,636	3,359
" " 1857	875	3,329	4,204
" " 1858	794	3,096	3,890
" " 1859	718	3,013	3,731
" " 1860	985	3,144	4,129
" " 1861	1,537	3,255	4,792
" " 1862	1,199	1,992	3,191
" " 1863	1,201	1,642	2,843
" " 1864	1,262	1,891	3,153
" " 1865	1,378	2,212	3,590

CHILDREN'S NURSERIES, RANDALL'S ISLAND.

	ADULTS.	CHILDREN.	TOTAL.
Remaining December 31st, 1864,	156	823	979
Admitted, 1865	143	1,544	1,687
	299	2,367	2,666
Discharged	122	1,463	1,585
	177	904	1,081
Elopements		8	8
	177	896	1,073
Died	4	113	117
Remaining December 31st, 1865	173	783	956

CHILDREN TAKEN FOR INDENTURE.
Boys........160
Girls........ 97
———— 257

CHILDREN RETURNED TO RELATIVES.
Boys........775
Girls........431
———— 1,206

1,463

APPENDIX.

NURSERY HOSPITAL.

Number of patients remaining January 1st, 1865					164
"	"	admitted during the year			1,582
"	"	treated	"	"	1,746
"	"	discharged	"	"	1,421
"	"	died	"	"	113
"	"	remaining January 1st, 1866			212

Included in the above summary of deaths are seventeen idiots, who were treated and who died in the Asylum. The whole number of deaths in the Hospital during the year is 96.

The percentage of mortality on the number treated is $5\frac{44}{100}$. The average weekly census has been $212\frac{20}{52}$.

COLORED ORPHAN ASYLUM.

STATISTICS.

Admitted since the opening of the Institution	1,884
Number of children at date of last report	209
Admitted: boys ... 39	
girls ... 35	
	74
	283
Present number of boys	119
" " girls	103
	222
Indentured	34
Returned to friends	10
Sent to Rhode Island to school, by Mrs. Stokes	2
Left without permission	1
Sent to the House of Refuge	3
Deaths	11
	283

COLORED HOME.

There have been received during the year (including those on hand at last report) 516 inmates, of which number 299 have been discharged, or have died, leaving at present 217 in the Institution.

LUNATIC ASYLUM.

The number of patients at the beginning of the year was 759. There were admitted during the year 525, making a total of 1,284. Of these, 127, or ten per cent., died, and 421 were discharged, leaving 736 at present in the Asylum.

Of those discharged, 142 were unimproved, 83 were improved, 192 had fully recovered, and 4 were improper subjects.

Of those admitted, 37 had attempted suicide previous to admission. Of these attempts, 11 had been by jumping from heights, 8 by drowning, 9 by cutting and stabbing, and the remainder by other means. A number of others were supposed to have suicidal propensities, although no attempt was known to have been made. Only two serious attempts at suicide were made at the Asylum—one by hanging and one by drowning. These occurred in cases shortly after admission, and were, unfortunately, both successful.

Of those admitted, 133 were native-born, and 362 were foreign. Of the foreign-born, 235 were from Ireland, 95 from Germany, 28 from England, and the rest from other countries: 280 Catholics, 224 Protestants, and 21 Jews.

OUT-DOOR POOR.

SUPERINTENDENT OF OUT-DOOR POOR.

NEW YORK, December 31st, 1865.

To the Commissioners of Public Charities and Correction:

GENTLEMEN:—The Superintendent of Out-Door Poor respectfully presents the accompanying statistics for the year ending December 31st, 1865, and by which it will appear that 3,743 adults and 7,462 children have been relieved by donations in money, and 15,481 adults and 25,572 children with fuel.

The total amount of cash disbursed by me for all purposes of the Department from 1st January to 31st December, 1865, was $102,783 24. A comparison with the years 1863 and 1864 is herewith presented:

	1863.	1864.	1865.
Donations, including Twelfth, Nineteenth, and Twenty-second Wards	$33,073 00	$39,957 97	$32,438 75
Children's Nursing	3,160 35	3,458 00	3,659 75
Transportation of Paupers and Children	2,269 15	2,198 17	1,583 65
Salaries	11,885 82	12,082 72	12,538 63
Coal, and Wood, and Cartage for 1865, including Twelfth, Nineteenth, and Twenty-second Wards	25,375 91	38,834 18	41,709 23
Expenses of Office, extra compensation, 1865, $1,975 stables, feed, horses, stationery, fuel, coffins, etc.	9,049 57	3,592 43	10,853 23
	$84,813 80	$100,123 47	$102,783 24
Less cash receipts	2,902 25	3,155 00	4,059 00
	$82,911 15	$96,968 47	$98,724 24

V. EDUCATION.

RECAPITULATION *of the Average Attendance and Whole Number Taught, for the year ending December 31, 1865.*

SCHOOLS.	AVERAGE.	WHOLE NUMBER.
Grammar Schools and Primary Departments	58,911	140,629
Primary Schools	15,255	38,155
Colored Schools	795	2,112
Evening Schools	11,487	24,056
Free Academy	......	788
Normal School	226	569
Total Ward, etc. Schools	86,674	206,309
New York Orphan Asylum	158	183
Roman Catholic Orphan Asylum	807	904
Protestant Half-Orphan Asylum	186	200
House of Refuge	840	1,475
Leake and Watts Orphan House	142	164
Colored Orphan Asylum	180	241
American Female Guardian Society and Home Industrial School	794	2,941
New York Juvenile Asylum	563	1,032
House of Reception of "	129	839
Ladies' Home Missionary Society	273	1,117
Five Points House of Industry	327	1,664
Children's Aid Society	784	2,680
Total	91,857	219,749

RECAPITULATION *of the Actual Average Attendance and Whole Number Taught by Wards, for the year ending the 31st day of December, 1865.*

WARDS.	ACTUAL AVERAGE.	WHOLE NUMBER TAUGHT.	WARDS.	ACTUAL AVERAGE.	WHOLE NUMBER TAUGHT.
First Ward	1,424	3,228	Thirteenth Ward	3,328	8,458
Second Ward	225	473	Fourteenth Ward	2,451	6,220
Third Ward	179	336	Fifteenth Ward	3,462	7,657
Fourth Ward	1,977	5,282	Sixteenth Ward	4,724	10,055
Fifth Ward	2,083	4,641	Seventeenth Ward	5,287	13,587
Sixth Ward	2,618	6,367	Eighteenth Ward	3,438	8,270
Seventh Ward	3,145	8,062	Nineteenth Ward	2,839	7,501
Eighth Ward	3,216	7,462	Twentieth Ward	6,114	18,942
Ninth Ward	4,635	10,929	Twenty-first Ward	3,783	9,032
Tenth Ward	5,144	12,485	Twenty-second Ward	5,560	13,495
Eleventh Ward	5,591	13,448			
Twelfth Ward	3,738	9,966	Total	74,961	180,896

APPENDIX.

EVENING SCHOOLS.

Average Attendance and Whole Number Taught in the Evening Schools for the year ending the 31st day of December, 1865.

WARDS.	MALE SCHOOLS.		FEMALE SCHOOLS.	
	AVERAGE.	WHOLE NUMBER.	AVERAGE.	WHOLE NUMBER.
First	192	607	199	360
Fourth	164	349	234	435
Fifth	320	684	173	456
Sixth	236	595	187	224
Seventh	243	596	127	213
Eighth	339	753	188	363
Ninth	336	1,251	201	471
Tenth	377	895	206	356
Eleventh	451	1,287	354	530
Twelfth, Harlem	110	287	32	65
" Yorkville	99	215	55	70
" Manhattanville	93	269	No Female	School.
Thirteenth	243	951	194	195
Fourteenth	311	746	236	359
Sixteenth	370	842	225	275
Seventeenth, Houston Street	464	894	360	439
" Twelfth Street	384	547	232	316
Eighteenth	361	926	182	252
Nineteenth	310	424	98	141
Twentieth	390	907	276	462
Twenty-first	316	850	277	433
Twenty-second, Fortieth Street	222	571	197	401
" Forty-fourth Street	352	594	No Female	School.
" Forty-seventh Street	254	565	175	233
Eighth, Colored	70	245	....	....
Sixteenth, "	72	157	....	....
	7,079	17,007	4,408	7,049

Average attendance—Male and Female Schools 11,487
Whole Number Taught " " " 24,057

CORPORATE SCHOOLS.

SCHOOLS.	NUMBER OF SESSIONS.	AVERAGE ATTENDANCE	WHOLE NUMBER.
New York Orphan Asylum	492	158	183
Roman Catholic Orphan Asylum—			
Male Department	494	449	502
Female "	493	358	402
Protestant Half-Orphan Asylum	60	186	200
House of Refuge—			
Male Department	506	673	1,119
Female "	506	167	356
Leake and Watts Orphan House—			
Male Department	231	74	85
Female "	468	68	79
Colored Orphan Asylum	500	180	241
American Female Guardian Society and Home Industrial School	459	794	2,941
New York Juvenile Asylum	573	563	1,032
House of Reception of "	514	129	859
Ladies' Home Missionary Society	482	273	1,117
Five Points House of Industry	512	327	1,664
Children's Aid Society	4,694	784	2,680
Total	....	5,183	13,440

Average Attendance and Whole Number Taught, in detail, for the year ending the 31st day of December, 1865.

SCHOOLS.	AVERAGE.	WHOLE NUMBER.
Ward Schools—Boys' Department	13,437	29,469
" Girls' "	12,439	26,306
" Primary "	33,035	84,854
Primary Schools	15,255	38,155
Colored Schools	795	2,112
Evening Schools—Male	7,079	17,007
" Female	4,408	7,049
Free Academy	......	788
Normal Schools	226	569
Corporate Schools	5,183	13,440
Total	91,857	219,749

STATE SCHOOL TAX.

The table annexed shows the State School Tax levied in each year, during the last thirteen years, on the taxable property of the State, the amount collected in the city of New York, with the sum re-apportioned:

YEARS.	AGGREGATE STATE TAX FOR SCHOOLS.	AMOUNT OF SCHOOL TAX PAID BY THE CITY TO THE STATE.	AMOUNT OF SCHOOL TAX APPORTIONED TO NEW YORK CITY BY THE STATE.
1853	$800,000 00	$241,553 19	$130,701 05
1854	800,000 00	257,616 11	131,808 48
1855	800,000 00	271,639 40	132,711 68
1856	1,072,862 83	383,805 37	146,522 41
1857	1,073,768 97	390,408 96	202,905 90
1858	1,052,853 75	398,416 98	212,889 55
1859	1,053,873 04	399,677 61	207,332 95
1860	1,064,473 15	412,550 00	207,990 35
1861	1,064,473 15	412,550 00	212,768 99
1862	1,081,325 57	428,309 40	245,080 84
1863	1,087,562 90	412,218 23	250,616 99
1864	1,090,841 11	410,562 02	252,265 54
1865	1,125,749 90	432,000 12	260,896 82
Total	$13,147,284 37	$4,851,307 09	$2,594,491 05

From the above statement it appears that the amount of
State School Tax paid by this city, during the last
twelve years, was.................................$4,851,307 09

The amount apportioned to this county by the State during the same period was, ... 2,594,491 05
Amount retained by the State Government for distribution in other counties............................ 2,256,816 04

COLORED SCHOOLS.

COLORED SCHOOLS.	NUMBER OF SESSIONS.	AVERAGE ATTENDANCE.	WHOLE NUMBER TAUGHT.	LOCATION OF SCHOOLS.
Colored School, No. 1—				
Boys' Department....	400	84	204	} 14th Ward, 135 Mulberry street, between
Girls' "	400	99	277	Grand and Hester streets.
Colored School No. 2—				
Boys' Department..	431	51	107	} 8th Ward, 51 and 53 Laurens street,
Girls' "	432	78	190	near Broome.
Primary "	431	124	370	
Colored School No. 4.....	425	13	37	12th Ward, 120th street near 4th av.
Colored School No. 5.....	432	60	159	5th Ward, 147 Franklin street.
Colored School No. 6.....	434	118	341	20th Ward, 1325 Broadway.
Colored School No. 7.....	432	128	327	16th Ward, 98 West 17th street.
Colored Primary School Nos. 2 and 3........	432	40	100	11th Ward, 2d street, near Avenue C.
		795	2,112	

THE CENTRAL PARK.

The Park has cost, up to December 31st, 1866, $9,763,895 98, and since it was begun the property in the vicinity pays an increased tax of $1,034,551 81, and has an increased valuation of $34,600,395.

The Drive and Ride are completed. Of the Drive there was completed previous to January 1st, 1865, 9 miles 176 feet; completed during 1865, 2,389 feet, or $9\frac{485}{1000}$ miles in all. Of the Bridle Road, completed previous to January 1st, 1865, $5\frac{503}{1000}$ miles. Of the walks, completed previous to January 1st, 1865, 23 miles 1,408 feet; completed during 1865, 2 miles 1,906 feet, or $25\frac{658}{1000}$ miles in all.

Allowing an average of three persons to each vehicle passing into the Park, the following will show approximately the number of persons who have entered the Park for the past four years:

```
1862............................................4,195,515
1863...  ......................  ..................4,327,409
1864............................................5,740,079
1865............................................7,593,139
```

The results are believed to be nearly correct; the probability is that they are under rather than over-stated.

APPENDIX.

THE FOLLOWING TABLE GIVES THE NUMBER OF VISITORS AT THE PARK DURING EACH MONTH IN THE YEAR FOR THE PAST FIVE YEARS.

	1861.			1862.			1863.			1864.			1865.		
	PEDESTRIANS.	EQUESTRIANS.	VEHICLES.	PEDESTRIANS.	EQUESTRIANS.	VEHICLES.	PEDESTRIANS.	EQUESTRIANS.	VEHICLES.	PEDESTRIANS.	EQUESTRIANS.	VEHICLES.	PEDESTRIANS.	EQUESTRIANS.	VEHICLES.
January	600,007	1,094	18,540	264,672	1,984	32,773	51,462	3,952	38,069	555,668	3,963	83,246	658,741	1,641	77,364
February	265,185	2,075	37,022	302,327	1,671	39,052	49,080	8,489	49,344	134,322	6,244	55,038	163,383	4,479	70,768
March	43,349	8,575	20,906	81,865	4,024	32,446	41,064	4,490	44,520	90,680	7,635	67,757	77,743	6,191	86,548
April	60,674	9,110	27,683	76,927	7,839	58,667	115,764	10,094	79,096	95,386	14,192	87,575	188,019	11,344	125,864
May	110,761	6,708	43,586	133,701	10,349	77,974	137,999	449	3,618	151,678	13,533	147,344	191,527	10,386	126,789
June	110,511	5,809	47,655	202,000	8,919	84,254	159,779	12,630	110,792	121,574	14,802	111,253	299,974	11,874	153,279
July	91,076	6,994	35,648	184,048	4,814	62,074	89,160	9,378	92,363	380,165	8,085	142,511	407,729	8,750	146,023
August	184,671	4,800	37,120	272,093	4,715	69,802	189,396	12,250	115,970	186,016	4,778	89,524	467,665	9,705	157,786
September	173,003	7,071	49,694	192,236	7,384	70,184	181,850	9,211	163,600	225,256	5,288	92,159	340,356	9,985	180,526
October	118,862	10,890	58,561	153,387	7,822	67,099	150,418	10,035	108,531	148,488	9,395	98,112	205,444	10,429	104,709
November	70,789	8,608	43,226	97,507	7,049	60,789	75,231	9,195	50,990	87,291	9,308	92,361	94,578	8,097	124,481
December	84,375	6,713	48,278	55,155	5,125	53,996	227,163	5,561	65,558	118,725	8,184	81,281	63,898	5,486	71,184
	1,863,263	73,547	467,849	1,993,918	71,645	709,010	1,469,835	90,724	922,450	2,295,199	100,397	1,148,161	3,219,056	98,380	1,425,241

The largest number of pedestrians entering the Park during any one month was, in January........ 658,741
The largest number of equestrians entering the Park during any one month was, in June........... 11,874
The largest number of vehicles entering the Park during any one month was, in September....... 180,526

VI. RELIGION.

NEW YORK CITY MISSION.

RESULTS OF THE YEAR 1865.

- 11 Mission stations.
- 43 Missionaries, and an average of 367 visitors.
- 64,314 Missionary visits.
- 840,591 Tracts distributed.
- 626 Bibles given, } On behalf of the New York Bible Society.
- 834 Testaments given,
- 2,652 Volumes loaned.
- 2,573 Children led to Sabbath-schools.
- 527 Children led to day-schools.
- 303 Persons to Bible classes.
- 5,980 Persons to church and mission.
- 437 Temperance pledges.
- 4,307 Religious meetings.
- 124 Backsliders reclaimed.
- 464 Persons united with churches.

RESULTS OF THIRTY YEARS, FROM 1835 TO 1864.

- 31,247,072 Tracts in English and other languages distributed.
- 34,196 Bibles supplied to the destitute.
- 40,080 Testaments supplied to children and others.
- 140,660 Volumes lent from ward libraries.
- 86,040 Children gathered into Sabbath, and
- 11,905 Into day-schools.
- 6,607 Persons gathered into Bible classes.
- 73,361 Persons induced to attend church.
- 32,016 Temperance pledges obtained.
- 58,548 Religious meetings held.
- 1,397 Backsliders reclaimed.
- 9,912 Persons hopefully converted: and
- 7,330 Converts united with evangelical churches.

NEW YORK ASSOCIATION FOR IMPROVING THE CONDITION OF THE POOR.

A Tabular Exhibit of the Operations of the Association, including the Receipts, Bequests, and Disbursements, since its Organization in 1844.

YEARS.	VISITORS.	VISITS.	RECEIPTS.	DISBURSEMENTS.	FAMILIES RELIEVED.	PERSONS RELIEVED.
1844....	244	10,042	$10,522	$8,704	1,560	6,240
1845....	276	18,044	16,692	17,338	2,896	11,554
1846....	297	25,963	24,644	24,327	5,200	20,840
1847....	298	26,435	24,659	24,040	5,580	25,110
1848....	299	28,040	25,078	25,483	5,340	24,030
1849....	300	30,590	28,753	26,551	6,672	29,844
1850....	317	27,180	25,807	23,821	5,725	25,762
1851....	324	29,277	33,656	32,327	6,202	24,992
1852....	337	27,284	34,577	33,866	6,307	25,922
1853....	357	25,203	31,359	29,692	5,468	24,606
1854....	361	28,142	35,637	34,661	5,977	26,896
1855....	378	55,898	90,445	95,878	15,549	62,396
1856....	378	43,244	48,811	51,059	10,879	43,516
1857....	378	32,294	42,480	42,085	8,154	32,732
1858....	382	48,173	66,578	67,094	13,842	54,268
1859....	377	46,944	44,592	44,855	9,281	44,577
1860....	362	40,886	37,986	40,565	8,031	35,942
1861....	364	44,569	40,516	43,725	8,532	38,394
1862....	364	36,732	33,382	33,461	7,583	33,815
1863....	364	13,482	36,293	32,934	4,357	19,532
1864....	366	18,106	47,788	47,416	4,696	20,810
1865....	366	22,309	43,975	49,300	5,573	22,285
1866....	366	24,222	51,643	45,089	5,115	19,878
Sundry Bequests		....	84,000	84,000	....	....
Total.......		703,104	$959,873	$958,271	158,519	673,941

DISPENSARIES.

NAME OF DISPENSARY AND DATE OF ITS INCORPORATION AND ORGANIZATION.

NAME.	INCORPORATED.	ORGANIZED.
1. New York........................	A. D. 1794.	A. D. 1791.
2. Northern	A. D. 1827.	A. D. 1827.
3. Eastern	A. D. 1832.	A. D. 1834.
4. Demilt..........................	A. D. 1851.	A. D. 1851.
5. North-Western...................	A. D. 1852.	A. D. 1852.
6. North-Eastern...................	A. D. 1862.	A. D. 1862.
7. Manhattan.	A. D. 1862.	A. D. 1862.

APPENDIX. 101

The most complete account of the workings of these institutions is from the report of 1862, which gives a good idea of their present value.

Number of male Patients in......1862...		59,513
" of female Patients....... "		86,085
" treated at Dispensaries.. "		118,409
" treated at their dwellings "		27,189
Whole number of Patients treated in 1862		145,598
Whole number of primary vaccinations in.......1862		13,841
" " Re-vaccinations .... "		4,537
" " Persons vaccinated........... "		18,408
" " Adult patients............... "		80,039
" " Infant Patients.............. "		65,529
" " Patients of American birth.... "		63,367
" " " of foreign origin...... "		81,231
" " " sent to Hospital...... "		6,437
" " Deaths of Patients........... "		863
" " Prescriptions dispensed........ "		274,648
General average number of prescriptions dispensed to each patient (excluding vaccinees—18,408=127,190 patients) in 1862..............		2.16
Aggregate amount of expenditures of the seven Dispensaries for the year 1862, excluding cost of repairs and management, or permanent improvement of property...		$21,199 19
General average cost of medicines, and medical, surgical, and vaccine service to each patient, for the year 1862.......................		14¼ cts.
Average number of years during which medical charity has been extended to the sick-poor of New York by the Dispensaries.........		22.8
Whole number of persons vaccinated by all the Dispensaries since the year 1804, or since the era of the discovery of the protective power of vaccine...		275,844
Whole number of the poor of New York who have received medicine, and medical, surgical, and vaccine service gratuitously, from all the Dispensaries since the organization of the first, in 1791, a period of seventy-two years		2,497,207
Aggregate amount of expenditures of the several Dispensaries during the same period, for medicine, salaries for medical and surgical service, etc..		$426,868 66
General average cost of medicines, and medical, surgical, and vaccine service to each Dispensary patient, from February 1st, 1791, to December 31st, 1862...		17 cts.
Average number of patients treated annually, for the average twenty-two and eight-tenths years that the Dispensaries have been organized and in operation		109,527

RECAPITULATION FOR 1862.

Total value of Dispensary medical service..............................	$215,190
Total value of the time saved to the sick-poor...........................	102,555
Estimated pecuniary value of the Dispensary system.....................	$317,745
Deduct amount expended in support of the system......................	21,199
Estimated saving to the public by the Dispensary system	$296,546

VII. IMMIGRATION

SHOWING THE NUMBERS AND NATIVITIES OF ALIEN EMIGRANTS WHO ARRIVED

COUNTRY OF BIRTH.	1847.	1848.	1849.	1850.	1851.	1852.	1853.	1854.	1855.
Ireland	52,946	91,061	112,591	117,038	163,306	118,131	113,164	82,302	43,043
Germany	53,180	51,973	55,705	45,535	69,919	118,611	119,644	176,986	52,892
England	8,864	23,062	28,321	28,163	28,553	31,551	27,126	30,578	22,938
Scotland	2,354	6,415	8,840	6,772	7,302	7,694	6,456	4,909	4,240
France	3,330	2,734	2,683	3,462	5,964	8,868	7,470	7,986	4,174
Switzerland	1,947	1,622	1,405	2,380	4,499	6,471	4,604	8,883	3,273
Holland	8,611	1,560	2,447	1,174	1,798	1,223	1,085	1,466	822
Wales	472	1,054	1,782	1,520	2,189	2,531	1,182	1,288	1,118
Norway	882	1,207	3,300	3,150	2,112	1,889	377	81	203
Sweden	139	165	1,097	1,110	872	2,005	1,630	1,859	304
Italy	197	321	602	476	618	359	558	785	667
Belgium	551	....	118	230	475	82	34	398	1,201
Spain	101	253	214	257	278	471	659	646	457
West Indies	299	392	449	554	575	265	....	11	19
Denmark	95	52	159	90	229	157	94	102	174
Poland	26	79	133	188	422	188	186	169	346
Sardinia	....	....	172	165	98	69	72	148	67
South America	....	31	33	104	121	120	175	111	112
Portugal	34	57	287	65	26	37	237	205	24
Nova Scotia	....	....	151	164	81	73	6	128	9
Russia	10	28	38	18	23	33	39	55	20
Canada	....	....	59	61	50	48	....	2	64
Mexico	....	12	23	41	42	23	51	34	20
Sicily	....	....	21	28	12	42	37	58	18
China	....	2	9	11	22	14	53	20	18
East Indies	23	....	34	32	10	18	....	....	5
Greece	....	1	6	4	1	11	1	7	3
Turkey	1	....	6	4	4	5	10	6	2
Arabia	....	....	8	....	....	....	....	....	....
Africa	....	....	....	....	....	....	....	....	....
Unknown	....	95	....	....	....	....	....	....	....
Australia	....	....	....	....	....	....	....	....	....
Central America	....	....	....	....	....	....	....	....	....
Annual Totals	129,062	182,176	220,603	212,796	289,601	300,989	284,945	319,223	136,233

APPENDIX. 103

TABLE.

AT THE PORT OF NEW YORK, FROM MAY 5, 1847, TO OCTOBER 1, 1866.

1856.	1857.	1858.	1859.	1660.	1861.	1862.	1863.	1864.	1865.	1866.	TOTAL.
44.276	57,119	25,075	32,652	47,330	25,784	32,217	92,157	89,399	70,462	73,258	1,483,311
56.113	80,974	31,874	28,270	37,899	27,139	27,740	35,002	57,446	83,451	81,287	1,291,640
23,787	28,622	12,324	10,375	11,361	5,632	7,975	18,757	23,710	27,286	28,624	427,609
4,723	5,170	2,718	2,325	1,617	659	692	1,937	3,126	3,962	3,917	85,828
2,984	3,069	1,786	1,532	1,549	1,200	1,187	1,303	1,804	2,059	2,390	67,534
2,559	2,454	1,315	791	1,442	1,398	1,254	1,194	1,652	2,513	2,769	55,405
1,666	1,734	348	261	440	831	456	407	615	729	211	22,384
1,376	887	566	500	811	697	1,062	1,143	659	505	494	21,816
438	62	3	36	53	93	22	238	88	158	484	14,879
918	619	237	318	361	382	663	1,370	1,516	2,337	3,818	21,630
690	596	669	399	542	750	487	444	475	591	674	10,895
850	444	253	57	76	165	195	456	186	97	120	5,988
330	263	146	234	228	190	124	202	196	224	250	5,721
225	330	344	416	523	165	156	256	236	283	201	5,699
469	453	284	493	495	612	1,689	1,580	565	427	1,458	9,977
142	245	88	114	80	43	50	137	198	423	207	3,464
426	405	324	164	89	67	39	....	....	....	....	2,305
163	66	92	138	110	88	92	60	124	109	134	1,983
30	93	27	45	19	14	13	3	34	42	93	1,385
30	40	18	81	23	11	67	77	40	77	34	1,110
19	11	13	13	22	36	46	47	37	93	130	731
57	30	17	25	25	19	33	17	35	43	27	612
19	11	13	13	22	45	13	38	92	70	54	636
10	26	19	1	4	1	9	1	3	3	....	293
8	11	15	4	13	10	15	5	41	36	13	320
....	....	7	....	4	2	1	3	1	7	15	162
2	8	2	6	2	1	6	2	13	5	3	85
4	....	6	3	3	5	3	2	5	5	8	82
....	....	....	....	....	....	....	....	....	....	....	8
....	....	....	....	....	....	....	6	....	....	14	20
....	....	....	....	....	....	....	....	....	....	....	95
....	....	....	....	....	....	....	....	....	18	11	29
....	....	....	....	....	....	....	....	....	....	10	10
142,315	183,742	78,583	79,266	105,123	65,539	76,306	156,844	182,296	196.352	200,711	3,542,705

APPENDIX.

TABLE

SHOWING THE AVOWED DESTINATION OF EMIGRANTS LANDED AT CASTLE GARDEN FROM AUG. 1, 1855, TO OCT. 1, 1866.

DESTINATION TO STATES.	1855. F'm Aug. 1	1856.	1857.	1858.	1859.	1860.	1861.	1862.	1863.	1864.	1865.	1866. To Oct. 1.	TOTAL.
New York	19,489	55,055	78,585	34,296	40,923	56,131	32,783	38,312	84,105	92,409	99,433	85,128	716,649
Pennsylvania	4,469	11,749	16,660	6,708	7,370	9,512	5,114	6,116	15,396	18,212	22,276	19,629	143,210
Illinois	3,444	11,064	15,750	6,690	3,940	4,077	4,010	5,009	8,435	11,631	17,177	18,393	109,520
Wisconsin	4,667	13,327	12,704	4,953	2,441	2,589	3,217	4,574	5,075	4,365	6,127	7,416	71,465
Ohio	3,250	7,085	10,054	6,178	4,668	5,195	3,863	3,942	6,574	9,267	10,316	9,830	80,210
Massachusetts	2,037	6,494	6,904	3,212	5,119	6,371	3,433	4,453	11,734	14,129	8,957	9,794	82,637
Canada West	3,346	8,526	9,673	4,218	2,202	1,872	1,546	2,788	3,000	2,600	1,300	1,300	42,371
New Jersey	1,119	3,242	3,806	1,922	2,621	3,414	1,892	1,483	3,744	5,306	5,395	6,303	40,247
Unknown	957	4,187	4,395	1,484	1,726	3,368		25					16,142
Michigan	1,648	3,296	4,108	1,697	1,305	1,478	1,521	1,900	3,062	3,167	3,178	2,897	29,257
Connecticut	829	2,292	2,974	1,227	1,929	2,579	1,416	1,248	3,339	8,603	2,323	8,103	26,862
Iowa	796	2,380	3,775	1,724	664	776	1,289	1,082	1,094	1,948	3,400	3,559	22,486
Missouri	434	1,064	2,366	1,690	1,598	1,614	911	850	2,188	8,379	5,016	3,656	24,746
Indiana	881	1,338	2,474	1,271	1,122	1,106	906	938	1,357	1,826	2,730	2,092	18,551
Rhode Island	551	1,354	1,389	510	1,001	1,291	530	481	1,696	1,848	1,353	1,878	13,882
Maryland	486	1,164	1,535	907	902	1,074	434	401	1,912	1,680	1,888	1,470	13,692
Uncertain	317	2,113	2,014	483	303	214							5,444
California	447	778	877	1,084	1,108	1,141	1,028	1,423	1,149	1,459	877	1,290	12,661
Minnesota	127	427	1,253	828	542	466	761	942	1,433	1,109	1,514	3,045	12,447
Utah	250	1,579	14	3	740	906	1,941	8,418	8,561	1,694	1,092	3,082	18,279
Virginia	292	687	702	548	575	452	102	585	187	334	560	817	6,617
Kentucky	183	460	660	520	546	650	301	215	593	910	1,060	1,287	7,385
District of Columbia	202	407	532	336	308	301	168	585	1,054	1,026	1,229	737	6,885
Vermont	198	250	297	172	198	270	135	153	297	362	263	208	2,773
Louisiana	60	171	206	240	265	321	180	50	240	327	266	364	2,680

APPENDIX. 105

Place													Total
South Carolina	80	...	178	157	168	185	296	45	2	...	6	77	125	1,319
Maine	143	...	148	186	210	122	142	176	121	340	609	413	290	2,900
Tennessee	72	...	178	127	165	147	269	62	56	190	398	39	440	2,148
Georgia	70	...	47	167	162	193	178	35	2	4	...	22	147	1,027
New Hampshire	71	...	177	179	69	131	123	89	63	110	562	202	141	1,917
Delaware	49	...	81	113	65	117	123	16	55	110	143	149	123	1,144
New Brunswick	2	...	...	97	75	82	42	98	43	99	89	50	44	721
Texas	5	...	76	55	43	52	63	88	3	6	2	41	66	449
Kansas	1	...	11	25	88	77	92	25	63	122	281	388	869	1,642
North Carolina	11	...	66	41	52	48	43	52	...	...	7	37	127	384
Mississippi	6	...	14	62	21	50	15	12	...	...	1	52	50	288
Alabama	7	...	30	21	24	39	46	11	...	7	...	27	45	256
Nova Scotia	30	...	2	42	53	14	21	14	149	65	43	45	82	610
Nebraska	...	...	2	27	42	31	46	3	42	89	13	116	16	493
South America	25	...	30	18	14	38	18	13	7	88	15	34	5	254
Cuba	...	...	12	25	32	46	29	20	17	29	29	50	20	282
Arkansas	8	...	12	9	10	16	21	6	6	...	...	4	8	127
Florida	13	...	...	5	11	32	17	4	3	1	4	5	11	120
Mexico	1	...	...	1	7	...	9	6	...	18	22	71	34	164
Oregon	2	...	11	7	6	6	13	4	7	2	10	18	15	103
West Indies	...	...	...	...	6	5	9	6	...	...	17	15	...	91
New Mexico	...	...	...	5	...	23	1	4	...	...	...	...	3	32
Central America	...	...	...	...	3	9	8	10	5	5	4	...	79	43
Canada East	...	...	...	...	...	10	6	8	6	89	44	67	5	344
Prince Edward's Island	...	...	...	...	3	3	5	8	42	...	...	...	...	20
Vancouver's Island	...	...	...	...	...	1	1	1	...	...	...	...	...	5
Washington Territory	...	...	...	...	...	...	...	...	...	...	...	...	...	3
Australia	...	...	1	...	...	1	1	1	1	2	1	...	...	10
Bermuda	...	...	...	...	...	...	1	...	...	...	...	...	...	2
Sandwich Islands	...	...	...	...	...	...	1	...	...	...	...	...	8	1
Russian America	...	...	...	...	...	...	...	1	...	...	...	...	9	1
British Columbia	...	...	...	...	...	...	...	...	...	8	22	7	9	341
Nevada	...	...	...	...	...	...	...	...	295	...	...	...	4	4
Colorado	...	...	...	...	...	...	...	...	...	...	...	...	26	26
	51,114	141,625	185,078	84,226	85,602	108,682	68,311	81,458	161,648	184,700	200,031	190,086	1,544,149

While there is no data or report to show the number remaining in the City of New York, it is to be believed that of the number destined for the State, from 25 to 40 per cent. remained in the City.

VIII. MISCELLANEOUS.

CHILDREN'S AID SOCIETY.

This Society has been in existence thirteen years, and has paid $304,190 99 in charity.

ANALYSIS OF DISBURSEMENTS FOR YEAR ENDING FEBRUARY 1ST, 1866.

Industrial Schools (13 in number)	$16,681 16
Donations by individuals for special purposes	1,712 99
Newsboys' Lodging-House	10,058 13
Girls' Lodging-House	7,356 44
Emigration Account	18,735 72
Refuge for Homeless Children (corner of Twenty-fourth street and Eighth avenue)	1,322 59
Salaries and Compensation to 13 different persons	9,422 06
General expenses, printing, rent, postage, etc., etc.	6,754 56
	$72,043 65
Balance on hand, February 1st, 1866	2,206 08
Total	$74,249 73

EMIGRATION OF CHILDREN.

The following table embraces thirteen years:

Sent, up to February 1, 1854	207
" February 1, 1855	863
" February 1, 1856	936
" February 1, 1857	742
" February 1, 1858	733
" February 1, 1859	779
" February 1, 1860	814
" February 1, 1861	804
" February 1, 1862	884
" February 1, 1863	791
" February 1, 1864	1,034
" February 1, 1865	1,235
" February 1, 1866	1,450
Total	11,272

Eleven thousand two hundred and seventy-two rescued from almost certain destruction! At least ten thousand of these may be regarded as saved, who, but for the interposition of the Children's Aid Society, would have been lost. If, as we are told, there is rejoicing over one sinner saved, have not the friends of the Society abundant cause for thankfulness and gratitude?

The report of the Children's Aid Society, from which these statements are taken, sums up the long and effective service of this institution to the welfare of the city, and proves the priceless worth of the ministry of Rev. Charles L. Brace among the children and youth of New York. His volume of Plain Sermons to Newsboys is the first fruit of what should be a new department of literature or oratory—the adaptation of great truths and duties to minds of little culture and many trials, wants, and temptations.

GIRLS' LODGING HOUSE.

STATEMENT.

DATE.	Number of Lodgers.	Number of Lodgings.	Number of Lodgings Paid.	Number of Meals.	Number of Meals Paid.
February 1st, 1865, in House..	39				
Since received	57	1,070	463	3,391	1,159
March, 1865.................	62	1,238	485	3,780	1,215
April, "	74	1,205	374	3,354	932
May, "	76	1,348	343	3,812	877
June, "	74	1,304	289	3,836	724
July, "	61	1,311	245	3,265	615
August, "	73	1,052	315	3 092	790
Sept., "	88	1,058	313	3,849	784
Oct., "	104	1,254	421	4,428	1,052
Nov., "	102	1,364	351	4,452	878
Dec., "	102	1,454	309	4,550	772
January, 1866...............	105	1,593	345	4,917	846
Total...	1,017	15,251	4,259	46,726	10,644

Average cost per meal. $5\frac{1}{4}$ cents.

     121 girls sent to situations.
      45 " found employment.
      21 " sent to other institutions.
      32 " gone West.
      35 " returned to friends.
About 3,000 garments have been made.

BOYS' LODGING HOUSE.

TABULAR STATEMENT FOR TWELVE YEARS.

YEAR.	NO. OF BOYS.	NO. OF LODGINGS.	NO. OF MEALS.	SUNDAY DINNERS.	RETURNED TO FRIENDS	EXPENSES.	PAID BY BOYS.	SAVED BY BOYS DURING THE YEAR.	
								BOYS.	AMOUNT.
1854 to 1855	408	6,872	......	......	......	$1,199 76	$397 56	......	......
1855 " 1856	874	7,599	......	......	......	1,431 82	891 26	16	$648 58
1856 " 1857	387	5,157	......	......	......	1,762 56	262 56	106	270 70
1857 " 1858	800	8,026	11,923	......	......	1,925 03	298 03	......	......
1858 " 1859	(about)8,000	(about)14,000	13,114	2,400	100	2,199 34	807 15	83	110 10
1859 " 1860	(about)4,500	(about)19,747	13,841	2,660	247	2,113 56	955 44	230	1,259 77
1860 " 1861	(about)4,000	27,390	16,873	2,790	......	3,420 57	1,036 98	388	1,376 59
1861 " 1862	3,875	32,954	19,809	......	396	2,786 08	1,138 88	847	1,315 10
1862 " 1863	3,000	(about)29,409	(about)20,000	......	437	3,402 82	1,102 33	405	2,080 06
1863 " 1864	6,325	36,572	25,506	......	576	5,758 16	1,559 10	499	2,505 92
1864 " 1865	6,793	42,446	30,187	3,640	683	7,159 95	1,944 22	599	2,486 43
1865 " 1866	7,256	43,797	32,867	3,640		10,058 13	2,127 44		
	40,718	273,969	160,570	15,130	2,389	$42,177 78	$12,020 95	2,558	$12,379 94

APPENDIX. 109

THE COOPER UNION FOR SCIENCE AND ART.

This Institution has now been in operation seven years. Its receipts have been $168,191 84, and its expenses $164,163 57.

TRADES AND PROFESSIONS OF THE PUPILS OF THE COOPER UNION

	Mathematics.	Chem. and Nat. Philosophy.	Architectural Drawing.	Mechanical Drawing.	Perspective Drawing.	Free Hand Drawing.	Draw'g from Cast and Life.	Totals.
Clerks and Bookkeepers	94	93	18	13	18	33	2	271
Machinists and Iron Workers	36	25	2	152	4	3	..	232
Teachers and Students	16	6	3	3	4	6	1	49
Carpenters and Cabinet Makers	4	8	35	21	..	5	..	73
Draughtsmen and Pattern Makers	6	4	1	7	2	..	..	20
Masons and Builders	..	..	8	1	2	..	..	11
Stone and Marble Cutters	2	..	11	2	..	5	..	20
Painters	..	..	1	1	..	16	1	19
Piano Forte Makers	1	1	3	1	..	4	..	10
Engineers	3	2	2	5	..	..	..	13
Carvers and Turners	3	1	1	1	2	35	1	44
Engravers and Lithographers	2	1	..	2	4	44	1	54
Photographers	..	7	..	..	..	2	1	10
Blacksmiths	1	2	..	5	..	..	..	8
Artists	..	1	..	..	1	..	4	6
Jewellers and Watchmakers	..	2	..	1	..	19	..	22
Printers	4	7	..	4	4	5	..	24
Gardeners	..	..	..	..	..	7	..	7
Bookbinders	2	..	..	..	..	3	..	5
Glass Stainers	..	..	..	..	..	7	..	7
Sundry Occupations	36	40	11	32	5	34	4	162
Totals	210	221	96	251	46	228	15	1,067

NUMBER OF VISITORS TO THE READING ROOM.

	1860.	1861.	1862.	1863.	1864.	1865.
January	18,532	24,240	19,866	17,389	16,365	15,862
February	20,044	24,113	18,359	15,602	15,021	15,371
March	23,696	22,543	20,593	15,911	15,296	16,735
April	18,735	20,470	19,327	13,835	15,992	14,038
May	18,739	19,597	15,996	12,962	15,430	15,283
June	16,230	17,956	11,936	12,786	14,442	13,529
July	15,098	16,459	13,331	11,676	13,986	17,607
August	6,299*	10,914*	8,501*	3,388*	4,701*	*5,692
September	17,888	17,546	15,796	16,270	18,045	20,898
October	20,371	19,884	17,970	16,762	18,320	19,024
November	17,234	19,630	15,288	16,871	19,368	20,956
December	21,344	15,244	17,889	18,919	16,460	19,662
Total	219,710	228,616	194,852	171,871	183,426	194,648

* Closed during part of the month.

MERCANTILE LIBRARY ASSSOCIATION.

The number of volumes added during the past year was,

By donation	170
By purchase	8,853
	9,023
Of which, were	
Folios and Quartos	85
Octavos	3,080
Duodecimos	5,858
	9,023
Less duplicate volumes sold	1,074
Net increase of books	7,949
Number of volumes in Library, as per last report	73,175
Present number of volumes	81,124
The additions are of the following classes:	
Theology	111
Mental and Moral Science, and General Literature	617
Political Science, Law, etc	292
History, Biography, and Travels	1,207
Natural Sciences	62
Medicine	49
Useful Arts	88
Encyclopædic	4
Fiction	6,593
	9,023
The number of volumes delivered from the Library was	118,842
From Up-Town Branch	36,110
From Down-Town Office	23,266
Total	178,218

NEW YORK SOCIETY LIBRARY.

This Library now contains over 52,000 volumes, and its annual receipts are, by the Report of 1866, $5,943 61, a poor and beggarly sum for the oldest institution of the kind in the city, and the only avowedly family library. The number of books taken out yearly has increased, since 1861-2, from 19,109 to 32,642. The yearly assessment has been raised from six to ten dollars, and the number of books may be expected to increase.

THE ASTOR LIBRARY.

This institution, which was incorporated January 18th, 1849, is one of the most significant facts that introduced this city to its rank as a cosmopolitan centre of learning. It does for the higher literature what the Cooper Institute does for popular instruction, and the two combine to provide our scholars and our people at large with priceless opportunities of improvement. The original endowment of the Astor Library was $400,000, which has been increased by over $300,000 by Wm. B. Astor, son of John Jacob Astor, $50,000 of the sum having lately been given, $20,000 of the donation to go for the immediate purchase of books, and the balance towards the endowment.

The present number of volumes in the Library, including pamphlets, is about 145,000. These are the main facts from the report of the trustees for 1866:

The Library continues to be largely and advantageously used by the public. The report of the superintendent exhibits in tabular form the number of readers monthly during the year, in the departments, respectively, of science and art, and of history and literature, arranged under fifty-three separate subdivisions. It is believed to be of general interest in showing the comparative tendencies of the public mind to different branches of knowledge.

The number of readers in both the departments was 19,540; of whom 11,282 were occupied with history and literature, and 8,258 with science and art.

In addition to these, 3,545 were admitted into the alcoves; 1,374 having been occupied in history and literature, and 2,171 in the various branches of science and art.

The whole number of books read during the year was 44,966.

By the treasurer's report it will appear that $8,375 53 was expended during the year for books and binding; that the income of the Library was $11,169 10, from a total investment of $184,868 39, and the expenses were $8,427 88.

The report of the superintendent shows that there were added to the Library during the year, by purchase, exclusive of periodicals and transactions of learned societies, 587 volumes and 63 pamphlets, and by donations, 196 volumes and 112 pamphlets.

NOTES OF THE ERIE CANAL.

NEW YORK CITY, *January* 18*th*, 1867.

MY DEAR DR. OSGOOD:—I have your kind note of yesterday, in which you ask for some facts illustrating the interest which your friend and fellow-laborer in the New York Historical Society—my father—took in the project of connecting the waters of Lake Erie with those of the Atlantic. Cadwallader D. Colden, in his elaborate *memoir*, has given so full an account of the building of the great work, and paid such ample justice to its originators, that, perhaps, I cannot better meet your wishes, than by confining myself to such topics as shall enable a younger generation to recall more vividly the painful agency of the Erie Canal in developing the internal resources of our State.

Great as was the assistance given to the canal project by the act of the New York Legislature of the 8th of April, 1811, the obstacles in the way of its successful completion were by no means removed. The same incredulity as to the practicability of the canal, and the same apprehensions as to the capacity of the State, continued to raise a fierce opposition in the Legislature against any appropriations for carrying on the work which it had itself authorized. Many attempts were accordingly made to arrest, or at least curtail and postpone the project; and often, during the progress of the undertaking, it seemed as if it would be utterly abandoned. Party spirit, at that time, ran high; and the greatest effort, on the part of its supporters, was required to persuade the people of the State to give it their support at the polls. In accomplishing this result, the *Commercial Advertiser*, of this city, gave powerful aid. That paper, which had always been the organ of the Federalists, became, upon Mr. Stone's assuming its management in 1820, a staunch advocate of the Clintonians. A strong personal friendship for Mr. Clinton, on the part of its editor, together with a firm conviction of the necessity for a canal through the interior of New York State, led to the position thus assumed. The trials and rebuffs experienced by Governor Clinton and his supporters in pushing the canal project, and the energy which fought it through to a triumphant end, are matters of history. The Erie Canal was completed in the fall of 1825. At ten o'clock on the morning of the twenty-sixth of October of the same year, the first canal-boat—the Seneca Chief—left Buffalo, having on board Governor Clinton; and the booming of cannon, placed at intervals of a few miles along the entire line of the canal from Buffalo to Albany, and thence along the banks of the Hudson to Sandy Hook, announced the successful termination of the enterprise. In New York City, especially, this event was celebrated by extraordinary civic and military ceremonies; and the citizens gave themselves up to the wildest demonstrations of joy. Nor was this joy ill-timed or excessive. "For a single State to achieve such a victory—not only over the doubts and fears of the wary, but over the obstacles of nature—causing miles of massive rocks at the mountain ridge to yield to its power—turning the tide of error as well as that of the Tonnewanda—piling up the waters of the mighty Niagara, as well as those of the beautiful Hudson—in short, causing a navigable river to flow with gentle current down the steepy mount of Lockport—to leap the river of Genesee—to encircle the brow of Irondequoit as with the laurel's wreath—to march through the rich fields of Palmyra and of Lyons—to wend its way through the quicksands of the morass at the Cayuga—to pass unheeded the delicious licks at Onondaga—to smile through Oneida's verdant landscape—to hang upon the arm of the ancient Mohawk, and with her, after gaily stepping down the cadence of the Little Falls and the Cohoes, to rush to the embrace of the sparkling Hudson—and all in the space of eight short years, was a work of which the oldest and richest nations of Christendom might well be proud." * Mr. Stone, as one of the most zealous champions of the canal, was appointed to write the NARRATIVE OF THE CELEBRATION, receiving a silver medal and box from the Common Council of New York City, together with the thanks of that body.

In connection with the Erie Canal, and its influence in building up the interior towns of our State, Mr. Stone was wont to relate the following anecdote: In 1820, he visited Syracuse with Joshua Forman, the founder of that city, and one of the earliest and most zealous friends of the Erie Canal. "I lodged for the night," says Mr. Stone, "at a miserable tavern, thronged by a company of salt-boilers from Salina, forming a group of about as rough-looking specimens of humanity as I had ever seen. Their wild visages, beards thick and long, and matted hair, even now rise up in dark, distant, and picturesque effect before me. It was in October, and a flurry of snow during the night had rendered the morning aspect of the country more dreary than the evening before. The few houses, standing upon low and almost marshy ground, and surrounded by trees and entangled thickets, presented a very uninviting scene. 'Mr. Forman,' said I, '*do you call this a village?* It would make an owl weep to fly over it.' 'Never mind,' said he in reply, '*you will live to see it a city yet!*'" Mr. Stone did, indeed, live to see it a

---

* Stone's Narrative.

city, when he wrote the above in 1840, with mayor and aldermen, and a population of more than twelve thousand.

Syracuse, however, was not the only town that vindicated the foresight of Clinton and Forman. In the fall of 1829, Mr. Stone made a tour of the towns and villages in the central part of the State, partly for recreation, but more especially for the purpose of observing for himself the great impetus given to internal improvement by the canal. Familiar, however, as he had been for the last four years with the progress which had been making, he was scarcely prepared for the signs of growth and prosperity which met him on every side. His amazement is pictured in a few extracts here given from the diary kept by him on this journey.

"Between five and six o'clock we entered Utica, which, nine years ago, the period of my last visit to it, ranked only as a flourishing village. It had now grown as if by magic to the dimensions of a large city; and it was with utter amazement that I beheld the long streets and rows and blocks of large, beautiful country seats, stores and dwellings through which our coach conveyed us in driving to the lodgings I had selected. I had heard much of the march of improvement in Utica, since the completion of the GRAND CANAL, but I had no idea of the reality. Rip Van Winkle himself, after his thirty years' nap in a glen of the Katsbergs, was not more amazed than I was at the present aspect and magnitude of this beautiful place. Bagg's Hotel, to which I directed my drive, was in the very heart of the village, and the centre of business at the period of my last visit. Now it was quite in the suburbs. The houses were then scattered, but now they are closely built, lofty and spacious, and the length of some of the streets, like New York, begin to look like a wilderness of bricks."

"*Tuesday, Sept. 22d.* Arrived at Syracuse at half-past ten o'clock, and had the unexpected pleasure of being greeted by my old and highly valued friend, Seth Hunt, a gentleman of extensive travel and vast general information. I looked upon the village as I stepped on shore with still more astonishment than at Utica. Another enchanted city! I exclaimed, as I glanced upward and around upon splendid hotels, and rows of massive buildings in all directions—crowded, too, with people, all full of life and activity. The prediction of my friend, Joshua Forman, when I was here nine years ago, is already realized. For if noble ranges of buildings, two or three large and tasteful churches, busy wharves and streets, and all the life and animation of a large commercial place, will constitute a city, then, most assuredly, Syracuse may be called by that name. And as the county buildings, now erecting upon an extensive scale, have been located midway between Salina and Syracuse, the two towns will be soon united, as Greenwich is to New York.

Within twenty years, therefore, Syracuse will equal the present size of Albany. Salt of the best quality can here be produced, at the cheapest rate, for the whole continent."

Leaving Syracuse, Mr. Stone visited successively the pleasant villages of Marcellus, Skaneateles, Auburn and Lyons, the rapid growth of which surprised him scarcely less than had Utica and Syracuse. "This village too," continues the diary, in speaking of Lyons, "was a wilderness at the period of my last visit; now it has grown into considerable importance. It is the shire town of Wayne County, and in addition to a number of shops and stores and the county buildings, it contains many respectable and some elegant residences. Among the latter is the seat of Myron Holley, Esq., formerly one of the leading and most able and efficient of our canal commissioners, whose names will be perpetuated as long as the lakes and the ocean are connected by the golden commercial chain forged under the direction of the great Clinton. Mr. Holley showed me through his grounds; and I was much surprised to find one of the richest and most beautiful gardens that I had ever seen. It contains some six or eight acres, which was forest at the time of my visit in 1820. Now it was elegantly laid out and cultivated, and planted with fruit-trees, plants, shrubs, and vines, in rich variety and profusion. The size to which cherry, peach, pear and plum trees, quince bushes, to say nothing of the beautiful shade trees in the lawn, had attained since this land was appropriated to its present purpose was truly wonderful. Cherry and apple trees, planted eight years since, now measure ten and thirteen inches in diameter, and every vegetable seems to flourish in this genial soil with the same unequalled vigor and thrift."

Rochester, however, seems to have completed his astonishment.

"*Friday, Oct. 2d.* And this is Rochester! The far-famed city of the west, which has sprung up like Jonah's gourd! Rochester, with its two thousand houses, its elegant ranges of stores, its numerous churches and public buildings, its boats and bridges, its huge mills of stone, like so many castles, its lagoons, quays, manufactories, arcades, museums, everything—all standing where stood a frowning forest in 1812. Here I am, near the very spot, where, in a thick wood, my namesake, Enos Stone, in the autumn of 1811, had a remarkable fight with an old she-bear, which, in anticipation of the present doctrines of Tammany Hall, was carrying out the agrarian principle by sharing his little patch of corn."

But I am already making this letter too long. On his return to New York, Mr. Stone gave his readers the results of this tour in a series of articles—the publication of which confirmed more strongly than ever in the public mind, the forecast and wisdom of the originators and executors of the GRAND ERIE CANAL.   Most cordially yours,

WILLIAM L. STONE.

116   APPENDIX.

P. S. I append a statistical statement of the Erie Canal, brought up to the beginning of the present year, the materials for which were kindly furnished me by my friend, the Hon. Nathaniel S. Benton, for many years our able Canal Auditor:

Length, Albany to Buffalo	363 miles.
Width at surface	70 feet.
" bottom	42 "
Depth	7 "
Width of tow-path	14 "
Burden of boats	80 tons.
Length of locks	90 feet.
Width "	15 "
Number "	84
Amount of tolls in 1823	$199,655 08
" " 1866	$3,966,522 52
Amount of tons going to tide-water from the Western States in 1836	54,219
Amount of tons going to tide-water from the Western States in 1866	2,235,716
Total amount of tons going to tide-water from the Western States, from 1836 to 1866, inclusive	40,485,738
Total amount of tolls from 1823 to 1866, inclusive	$90,153,279 19
Amount of tons going to tide-water from New York State in 1836	364,906
Amount of tons going to tide-water from New York State in 1866	287,948
Total amount of tons going to tide-water from New York State, from 1836 to 1866, inclusive	12,276,229
Amount of tons going from tide-water in 1836	133,796
" " " 1866	626,974
Total amount of tons going from tide-water from 1836 to 1866, inclusive	10,334,311
Estimated value of all property transported on Erie Canal in 1837	$47,720,879
Estimated value of all property transported on Erie Canal in 1865	$186,114,718
Total estimated value of all property transported on Erie Canal, from 1837 to 1865, inclusive	$3,439,407,522
Amount of tons going to New York by canal-boats, on different canals in the State, without breaking bulk, for 1857	381,390

Amount of tons going to New York by canal-boats, on different canals in the State, without breaking bulk, for 1866..	1,633,172
Total amount of tons going to New York by canal-boats, on different canals in the State without breaking bulk, from 1857 to 1866, inclusive................	11,775,396
Amount of tons arriving at tide-water, the product of New York State, on the Erie Canal, for 1836.......	364,901
Amount of tons arriving at tide-water, the product of New York State, on the Erie Canal, for 1865......	173,538
Total amount of tons arriving at tide-water, the product of New York State, on the Erie Canal, from 1836 to 1865, inclusive...............................	11,792,314
The original cost of the Erie Canal was...............	$7,143,789 86
Cost of enlargement......................................	$33,080,613 80
Total...	$40,224,403 66

Wm. L. S.

SPEECH OF HON. J. B. VARNUM ON THE GOVERNMENT OF THE CITY.

Mr. J. B. Varnum, Jr., desired to refer the committee to a report of the Committee on Cities and Villages of the Assembly on the subject of the present city charter, which report would be found in the Assembly Documents for 1857. It states, in a very concise form, what portions of said charter were derived from former charters, and the reasons for those sections which were new. A perusal of it would, he believed, materially aid the committee in deciding what the defects were in that instrument, and what recommendations to make. The year 1857 was one during which a great excitement prevailed in New York city on the subject of reform in the city government and police, an excitement which gradually extended to most of the other cities in the State, so that the Committee on Cities were overwhelmed. It was in that year that the Metropolitan Police bill, the City Charter, and the Supervisors' bill were passed. That committee had not the advantage of sessions in the city of New York; but large numbers of persons appeared before them with drafts of charters, and suggestions which embodied much reliable information; but comparatively little of this material was in a very available, systematic form, and the committee found themselves unable to agree upon any one of the plans proposed. They therefore decided to make a charter which should combine, as far as possible, whatever was good in former charters and in the suggestions laid before them. The result of a compromise of opinions among themselves was the present charter, which was amended in the Senate by the insertion of Aldermanic Districts, and which was at the time generally received as a great improvement upon its predecessors, although time has shown it to be by no means free from the defects incident to everything human. Still, he believed very slight amendments were all that were required. Others have commented upon the absence of any proper system for examining accounts. He would advert to one or two other points. *And first as to the Legislative Department.* It would be found that a large proportion of the plans which were being presented in the newspapers, and some of which he presumed were laid before the committee, had heretofore been tried in one form or another. He had recently seen an earnest recommendation that the Board of Councilmen should be composed of a large number representing small districts, the writer apparently not knowing that *we once had a board of sixty councilmen*, established by a law passed in 1853 (*Laws of* 1853, *p.* 410). *Prior to that time the two Boards, or the Aldermen and Assistant Aldermen*, were each composed of the same numbers, chosen by the same constituencies, with only the difference that the Aldermen were chosen for two years, so that one formed scarcely any check upon the other. A number of most respectable and public-spirited citizens proposed and carried through the Board of Sixty. The idea was, that in small districts electors would be more likely to know the man who was presented for their suffrages, and that political parties would have to be more particular in presenting men who were favorably known. However plausible this theory might be in a country district, it proved to be entirely fallacious in a city, where four-fifths of the voters never can be induced to look at such a ticket until they go to vote on election day, and where, owing to the constant changes of residences, there is scarcely any such thing known as neighborly association. Its operation was precisely the reverse of what was anticipated. Men who could not have had influence or character enough to obtain a nomination in a whole ward, managed to pull the party wires so as to secure it in a small section, and the consequence was, we had, with here and there an exception, a class of men inferior to those who had previously been chosen—small fry, hoping to swim in deeper waters—men who expected to live by politics. It operated precisely as the single district system is said to have operated, in sending to the Legislature men inferior to those who had been elected under the general ticket system. The people became thoroughly sick of the board, and there was no hesitation about abolishing it; but what should be substituted was not o clear. Arguing from the experience in regard to Assemblymen before referred to, a board elected by general ticket was strongly urged; but that was objected to because the board thus constituted would always be composed entirely of one political party. *The committee adopted the present plan as a compromise—four general tickets, one in each Senatorial District.* They also introduced the system of *classifying the terms of Aldermen,* so that those from the district having odd numbers go out one year, and those from the even numbers the next. It is doubtful whether any improvement can be made upon this system, unless, perhaps, by increasing the number of Councilmen on each general ticket. He did not believe that any legislation would secure the choice of better men. The object of a second board is to furnish some check upon hasty legislation, and to that end it is desirable that it should be chosen by a different constituency or in a different way. *Secondly, as to the Board of Supervisors.* That board had formerly consisted of the Aldermen, Mayor, and Recorder, and he, the speaker, had never been entirely satisfied that there was a necessity for substituting the present board for the purpose of settling accounts, although at the time he concurred in it, deferring to the judgment and larger experience of others. *The idea originated in the manner in which our Alms House department was formerly managed by ten governors*—half of them elected, and half appointed from those having the next highest number of votes. *The first ten governors were named in the bill (Laws of* 1849, *p.* 367),* and being mostly men of well-known philanthropy, character, and means, so long as they remained it worked very well, and it was hoped to continue a class of men who would be actuated by the same motives which control the managers of the House of Refuge and other charitable institutions. But by degrees, as one term after another expired and others were elected by the people, many men were introduced who only cared to use it as a stepping-stone for some other position, and made it more a means of frolic than of doing good, the temptation to enter this board being greater, because a nomination was an election; and so it happened, in course of time, that this system was wiped out, and a *board of four, to be appointed by the Comptroller, established (Laws of* 1860. *p.* 1026), which he believed had thus far been in good hands. He wished to make no reflection upon the members of the Board of Supervisors; but he thought the committee might understand how the mode of their election must inevitably result, eventually, in the same way as had the experiment with the ten governors.

Thirdly, in reference to the executive power:

That was formerly vested mainly in the Mayor. But the same mania for decentralization, which pervaded the State and led to the

---

* This was the first interference (so-called) at Albany.

Constitution of 1846, entered into the plans of all who were reforming city charters, and they went from one extreme to another.

In the State, it resulted in depriving the Governor of any voice in naming his cabinet, so that the Comptroller, Secretary of State, Treasurer, and Attorney-General were to be elected. Even the State Prison Inspectors were to be chosen by the people. With as much propriety might you choose in that way the directors of Lunatic and Idiot Asylums. So it was in the city. *The Mayor had the policemen, as well as other offices, in his gift, which was supposed to give him too large an army by which to secure his re-election, especially as the police were appointed for short terms,* instead of as now during good behavior. *And so, in 1849, we passed a law providing for the election of six heads of departments by the people,* and as the city election then took place at the same time with that of the State, it happened that we sometimes had fourteen ballot boxes at one election, and people were bewildered by the multitude of tickets. So we had six heads of departments, sailing on together, each responsible to no one but the people, which was really no responsibility at all, and when the subject came to be considered in 1857, there were few who could say a word on behalf of this system. Mr. Varnum had voted for it in 1849, and was in 1857 so well convinced of his error, that he was ready, as one of the committee, to vest the whole appointing power in the Mayor; but the majority were impressed with the argument that the Comptroller, who had charge of the finances, and the Corporation Counsel, who was the adviser of the city, should be made independent of the Mayor and Councils, so that they might not be influenced in their actions by a desire to retain their places. Reference was made to the changes made by General Jackson in the offices of Attorney-General and Secretary of the Treasury, in order to secure the removal of the deposits. But these arguments were, after all, more plausible than real, at least so far as the Comptroller was concerned, who must keep his accounts and make payment according to law, and, if the Mayor does not appoint this officer himself, let it be by the two boards, as United States Senator is chosen by the Legislature, and so with Corporation Counsel. *It is quite enough to ask the people to elect Mayor, Aldermen, and Councilmen, which is more than they can well manage;* but which there was, he supposed, no other way of doing except by the people, or rather by the party conventions. We might, however, hope occasionally, by a spasmodic effort, to revolutionize the city, and elect a respectable man for Mayor. We have had many such. And we ought to impose on him the same kind of responsibility which is imposed on the President of the United States. Give him the appointment of all his assistants, with or without the approval of the Aldermen—he rather thought without it—certainly, without "their advice." Give him these appointments, and then you can blame him if anything goes wrong. Better have one bad man, whom we can call to account for his stewardship, than have to deal with half a dozen, each of which will shift the burdens on to the others. The idea that the Mayor would use this patronage to keep himself in office is not sustained by past experience in regard to executive stations. Neither President nor old-time Governors have found that patronage helped them much; for every man they appoint, hundreds are disappointed. Besides, *the Mayor no longer controls the police, which are now, very properly, appointed by Commissioners, in the choice of whom the men had no agency.* The charter of 1857 *did not give the power of removal, except by consent of the Aldermen, and for cause. This was a great mistake.* A man might be utterly inefficient in the judgment of the Mayor; but he could not assign that as a cause, without going into particulars which would, perhaps, not impress another as sustaining the charge. It often occurs in private business, that you may wish to get rid of clerks and employés, with whose work you are not exactly satisfied, yet you would hesitate about making charges against them. And so it is here. The Mayor, being responsible, should be the sole judge, as the President is, and should be required to give no reasons to Aldermen or any body else. If he appoints bad men or removes good ones, let the people remove him; but don't ask the people to watch Comptroller and Counsel as well. The charter of 1857 *did authorize the Mayor to suspend; but, by an amendment which was slily introduced at a subsequent session, this power had been rendered doubtful,* and this brought the speaker to say, *lastly, that some action should be taken toward securing a constitutional check upon this constant tinkering of charters.* He could think of no other way, except by a provision that no amendment of city or village charters should take effect as laws, until they have been submitted to and approved by electors of the city or village. Such alterations would not be so readily asked for, or, if asked, would not be as readily passed, if they were in each case to go through the ordeal of submission to the people. As it is now, we often hardly know what is proposed before we hear that it is passed. If it were to be submitted to the people, it would at least have to be published, and the motives of the authors, whether good or bad, explained. At least the assent of two successive legislatures should be required.

Since the above remarks were made, my experience as an Alderman has satisfied me that the only real relief must come from a Constitutional amendment, so as to confine voters *at municipal elections in cities* to the holders of real estate, or to those who can read and speak the English language. *There is now one member of the Board of Councilmen who cannot read, and cannot even write his name.* The real estate qualification is the best; but I suppose it is useless to expect either. The only other remedy is to have the corporation authorities appointed at Albany. The commissions appointed at Albany have worked pretty well thus far; but, by degrees they will be corrupted, I fear, by the same influences. There must be some central power to keep them all in check. At the last Legislature a Board of Control was proposed; but it left the Supervisors and Common Council in full operation, because the former could not be abolished under the Constitution, it was thought.

J. B. V., Jr.

DANGERS FROM MISRULE.

The Discourse favors the general belief of our citizens, that the city has a larger population than ever before, and that the census of 1865 was wrong, or recorded the results of temporary depression. It is hard to resist the impression that the city is overflowing with people, alike with visitors and residents, and every tenement is occupied, and there is a call for thousands more of houses. It is but just, however, to present the other view of the subject, which is effectually given in this article from the *New York Times:*

A LESSON FROM STATISTICS.

Our readers will bear witness that we have never refrained from predicting unpleasant things in regard to the consequences of our municipal disorders and bad government on the prosperity of our city.

We have said again and again—we fear to the weariness of our readers—that our citizens would not bear forever this atrocious misgovernment, these incessant jobs, this heavy taxation, the horrible condition of our streets, and the discomforts of the city. It was plain to any one who looked below the surface, that all these shameless jobs of the Common Council were not mere amusements of these representatives, which injured nothing except our moral sense, but that they included definite sums taken out of the pockets of every rent-payer or consumer in the city. For every dollar squandered by Aldermen and Councilmen, each mechanic and day laborer, every manufacturer and merchant, every man and woman, and child must pay—either in rents or in increased prices depending on rents. The consequences of this jobbery have been that the expenses of living have arisen in this city more than in any other large city of the Union, as is best shown by the rate of rents; for provisions and imported products are undoubtedly afforded to the wholesale dealers cheaper here than in Philadelphia or Boston, for instance.

The increased cost of the consumers is in the necessary expenses of the retailers, and these expenses come in great part from the taxation. Moreover, the gradual influence of the annoyances of New York, our execrable streets, the filth and odors prevailing, the sanitary evils dreaded, the bad accommodations on the railroads, and the other *desagrémens*, was inevitably to force the middle classes from the city. The very rich could somewhat guard themselves against these evils and annoyances, especially by removing to the country in the summer season; the very poor and the laborers must remain near the market of labor; but persons with incomes from $1,000 to $5,000 per annum soon found it very injurious to their families, and too expensive to remain in the city, and these, by the thousands, scattered themselves in all the region around New York—in New Jersey, in Westchester County, on Long Island and Staten Island, and on the borders of the Sound. Here, though they must add to their rents the expenses of a daily journey of twenty or forty miles, and though provisions are more expensive in the suburbs than in the city, the saving from taxation and increased rent, and the sanitary advantages to their families, kept them constant residents, and added to their numbers.

Following them, have emigrated numbers of manufacturers who really belong to New York, but who find it cheaper to carry on their factories away from city taxation, so that the banks of the Hudson and the railroads of New Jersey find themselves more and more lined with huge factories, surrounded with laborers' shanties or cottages. The result is what we have uniformly predicted—that New York is decreasing in population, while the suburbs are increasing, and that marvellous growth in population, which was so long our pride, seems temporarily checked. Thus, in 1855, the population of New York was 629,810, and in 1860, 814,254, or an increase of more than five and a half per cent. per annum. In 1865-66, the population is only 726,386, being a decrease of some 87,000 since 1860, instead of the old increase of some twenty-nine per cent. Brooklyn, in place of its supposed 500,000, has only 296,378. But the whole Metropolitan Police District, containing the counties of New York, Kings, Westchester, and Richmond, and six towns in Queens County, embrace a population of 1,224,879, of which Westchester has 101,197; Kings, 311,090; Richmond, 28,209; and the six towns in Queens, 57,997. Some of the suburban villages have become considerable cities, thus: Morrisania has 11,691 inhabitants; Yonkers, 12,756; Flushing, 10,813; Hempstead, 11,764; Newtown, 13,891; Oyster Bay, 9,714; Cortland, 9,393, and so on with others.

The *foreign born* in New York number nearly half (313,201), and with their children must constitute some two-thirds of our population. In Brooklyn they amount to 107,851, or a less proportion. In Westchester they are only about one-quarter (26,394); in Richmond about one-third (9,142). In the matter of sexes, New York has some 38,000 more women than men, and Brooklyn some 13,000.

The poorer wards of this city contain enormous numbers; thus, the Seventeenth has 79,563; the Eleventh, 58,953; the Twentieth, 61,884; the Eighteenth, 47,613; the Twenty-second, 47,361, while the wealthy Fourteenth and Fifteenth have respectively only 23,382 and 25,572 inhabitants.

If this exodus be not checked by an honest and faithful management of the city affairs, New York will be delivered up to the very rich and very poor, and its prosperity receive a fatal blow.

AUTHOR'S NOTE.

I would acknowledge the great kindness of these gentlemen in assisting me to obtain the facts for this discourse. I might name many others who have shown good will and given information:

GEORGE H. MOORE,	JACKSON S. SCHULTZ,
ANDREW WARNER,	J. B. VARNUM,
GEORGE BANCROFT,	GULIAN C. VERPLANCK,
ELISHA HARRIS,	WILLIAM L. STONE,
CHARLES P. KIRKLAND,	EDWARD BILL,
J. S. HOMANS,	HORATIO ALLEN,
D. B. EATON,	B. F. VARNUM, JR.,
BROWN BROTHERS,	MAJ. GEN. BARLOW,
D. T. VALENTINE,	HENRY B. DAWSON.

I have consulted freely the well-known works of Dunlap and Hammond on the Political History of New York, Dr. O'Callaghan's New Netherlands, and have found some valuable information in Miss Booth's History of the City. The publications of the New York Historical Society have been of constant service, and especially Benjamin F. Butler's Discourse on the Constitutional History of New York. The histories of Bancroft, Brodhead, Hildreth, Motley, and Palfrey have been relied upon for important statements. I must say, also, in sincerity, that no man can study any important American subject, without finding constant help from Appleton's New American Cyclopædia and Annual Cyclopædia. These manuals are full of our national and local history, and their biographical sketches are ample and reliable, and many of them give materials nowhere else to be found in print.

This appendix, of course, does not aim to give a complete body of statistics of the city; but only to put in permanent form the chief facts that were furnished me up to the date of the Discourse, and so to contribute something towards a sketch of the present state of affairs. The outline of the speech of Hon. J. B. Varnum is inserted mainly on account of its valuable facts, and is a fitting contribution from one of the worthiest members of our Historical Society.

I am well aware that the whole subject is too great for a single discourse, and that a man not a native of the city labors under some peculiar difficulties in undertaking such a task as this; yet both natives and new comers must both acknowledge that the city is constantly showing new growths and aspects to them. I am content to appear as a learner more than a master; and I trust that friends and fellow citizens will deal gently with the defects of this little offering of public spirit.

S. O.

Printed in Dunstable, United Kingdom